LIFE IN THE STOCKS

RARE BIRD
LOS ANGELES, CALIF.

LIFE IN THE STOCKS

VERACIOUS CONVERSATIONS WITH MUSICIANS & CREATIVES

VOLUME ONE

MATT STOCKS

FOREWORD BY JESSE MALIN

THIS IS A GENUINE RARE BIRD BOOK

Rare Bird Books
453 South Spring Street, Suite 302
Los Angeles, CA 90013
rarebirdlit.com

FIRST TRADE PAPERBACK ORIGINAL EDITION

Set in Dante
Printed in the United States

10 9 8 7 6 5 4 3 2 1

Publisher's Cataloging-in-Publication Data available upon request.

For Amie Harwick

CONTENTS

FOREWORD

I FIRST MET MATT in one of my favorite places in the world: the fair city of London. It was 6:00 p.m. at a sound check, and I don't always enjoy doing interviews at these things, due to the fact that they usually run pretty long—all the "kick, snare, hat, more monitors please," etc.—and that leaves me with very little time to grab a bite, change my shirt, write up the set list, and take a breath.

On this occasion, though, I didn't mind at all. My road manager had informed me that I had an interview with a journalist to discuss my favorite songs by The Jam, a group I've loved since I was a kid. Being in England, drinking lager in a piss-stained dressing room with their songs running through my head seemed like a perfect thing to do.

I was expecting an older bloke—as they say over there—and someone who might have seen or known The Jam back in the day, when into the room walked this young kid with great, upbeat energy. It was Matt Stocks. He knew a lot of my music, and also every Jam song that I began to babble on about. It was a really fun hang; just sitting there talking to him got me even more amped up to do the show, and reminded me *why* I do this, and *why* I love it.

About a year later, I stumbled upon a podcast with Blondie's drummer, Clem Burke, who is one of my favorites, and has recently become a good pal. I thought I knew a lot about Clem, and about Blondie in general, but as I listened to this interview I was totally taken in. The host had great questions, and he really knew his shit. I could tell he put Clem at ease, too. And he got him to tell stories I'd never even heard before.

I called my publicist and said I'd heard this "Life In The Stocks" podcast, and that I was blown away by it. I asked him if there was any possible way I could be a guest on this guy's show, to which he laughingly informed me that I'd already been interviewed by him before. And he didn't seem to think it would be a problem getting me on the podcast—incidentally, "podcast" was a word I'd been hearing for years, but still wasn't really sure what it meant. In my mind, I pictured Spinal Tap busting out of their pods on stage.

It was a sticky summer day in 2017, and I was coming down from this crazy show we'd just played in Hyde Park, London, with Green Day. Matt and I had plans to meet up in the lobby of the infamous Columbia Hotel across the street. I walked into the dining room/bar area—a place I'd spent many nights trying to rid the UK of its alcohol by drinking all of it—and I instantly recognized Matt as the guy I'd had beers with at The Borderline a year prior, who'd listened as I gushed over Paul Weller's lyrics.

The next two hours would fly by, as we talked about the current state of the world, my new record, our childhoods, and where this whole music thing was going. Interviews can often be the same old boring questions over and over again, but this one was different. It was really fun, but also, in some way, felt therapeutic. Before I knew it, the van pulled up out front and it was time to hit the road. We raised our teacups, said goodbye, and I left to ride down the motorway, checking out the rest of Matt's podcast episodes along the way.

I was impressed with his choice and range of guests, from Gene Simmons and Johnny Rotten to Little Steven Van Zandt, and the wide mix of actors, comedians, and artists like Ralph Steadman, whose work had been engraved in my brain since Junior High School when Pink Floyd's *The Wall* was on every kid's denim jacket.

He covered everything from hardcore to arena rock, nineties emo to classic punk, and could talk to Joe Elliot of Def Leppard one week, and Eugene Hutz of Gogol Bordello the next, without missing a beat—and somehow make it all fit together. It also seemed like he was never afraid to ask a question that might be heavy, personal, or controversial. And he knew when to sit back and listen, and not over-insert himself like so many podcasters do ad nauseam.

Matt's podcast seems to bring out the humanity, vulnerability, and true passion of the artists that he interviews. He lets us know that we're not alone on our journey, and that there's beauty in the struggle, which is what makes the real art happen. Listening to his show has been motivating and inspiring, and Matt has a real warmth and a magic that brings out the best in people. We "open up and bleed," as Iggy Pop once said.

Over the years, Matt and I have stayed in touch and met up in many different cities, pubs, gigs, and hotel lobbies to talk about what we're listening to and what we're up to. And when I don't see him, I always know where to find him: on another *Life In The Stocks* podcast, because this guy never stops.

I believe our rock and roll culture—both past and present—is important, and guys like Matt are keeping it alive.

Life is for the living, kids, and we're staying up late to get the whole picture.

—**Jesse Malin**, New York City, June 2020

INTRODUCTION

O N NEW YEAR'S EVE 2016, I landed back in the UK after spending Christmas in Cuba with my ex-partner. Wi-Fi is basically nonexistent in Cuba, or at least it was back then, and there was no way I was paying for those roaming charges, so my ex and I made a pact: to leave our phones on airplane mode for the duration of our trip. The plan was to lose ourselves in the revolutionary charm of Cuban culture and the bygone beauty of a world pre-smartphones.

We both upheld our end of the bargain, and for two weeks we were completely off-grid in one of the most romantic and exciting countries in the world. It was a magical adventure. But the moment we got back home, everything turned to shit.

Unbeknownst to me, whilst we'd been swimming in the ocean in Varadero, hiking up the mountains in Viñales, and cruising along the Malecón in a 1950s Cadillac Convertible, the two companies that I worked for had both gone out of business. And I was none the wiser. Why would I be? My phone was totally out of action. Sometimes, ignorance really is bliss.

The second we touched down in London, however, I rejoined the world I'd been so happily disconnected from, and all the texts, emails, and voicemails came flooding in. "Dude, what's happened to Team Rock?" "Mate, have you seen the news about Team Rock?" "I hate to tell you this, but the Brooklyn Bowl is also closing down." "I'm sorry to hear about the Brooklyn Bowl, mate." "Are you okay?" "What are you going to do now?" Worst. New Year's. Ever.

At this stage, I'd been working as a freelance writer for Team Rock—a publishing company that owned the rights to *Metal Hammer* and *Classic Rock* magazine—for the last two years. And I'd served as resident DJ at the Brooklyn Bowl in London for the same amount of time. I was self-employed, but 90 percent of my annual income came from those two companies, and now they'd both gone bust. It was game over.

Now, I'm no stranger to the joys of unemployment. I've been let go without warning by every media company I've ever worked for: *Kerrang! Radio, Team Rock Radio, Metal Hammer, Scuzz TV*—they've all gone out of business at one point or another, and I've been laid off by all of them at the drop of a hat, without severance pay. But after losing four gigs in three years due to constant cutbacks in the music industry, this was the final straw. I was tired of having the rug pulled out from underneath me. And I'd completely lost faith in every rock-based website, magazine, radio station, and TV channel. I was done. The time had come to go it alone.

Coincidentally, I'd already planned to launch my own podcast. The show was originally intended to be a side hustle to my more permanent, albeit shaky position as a freelance writer and DJ. But when the company *and* the venue that I did all my writing and DJing for *both* went out of business, the podcast took on a life of its own.

Following its launch on January 31, 2017, *Life In The Stocks* became my primary focus and sole source of income. It would be a long time before the podcast made me any money, of course. It still doesn't, to be honest. But what it has done is open the door to lots of other creative ventures, like touring with my favorite bands, hosting a wide range of live Q&A events, and directly inspiring me to write this book.

It's pretty amazing when I think about it. And I still find it hard to believe. But for nearly four years now, *Life In The Stocks* has allowed me to continue to do what I love for a living. It's also 100 percent mine and no one can take it away from me. That level of freedom, independence, and creative control is almost unheard of nowadays. In this line of work, it's the holy grail.

It hasn't all been plain sailing, though. Building something from nothing entirely off your own back is fucking hard work. The full-time hustle takes its toll on your bank balance, your mental health, your friendships, and your romantic relationships. And I've taken hits in all of those departments to get to where I am today. But the struggle and the hardship has all been worth it.

I believe in fate. And I believe that everything happens for a reason. I also believe this podcast came into my life at *exactly* the right time. It's not only given me a career; it's also given me a life. And I don't say that lightly. If it wasn't for the opportunities and experiences that *Life In The Stocks* has afforded me, I hate to think where I'd be today. I certainly wouldn't be writing this book, that's for sure. So I have a lot to be grateful for.

Most of the guests that feature on my podcast are musicians, actors, and comedians, and they're often people who've inspired me through their work. During times when I've felt depressed, broken, lost, and alone, they're also the people whom I've turned to for words of guidance, encouragement, and support, and those conversations have often given me the strength and motivation to carry on.

To paraphrase Tim Armstrong of Rancid, I've always felt an urgent need to belong. I have an almost compulsive desire to connect to people. And nothing in the real world has ever fully satisfied that deep sense of longing or disconnect inside me. That's why I turn to movies and music, and the people who make them, to give my life purpose and direction. *Life In The Stocks* has been an absolute godsend in that regard.

Whether it's talking to Dave Hause about sobriety, Joe Cardamone about grief, Tom Green about our near-death experiences, Andrew W.K. about the meaning of life, Jesse Leach about our mutual struggles with depression, Laura Jane Grace about gender dysphoria, or my dearly departed friend Amie Harwick about feminism and how to be a better man, these discussions have helped shape me into the person that I am, and I'm eternally grateful for all of them.

You can listen to these conversations in their entirety any time you like—just search "Life In The Stocks" wherever you listen to podcasts. But for the purpose of this book, I've pulled out the highlights from my own personal favorite episodes and presented them in a way that tells a story. Hopefully, they'll have the same positive effects on you as they've had on me, and you can come back to them time and time again.

On a personal level, I really enjoyed going back and listening to these conversations. A lot of crazy memories came flooding back, both in regards to the events surrounding the interviews and, in a more general sense, what was going on in my life at that time. What a trip! Now it's your turn: you've bought the ticket, it's time to take the ride.

(Note: all the guests that appear in this book are American or Canadian—or at least live in America now, or have lived there for an extended period of time in the past. For that reason, I've chosen to present their words in American English. To all my UK friends reading this back home: don't be alarmed if you spot lots of z's and not enough u's. This is the American way.)

—**Matt Stocks**, London, July 2020

ADOLESCENCE

"I was a difficult teenager"

THE IRISH PLAYWRIGHT GEORGE Bernard Shaw once famously said, "Youth is wasted on the young." But he was also a fan of bastard dictators like Mussolini and Stalin, and he's been dead for seventy years, so what does he know, *really*?

One thing I can say for certain is this: I made a hell of a lot of mistakes growing up. But if I had possessed the mind of an older, wiser human being as I attempted to circumnavigate the stormy seas of youth, I probably wouldn't have made those mistakes in the first place, and therefore never learned from them, or matured in the ways that I have.

It's important to make mistakes in life. And it's important to learn from those mistakes, and try to make sure that we don't make the same ones again. Of course, we don't always succeed in our attempts. But as long as we keep trying, then we're on the right track.

Here's something else that I know to be true: whether we like it or not, we are all products of our upbringing. That's not to say we can't transcend the circumstances of our upbringing. But whatever those circumstances are, you can be damn sure they're coming with us into adulthood. It's just up to us whether we turn them into a positive or a negative force that drives us along.

The more I talk to people about their family lives and upbringing, the more I realize we all have our own struggles. One of my favorite things about hosting *Life In The Stocks* is getting the chance to chat with people that I respect and admire about their past, and learn about how their childhood impacted their life and shaped their worldview as an adult.

As a naturally curious conversationalist, people's backstories fascinate me. Whether it's talking to Laura Jane Grace about the devastating effects of divorce, or listening to Robb Flynn explain how being adopted informed his views on race and nationality, I find these revelations both comforting and enlightening: we all have our own issues, and we're all trying to process them in our own way.

The other cool thing about talking to creative people about their childhood is you get to hear all kinds of insights into trailblazing art scenes; whether it's Nick Oliveri recalling the birth of desert rock in Palm Desert, California, or the old New York stories courtesy of CBGB celebrities like Tommy Victor, Jesse Malin, and CJ Ramone, these are the rock 'n' roll anecdotes that I live for.

Let's kick things off in the swinging sixties, with the tale of how a little-known band from Liverpool made a guest appearance on American television and unwittingly changed the course of musical history—forever.

STEVEN VAN ZANDT—*BRUCE SPRINGSTEEN AND THE E STREET BAND, SOLO ARTIST, PRODUCER, RADIO HOST, ACTOR, ACTIVIST*

STEVEN: I grew up in the middle of a renaissance period. Our standards were set very high, being that close to the roots of gospel and soul. There was an intensity that just doesn't exist anymore.

MATT: It was a golden age, and you were obviously at the right place at the right time.

STEVEN: Well, I was sort of just after it to be honest. We were the third generation of rock 'n' roll, and it was the first two—the 1950s and 1960s—that were the main thing.

MATT: You were a teenager when The Beatles exploded, though?

STEVEN: I was thirteen.

MATT: Was *The Ed Sullivan Show* the light-bulb moment for you?

STEVEN: For me, and everybody else. The day before that show, there wasn't a single band in America. The day after, everybody had one. Of course, not all of them got out of the garage—in New Jersey, only about a dozen of us did. But everybody had a band the next day, and there was no such thing as bands in America before then.

KYLE GASS—*TENACIOUS D, THE KYLE GASS BAND, ACTOR, COMEDIAN*

KYLE: I look back on my childhood in California in the 1960s and 1970s, and they were extremely formative years. I was born in 1960, and I had two older brothers who would turn me on to the sixties rock groups of the time. I was absolutely fixated on them; I remember just staring at a Bob Dylan album cover for hours. That was where my interest in music began.

Politically, it was an interesting time, too. In 1968, both [Robert] Kennedy and Martin Luther King [Jr.] were shot, and there was the war in Vietnam. There was so much upheaval, and it seemed like such a crazy time. Then you had Watergate in '74. I was fourteen at that time, and I just remember being glued to the TV throughout all of it. I've been fascinated by politics ever since.

MATT: Were you aware of a nationwide loss of innocence at a young age?

KYLE: I think I was, yeah. It seemed like we went from *Leave It to Beaver*—which was a famous suburban TV show back then—to this multi-cultural revolution where everything was changing. It was really quite a heady time.

STEVEN VAN ZANDT

STEVEN: The Beatles revealed a whole new world, and it really was a *whole* new world. It was equal to a spaceship landing in Central Park: everything about them was alien and beautiful and perfect. It wasn't until about four months later, when The Rolling Stones came around, that it seemed accessible or attainable for everyone else.

I think one of the biggest life-changing moments for me was watching Mick Jagger; he was the only performer I had ever seen in my life—at that point—who didn't smile when he performed. That, believe it or not, was the most important moment for me—or certainly the second most important, after The Beatles on *The Ed Sullivan Show*—because it took it from show business to lifestyle, and that's when I really felt, like, "This is where I belong."

At that age, you're searching for an identity, and it was quite an epiphany for me to realize that this thing could be a lifestyle and not just something that you do on stage as part of an act. You're looking for that truth when you're a kid.

As it turned out, The Beatles would literally become the kings of the pop world, whereas The Stones would take it down more of a rock 'n' roll, blues-based route. But they're both equally important; they were the two sides—the yin and yang—of the renaissance. Then, of course, you had all the other British Invasion bands, and the British Invasion in general was the beginning of my whole life. My whole radio format is based on it.

MATT: What about the US garage rock bands of the 1960s? Or was it predominantly about the British bands for you?

STEVEN: It was almost exclusively about the British bands at first: The Beatles, The Dave Clarke Five, Herman's Hermits, The Kinks, The Animals, The Yardbirds, The Who, The Hollies, etc.

MATT: There was a strong transatlantic relationship that existed during the early days of rock 'n' roll that's worth talking about here: you had these young British kids listening to soul and rock 'n' roll music from the States, then translating it in their own way, and almost giving it back to America.

STEVEN: Not almost—*literally* giving it back. I'd never heard of Chuck Berry or Muddy Waters before. We had The Beatles, The Stones, and The Yardbirds telling us about our own music, and the way they interpreted it was just extraordinary. When I use the word renaissance, I don't use it lightly; I really feel that period will be studied for hundreds of years to come. It was a total separation, at that point, between the past and the future.

Everything changed in the 1960s, in terms of our consciousness and sensibilities. It was also the beginning of mass media, civil rights consciousness, women's rights, gay rights, ecological concerns—you name it. Before then, everything the government did was supposedly always right: you did what they said and you followed the rules. Suddenly, all of that was out the window and a huge change took place.

TROY VAN LEEUWEN—*QUEENS OF THE STONE AGE, A PERFECT CIRCLE, FAILURE*

TROY: I'm a child of the 1970s, and I was probably three or four years old when my dad first played me Chuck Berry and Jerry Lee Lewis. That's when it all started. It was all about the energy for me. I don't remember much before that, to be honest.

MATT: Was your dad a musician, or just an avid music fan?

TROY: Both. He played trumpet in the army band. But he never read a note of music: it was all by ear. I definitely got my ear for music from my dad. He bought 7-inches every weekend.

MATT: What was the first instrument you learned to play?

TROY: Mine was the drums. And the records that I started playing along to were Cheap Trick, AC/DC, and Black Sabbath. But when I listened to Led Zeppelin, I realized I couldn't play drums anymore. I just couldn't figure out what he [John Bonham] was doing with his kick drum. So I started playing guitar at that point, which was a lot easier for me to figure out. I stuck with the Zeppelin, though: "The Rover" was the first solo that I ever learned to play.

EUGENE HUTZ—*GOGOL BORDELLO*

MATT: What first took you to America?

EUGENE: A Boeing 254—or whatever the name of that model was.

MATT: And what was your reason for moving from the Ukraine to the United States?

EUGENE: I think my family was always destined to go. My father was on such a pro-Western wavelength. He always spoke great English, whereas I didn't speak any English until I got to the States. He was very pro-Western in his tastes in music and all that kind of stuff.

We were like an oasis of freakaholic fantasies in Ukraine. Our weekends were unlike any of my schoolmate's family weekends. We were always out for a hedonistic picnic, or listening to rock 'n' roll music, or having some kind of party where spontaneous theater was involved. I mean, we were listening to Parliament-Funkadelic. Who the fuck does that in Ukraine? Nobody—not even now. But my father was friends with a lot of diplomats and foreign exchange students, so he was always picking up records from really cutting-edge bands.

My father's brother is a painter, too, and his wife was a psychiatrist, so I could always get my hands on something that wasn't on any of the bookshelves or in any of the stores. In a state of dictatorship, which the Soviet Union was at that time, you weren't allowed to read Carl Jung or Friedrich Nietzsche. That just wasn't available. Nobody even knew those people existed, unless they had access to a special library for research. Otherwise, those schools of thought were out of the question. You couldn't have conversations with anybody about that stuff.

MATT: Were you the only kid, that you knew of at least, that had access to all this reading material?

EUGENE: There was one other friend that I had. His name was Sergei, and his family had an encyclopedia that was published in 1905, or something like that. It contained writings from Nietzsche, Arthur Schopenhauer, and Immanuel Kant—all these philosophers who were fundamental. I could talk about all that stuff with him.

MATT: Did you move to the States with your family, or did you move there alone?

EUGENE: No, no, I moved with my family. I had no power to execute anything like that when I was seventeen.

MATT: Was New York where your family originally settled?

EUGENE: We were hoping to move to New York, but we quickly got relocated to Vermont, and my first seven years in the States were spent there. And Montreal was only an hour and a half away, so that's where I saw most of the great shows.

MATT: Who did you see during that time?

EUGENE: Well, just about everybody that came through: Jon Spencer, Beck, Fugazi, Nirvana, Nine Inch Nails, and, most importantly, Nick Cave. The first time I saw The Bad Seeds was in broad daylight in this horrendous parking lot, but that didn't matter to me: I was completely focused on the experience of watching them play.

MATT: He's a special guy, that Nick Cave.

EUGENE: I think he's the greatest songwriter alive, and I'm not the only one who is of that opinion. There's a lot of spirituality around these days that's packaged up nicely, but Nick Cave is connected to a raw form of spirituality that's loose and gnarly—and quintessentially Australian. It's hard to put into words, but the spirituality and energy of his pursuit really reminds me of people like August Strindberg, who just have this drive and can undertake just about anything and turn it into gold.

Initially, I hated being stationed in Vermont by the refugee program, but then I kind of eased into it and was like, "Actually, this is not so bad." Plus, Bernie Sanders is from Vermont, so it kind of has a streak of progressive tradition.

MATT: Was it a good place for you to nurture your artistic personality?

EUGENE: You know, maybe I just got lucky as far as that goes. I did a lot of my homework there, and I had a great library at my disposal: UVM [University of Vermont] is one of the oldest and biggest universities in the country. And it's a great school: people like Ralph Waldo Emerson lectured there. It has this whole Rosicrucian vibe to it, and I was going there on a regular basis. They could've handed me about three diplomas from UVM by the time I left Vermont, without ever filling out an application form.

MATT: Did you ever get lonely or feel estranged, growing up as an outsider in a foreign country?

EUGENE: There was a lot of aloneness and seclusion, yeah. So not all of it was great. And the winters in Vermont are fucking miserable and intense—almost to the point of being paralyzing. But I think all the ideas that I had brewing up formed there because of all that solitude.

CJ RAMONE—*RAMONES, SOLO ARTIST*

CJ: I was born in Queens, New York. My dad worked at a gas station and my mom was a stay-at-home mom. We were a very blue-collar family, and we lived in a neighborhood called Fresh Meadows, in an apartment building set right on a major highway. We lived there until I was about two, so I don't have a lot of memories of it, but I've seen all the pictures and everything like that.

We eventually moved out to Long Island, and that's pretty much where we set down our roots. The town that we settled in—Deer Park—was right next to an aircraft factory where everybody in the area worked. My dad worked there for a while, and I started working there almost directly out of high school.

Then, while Ronald Reagan was in office, the Air Traffic Controllers went on strike and Reagan gave the companies permission to fire them and hire new people, which kind of weakened the unions. Long Island's entire economy at that point was basically aerospace and fishing: either you worked on fishing boats and clamming boats, or you worked for the aerospace industry, or at one of the machine shops that supported the aerospace industry.

All the people who worked for these companies were union workers with good-paying jobs for blue-collar people. But when all factories shut down, the companies packed up and moved down south to right-to-work states where there were no unions, and I lost my job.

When the factories closed down, the jobs in Long Island just dried up, and we went into a severe depression. It was really bad: at one point on the main street in my town just about every store front was closed down.

MATT: Is that what pushed you to join the Marines?

CJ: Yeah. I woke up one morning, I was twenty-one years old and working as a landscaper, and I said to myself, "I'm not going to live and die in my hometown. There's no way." And my dad's family was a military family: my dad and all his brothers served. So it was a pretty easy decision. I went down, signed up, and when I got the date that I was set to leave for boot camp, I finally told my parents I'd enlisted. My mom was totally against it, though.

MATT: How come?

CJ: She found out she was pregnant whilst my dad was in the navy, and it would've been an older sister, but the baby died. My dad went UA [unauthorized absence] and deserted from the navy to be at home with my mom and bury my sister, and he got into a lot of trouble for it. My mom always had a bad taste in her mouth about the military after that.

MINA CAPUTO—*LIFE OF AGONY, SOLO ARTIST*

MINA: I grew up in New York City. I'm from an old-school Italian upbringing. I lived with my grandparents and my grandfather fought in World War II. I never knew my mom: she OD'd at the age of twenty, when I was one. And my dad was a professional junkie his whole life. He died in 2002, at the age of fifty-six.

MATT: Was their connection drugs? Is that how they met?

MINA: I've heard many truths about their life, and I still don't know what to believe. I've heard my father's view, my father's sister's view, and my father's brother's view of who was who, and who behaved how. Every once in a while, I think I can still taste the trauma of what I went through in my mother's belly, and how she felt as a human being. And I basically mothered and fathered my father throughout his life, by putting him up and paying for his wake and his funeral. But he was an amazing man. I don't wish to deceive people into thinking that I'm hating on my dad.

I love my dad very much. He was an incredible artist. He built boat engines and jet parts in the Air Force, and he could come into the backyard with a nut and a bolt, and a month later have a Harley-Davidson built. He ran with the Hells Angels, too. I had Hells Angels in my backyard every Sunday, which was surreal and amazing. He also painted murals, he pinstriped, and he tattooed in jail. He was amazing. I think he's where I get a lot of my creative side from, only I use it to write songs and poetry.

JESSE MALIN—*HEART ATTACK, D GENERATION, SOLO ARTIST*

JESSE: My mom passed away when I was in my late teens and my sister was in her early teens. She was a single mom, and she was forty-three when she died from breast cancer. There was a five-year lead-up, too. I'd been living in the city prior to that. I left Queens to be in Manhattan and do my music, and I lived in my rehearsal studio and crashed with my friends. I wanted to be downtown because you could be freethinking, it was cheap to have a space back then, and there were cool clubs and movie theaters everywhere. I also preferred all that to going to school in a mainstream middle-class borough. So at that point I was in the city doing the band Heart Attack, just touring and putting out records.

When my mom got sick, it was a real shock and it was very upsetting. During those five years, I had to move home to help out and take care of her, and it just got worse and worse. When she eventually passed, I stuck around to take care of my sister, and we had to figure out where we were going to live. We go through these things in life, I guess. And it was a difficult time, but we got through it.

TOMMY VICTOR—*PRONG, DANZIG, MINISTRY*

TOMMY: There's a Spike Lee movie called *Summer of Sam* that perfectly captures what New York City was like in the 1970s. It was pretty bad back then. There was an onslaught of street violence, graffiti, and drug addiction, and that was all during the time that I grew up.

MATT: Do you remember being exposed to all that as a young kid?

TOMMY: Absolutely. Growing up in Queens, I saw all of it. I used to frequent bars at a very young age, and back then it was unheard of for anyone to be sober.

MATT: How old were you when you started drinking?

TOMMY: Probably about eleven. That was what everyone was doing, for the most part. The smart kids, and the ones who had parents who were watching what they were doing, were shut indoors and you never saw them. They were in their houses and apartments, studying and paying attention, and they were the ones who probably succeeded in life. Everyone else fell into a whole other life entirely.

MATT: What do you remember about your childhood?

TOMMY: My childhood was pretty tumultuous. I'm the youngest of five, and everyone else got out of there and went off to college, so I was sort of left on my own. My mother was the only one around, but she was working all the time, and whenever I wanted to leave the house, I'd have to look out the window to see who was around, just so I could try and avoid getting my ass kicked.

I was constantly paranoid about getting beaten up by the older kids in my neighborhood. I had this Lou Reed T-shirt when I was about twelve or thirteen, and I got so much shit for wearing it. They'd all say, "Who the hell is that? You faggot!" I'd even get shit for wearing a Deep Purple T-shirt because no one knew who the hell they were. People don't understand what New York was like back then. You really had to earn your cool. It was tough down there: I was under constant attack from everybody.

CJ RAMONE

MATT: Were there a lot of drugs in New York when you were growing up?

CJ: Absolutely. Just about everybody I knew smoked weed, took hallucinogens, and did heroin and cocaine—the whole gambit. It was all available.

MATT: It was obviously a very different city back then, too. What are your memories of being a teenager in New York?

CJ: I remember New York City when it was really bad, when it was on its knees. In the early 1970s, after President Nixon was impeached and President Ford came in, New York City was completely broken and falling apart. They'd stopped picking up garbage and things got really bad. There's a famous headline from the *New York Post* from that time, that says, "Ford to City: Drop Dead." Apparently, that's literally what he'd said.

New York was just a wasteland back then; parts of it looked like a warzone. A lot of buildings had been vacated and were falling down, and a lot of them had been knocked down and burned down. That's kind of my earliest memories of New York. But there was still something cool and gritty about it that I was always attracted to.

EUGENE HUTZ

EUGENE: I learned very recently that Manhattan Indians, who were living in that area before the invasion, dealt a lot of business on the island of Manhattan. But they were not residing there, and that's because they thought the energy of the island was too intense—it was really just for doing business.

MATT: Get in. Get out.

EUGENE: Yes. Because the soil and the geography of that area is a power point.

MATT: Maybe that explains why so much great art and music has come out of there.

EUGENE: And the rest of all the good and the crap that takes place there, too. It has this ongoing, cosmically given power. And if you're the kind of person who has a germ inside you that resonates with that, you will always stick out as this wounded, ugly duckling in other areas that don't have that factor. But as soon as you go to New York, it clicks, and you become something else; you don't feel debilitated anymore.

MATT: When you moved to New York, you became the swan—as it were.

EUGENE: Exactly. I was just like, "This is my place." Whatever your cosmological elements are, you have to go to where your friendliest environment is. And I think New York, despite its miserable winters, has a lot of other vitamins that are great—for me at least.

NICK OLIVERI—*QUEENS OF THE STONE AGE, KYUSS, MONDO GENERATOR, DWARVES*

NICK: When I first moved out to the desert [Palm Desert, California] in 1983, there was nothing out there. There were no venues for bands to play. There wasn't even a sewage system in place. It was backward living, and I hated my parents for moving us out there. But when I look back on it now, I'd never have played in any of the bands that I've played in had I not started in Kyuss. That's what got it all started, and if I hadn't moved out to the desert then it would've never happened.

MATT: What were you like as a kid?

NICK: I was pretty hyperactive to say the least. I still don't know how to go to bed at night. I don't know how to lie down and tell myself, "I'm going to sleep now." I don't know how to set the alarm and go to sleep. When I was a kid, I'd fall asleep standing up because I'd sooner go outside and hide in the bushes than go to bed. Brant Bjork always says, "I guess you're one of those kids who doesn't want the chocolate bar—you'd rather stick the spoon in the sugar and eat it pure, then run around like crazy." I was like that then, and I'm like that now.

MATT: You've known Brant Bjork a long time, then?

NICK: I used to play baseball against his team when we were kids. He turned me on to a lot of great music growing up. I saw his first band, Today, when he was thirteen years old. They played with DI: Doggy

Intercourse and Zezo Zece Zadfrack and the Dunebuggy Attack Battalion, which was Sean Wheeler from Throw Rag's first band. And Brant was great. We got to talking after the gig, and he said, "You should come over to my house and jam some time."

I'll never forget the first practice that we had together. We played a bunch of covers, and Brant had one original song, too. Josh [Homme] played lead guitar, I played second guitar, and this guy Chris Cockrell played bass. He lives in Berlin now—I actually just saw him. I sang vocals to begin with, then John [Garcia] showed up later. We had to kind of force John to sing at first.

MATT: Do you remember your first gig as Kyuss?

NICK: I do. Kyuss played their first ever show on Halloween night in 1987. All the older kids were watching us play, and we had to start without John because he was back in the car still reading the lyrics. He shows up at the end of the last song, like, "Fuck, I'm late. Sorry guys." And the older kids said, "We want to hear it again, but with you singing," because they liked us instrumentally, but they wanted to hear the songs with vocals on top. So we got to play twice. And John was so nervous. But he kicked ass. That was in the backyard of our friend Chris Baker's house on Primrose Avenue, near Palm Desert Middle School. That's where it all began: Palm Desert, California.

ROBB FLYNN—*MACHINE HEAD, PODCAST HOST*

ROBB: I grew up three blocks away from the trailer park that my dad lived in. In that sense, we were better off than he was because he was in a goddamn trailer park. But it was a constant reminder that I was just one generation away from white trash. And I was adopted, which meant we didn't even know what race I was. My parents just went in and asked for an Irish-Mexican baby, because my dad was Irish and my mom was Mexican. They were like, "Sure. Here you go." Because that's so common in California—an Irish-Mexican baby.

I never really had any identity with race or nationality, or anything like that. I think that tripped me out for a while while I was growing up because I felt like I wasn't part of anything. But when I look at the world now, I'm so fucking glad that I didn't have any of that bullshit in my head growing up. I look at all this crazy nationalism that's happening all over America and other parts of the world, and I'm like, "Who fucking cares?" I never fucking knew. I'm just a mutt, and I'm fine with that.

MATT: Did you spend your whole childhood living next door to your dad's trailer park?

ROBB: We lived in that area of San Lorenzo for a while, which was very lower-middle class. But by the time I was a teenager, we moved to a Californian suburb sixty miles away from the city. It was full of skateboarders and rife with that whole eighties suburban culture of vandalism and teenagers getting into trouble. And that's what we did: we got into a lot of trouble.

MATT: What kind of trouble are we talking?

ROBB: We were complete assholes. We used to do the dumbest, most ignorant shit. I used to steal my dad's car because he went to sleep really early—he was a baker, so he'd wake up at 2:00 a.m., which meant he'd basically be asleep by 7:00 p.m.—and we'd load up his car with rocks and just drive through the neighborhood throwing rocks through people's car windows. I can't even believe some of the shit we used to get away with.

DR. AMIE HARWICK—*THERAPIST, WRITER, MODEL*

AMIE: I found my biological mom when I was eighteen, and I met her, which was interesting because she doesn't look anything at all like me. I found my biological father when I was in my late twenties, and I haven't met him in person, but we keep in touch on Facebook. It was interesting: I think when you're adopted you grow up wondering or fantasizing about who these people could be, and then when you find them you typically realize, "I'm really glad that I was adopted." But I have like a friendly relationship with both of them at this point.

What's really interesting, though, is I have a biological brother, and in Pennsylvania, especially where I'm from, it's very conservative and a lot of people are very Republican and Christian. Being into the things that I was into as a teenager, I was really an outcast: there weren't many people that liked the things that I liked. But my biological half-brother has almost all of the exact same interests as me: he's really into metal, he loves horror movies, and he's pretty dark, just like me.

Before meeting my biological parents, I always thought that nurture or environmental factors were the most influential things on people—even though I know that there's a balance. But now, after meeting my biological brother and finding my biological parents, I have a very different perspective on how nature impacts our personalities; the biological impact is a lot more significant than I had previously thought.

MATT: That's fascinating. I've always thought that I'm very different to both my parents, but whenever I've been in a long-term relationship in the past, my partner has always pointed out that I'm basically an amalgamation of my mother and father.

AMIE: Well, parents are our behavior models: they're our models for how a man and a woman are supposed to behave. Then, as we become teenagers, we suppress these ideas and our peers and our friends become more important. But the influence that our parents have from age zero to twelve, thirteen, or fourteen years old is monumental.

LAURA JANE GRACE—*AGAINST ME!, SOLO ARTIST, AUTHOR*

LAURA: My dad worked for NATO, and we lived in Italy from when I was seven to twelve years old. It was like a different world. We did sports in this extinct volcano called Carney Park. You drove up the volcano and went into the center of it, and there were sports fields and golf courses and swimming pools—and you were inside a volcano. They also sent us on all these amazing field trips to places like Rome and Siena. It was unreal. It was a really magical time and place for me. We existed in a bubble, in a way. There was only one channel on our

TV, which was the Armed Forces Network, and the programming was like a year behind everyone in the States. In the pre-internet age, we were really cut off from the rest of the world.

MATT: When did your parents split up?

LAURA: My parents divorced when I was twelve. I moved to Florida with my mother and my brother, and I didn't really connect well with other kids when I moved back to the US.

MATT: Divorce is rough on anyone, but you obviously had the added upheaval of being moved to a different country. It must have felt like your whole world had been turned upside down.

LAURA: Completely, and that wasn't something that I realized until I was out of the military environment. There was privilege that went along with the military world because my dad was an officer and he was so high-ranking, and there was respect for my family that went along with that.

MATT: How was your relationship with your dad?

LAURA: I really respected him. I was kind of in awe of him, actually. It's hard not to be when your dad is like G.I. Joe. He had his boots and his fatigues, and people saluted him whenever he walked by. But there's also a certain amount of coldness that comes with military life; they're trained to be a certain way, and that's not just me imagining it.

MATT: My dad was in the army, and there's definitely a psychological process that they go through to toughen them up and make them harder.

LAURA: To make them soldiers—sure. But at the same time, I loved my dad. And while he was often really involved with work and that meant he'd be away a lot, when he was around we had whatever relationship we had—we used to play catch and build models together, stuff like that. But after my parents divorced, that drove a real wedge between us, and we never reconnected after that.

MATT: What about your relationship with your mother? From reading your book [*Tranny*], it sounds like you put her through a bit of a hard time during the turbulent teenage years.

LAURA: I did put my mother through a bit of a hard time, yes. That's an understatement. But to her credit, she was always there to bail me out of jail, and she always had my back. I was a difficult teenager; I got arrested a lot; I got beat up a lot; I got expelled from school all the time. But I was always close with my mom. Even when we fought, we were always close.

CHUCK RAGAN—*HOT WATER MUSIC, SOLO ARTIST*

CHUCK: Everyone has their own moments growing up where they literally feel like it's the end of the world. I think that's a part of growing up, and I think it's important to feel and understand that, and find our own way out of it. It's part of maturing and becoming a young adult. I look back on my childhood, and in the grand scheme of things it was all first-world problems; I had it pretty damn good.

I had two very loving parents who were wonderful to me, for the most part. There were times where they definitely didn't support what I wanted to do, and there were times when they may have been wrong in the way that they disciplined me or tried to veer me away from something that I wanted to do that might not have been so bad. But when I look back on it, especially now, being a parent myself, I understand that their primary goal was just to care for me and to try to keep me safe and on the right track.

My mother even said it when I was a kid: "I don't want you in bars. I don't want you playing this punk rock music. I don't want you playing rock 'n' roll. It's a dark path, and it will lead you to a dark place." In a lot of ways, I can't blame her one bit. If my son brought home some of the kids that I brought back to my parents' house, I'd be like, "Get that kid out of my house, and you're not hanging out with him anymore." So I don't blame them one bit. They were just looking out for me.

TIM McILRATH—*RISE AGAINST*

TIM: I grew up in the 'burbs, probably about fifteen miles outside of Chicago. My grandparents lived in the same neighborhood as the *Home Alone* and *Uncle Buck* house, and my cousins all lived in the area where they filmed a lot of *The Breakfast Club.*

Chicago is like a lot of big cities: the trains connect the outlying suburbs to the main city. And before I or any of my friends could drive, we'd make use of the trains and get them into the city to go skate, or go to a record store or the cool clothing shops, and to go see shows.

MATT: At what age did you start making those trips into the city?

TIM: Probably about fourteen or fifteen years old. And the second I was able to, I moved into the city—pretty much as soon as I got out of high school. As soon as I turned eighteen, I was like, "I want to live in a house in the city with a bunch of punks, play music in the basement, and go to shows every night." And that's exactly what I did.

JOE CARDAMONE—*THE ICARUS LINE, SOLO ARTIST, PRODUCER*

JOE: My dad worked through the 1970s as a jobbing actor, and he was in some things here and there. He starred in this B-movie horror flick, and he was an ape in *Planet of the Apes*—shit like that.

MATT: That's a pretty cool gig.

JOE: Totally. Then he finally got a call from Francis Ford Coppola to be in *Apocalypse Now.* He was cast as "mustached dude on the boat." Then my mom got pregnant. The choice was either go to the Philippines for however fucking long this crazy film was going to take—

MATT: Which wound up being about two years, right?

JOE: Exactly. Or stay home and take care of your family, and see your son be born. And that's what he chose to do. After that, he never went out for anything again.

MATT: Assumedly, you were that son?

JOE: Yeah. Wild, right?

MATT: Really wild. What a lovely story, though. Family over everything.

JOE: Family over everything. And he's a really dedicated father. He went from acting to working behind the scenes in films, doing hard labor in a union.

MATT: Building sets and things like that?

JOE: Yeah. He did hard labor for ten years to take care of his family.

JUSTIN SANE—ANTI-FLAG

JUSTIN: Pittsburgh was a really working-class steel town when I was growing up. Most of the industry left when I was in high school, and then it became a really depressed town; there was tons of unemployment and a lot of alcoholism. Half of our population left in a very short space of time, and Pittsburgh became a ghost town of really young people and really old people. Anybody who needed a job just left.

Our football team are the Pittsburgh Steelers, and in the 1970s they won four championships, so they became the rallying point for everyone in the city. In the 1980s, when everybody left Pittsburgh, so many people left town that there's now what we call the Steeler Nation, which is people from Pittsburgh who live all over the country but still support the Pittsburgh Steelers. Pittsburgh is probably the most represented football team in America because there's so many people from Pittsburgh living in other places. In almost every city you go to, there's a Steelers bar. And what's amazing about that is it's a reflection of how devastated the town was when the steel industry shut down. All that labor history, and all that working-class history, means Pittsburgh has always been an incredibly political town.

MATT: What sort of an impact did that economic environment have on your family when you were growing up?

JUSTIN: It was a very Charles Dickens kind of childhood. But that's okay.

MATT: Do you have any siblings?

JUSTIN: I'm the youngest of nine.

MATT: *Nine?* That's the largest family I've ever heard of.

JUSTIN: Yeah, my parents were Irish Catholic and they took it very seriously. It was chaos, but it was great. We were like the Weasleys of Pittsburgh—straight out of *Harry Potter.*

MATT: Is it not difficult maintaining a relationship with nine siblings? I have enough trouble keeping in touch with one.

JUSTIN: I think because I'm the youngest, I have a great relationship with all of them. I don't think anyone should have nine kids, though. Somebody is always going to get neglected because how can you realistically keep an eye on nine kids?

Both my parents worked their assess off; they were dedicated to the family; they worked really hard, and when somebody needed one of them they were always there. But when I look at religion and the way that religion controls people and pushes them to do things that are not in their best interests—like having nine kids because they think they shouldn't use birth control, otherwise they're going to go to hell—then I really think the Catholic church has a lot to answer for.

FRANK IERO—*MY CHEMICAL ROMANCE, LEATHERMOUTH, SOLO ARTIST*

FRANK: I'm an only child. I desperately wanted a sibling as a kid, though. I really wanted that sense of companionship, and I envied people that had it. But later in life, when I met people who were multiples and had loads of siblings, they'd always say, "I wish I was an only child." Go figure.

KYLE GASS

KYLE: My brothers reminded me every day how I wasn't as smart as them. But one of them is a computer tech guy in Silicon Valley, and the other is a very successful engineer, so they are smarter than me—they were right. That kind of helped me go in a different direction: the class clown. It was always about gaining favor to get our mom's attention; we were always sort of battling for that.

My mom had a weakness for show business, so actually my whole career is just an attempt to get her approval. She had this brilliant skill—I don't think she even knew that she had it—where she would slightly withhold her approval, and in doing so she created this achievement machine where it was never enough. Even now, I'll be like, "Mom, I won a Grammy, and I'm playing in front of two hundred thousand people." And she'll say, "That's very good, dear. But you could do a little bit better." Basically, I'm extremely unhappy and I need a lot of therapy. But this is helping, so thank you.

DOUG STANHOPE—*COMEDIAN, AUTHOR, PODCAST HOST*

MATT: Do you have any brothers and sisters?

DOUG: I just have one brother, who's a little bit older than me.

MATT: Are you guys close?

DOUG: No. Not anymore. But that's fine. Life's too short to surround yourself with people who don't fucking laugh at the joke.

ROBB FLYNN

MATT: Did you have any brothers or sisters growing up—either from your adopted or your biological family?

ROBB: My parents couldn't have kids, which is why they adopted me. But my whole extended family was really dysfunctional. My dad has a twin brother who joined a cult when I was really young, so I grew up with cousins always living at our house. If you were having a problem with your crazy uncle or my crazy aunt, you came and stayed with us. For long periods of time, I'd have three brothers, or two sisters and a brother, and then they'd go away. Then they'd come back. Or I'd have another set of cousins come and live with us. It was a trippy upbringing; I got used to having lots of other kids around.

MATT: What cult did your uncle run off and join?

ROBB: He's actually still in it. It's some crazy religious cult where you tie all your money to the main Jesus guy, and they all work and he doesn't. He basically just up and left his family and kids. I remember going up there with my parents to try and get him out. I wasn't really clear on what we were doing at the time, but my dad told me later on why we went up there. It was some crazy hippy commune in the middle of fucking Oregon—everyone was smoking weed. We tried getting him out but it didn't work, and he's still there now. They all think this dude is some disciple.

MATT: That's mental.

ROBB: Right? I've always had this disconnect to race and nationality, and a real disconnect to religion after seeing that shit and what it did to my cousins. From a very young age, I was like, "I don't know about all this stuff."

DR. AMIE HARWICK

AMIE: When I was adopted, they gave my parents these papers that gave limited information without identifying who these people were. They said that my biological mother was a carnival-ride operator, and that my biological father was a criminal, which is kind of true on both ends. So at first I was like, "Oh, my God. My mom's a carny. That's actually really awesome." But it turned out that's just what she did when she was in high school.

MATT: Like a summer job?

AMIE: Exactly. A summer job at a local fair. She works in an office now. But what's interesting about her—and, like I said, I come from a very conservative place, where the older people especially aren't listening to rock and metal music—is the first day we met, when I was eighteen, I asked her, "What kind of music do you like? What's your favorite movie? I want to know who you are." And she said, "Well, my favorite musical group is Suicidal Tendencies, and my favorite movie is *Pink Flamingos* by John Waters." I was like, "Yeah, I give up. We are obviously of the same breed."

MATT: What's the story with your biological father? How did you track him down?

AMIE: He was in prison, and my best friend back home is a social worker, and at the time she was working for child support. She said, "Look, I think I can find him. If he's currently incarcerated and he's had a child support order against him at some point in time, I could probably figure out who he is." Within an hour of her getting into work the next day, she was like, "I found him." And she sent me his mug shot. Do you know who Tom Savini is?

MATT: Of course. He's the guy in all the Robert Rodriguez films.

AMIE: He could be a clone of him. And of course, I'm a horror movie nerd, so I was like, "Oh, my God. My birth dad looks like Tom Savini." And that was interesting because he looked like someone that I'd hang out with.

So, we started writing letters back and forth. He was in and out of jail, mostly for theft and drugs, but he just kept ending up back in the system. Basically, he had no hope. But I told him all about school and how I was studying for my Master's program, and that I was a functioning human being, and he became motivated, then, to be held accountable to someone. I think he just wanted someone to know that he was working on himself.

Eventually, he got out of jail, and he's been out of jail ever since—this was about six or seven years ago now. He also has a job and his own place to live, and he started a painting business. And because I'm a crazy cat person, he got himself a black cat, too. So he's doing really well. And even though we've never met in person, we write back and forth, and he's actually now a pretty functional guy.

DOUG STANHOPE

MATT: You talk about your mother in a lot of your stand-up. Did she have a dark sense of humor, too?

DOUG: Yeah, she was fairly caustic. She wasn't nearly as dark as I became, though. The student became the master there. But when I was growing up, she'd let me smoke cigarettes and read *Hustler* magazine, which is probably why I'm so desensitized and asexual now.

I was jerking off to fucking spread beavers when other kids were stuck looking at the *Sears* catalogue.

MATT: What about your dad? Did you have a good relationship with him?

DOUG: Yeah, he was a soft touch. He was eighteen years older than my mother. He was a nice guy, just a big, fat sweetheart. He didn't really have any range of emotions. He never belly-laughed in his life, and he swore he'd never been in love—said he didn't know what that meant. He used to say, "I really thought your mother only divorced me because it was a popular thing to do at the time." And when I asked her about it, she said, "Yeah, that's true."

FRANK IERO

FRANK: My parents split up when I was around three, and they eventually divorced when I was six or seven. So I don't ever remember having both parents at home. But I do remember whenever they were together, it was toxic and hard. They just couldn't get along, and it was better for them to be apart.

MICHAEL MONROE—*HANOI ROCKS, DEMOLITION 23, SOLO ARTIST*

MICHAEL: My parents broke up when I was eleven, but I'm glad that they did; I think it's better that they broke up. Some people say, "Stay together for the kids," but I think it's bad for the kids if you have to listen to people fighting. I actually had a happy childhood, though, despite my parents getting divorced.

MATT: How old were you when you left home?

MICHAEL: I left home when I was seventeen. I was underage, and my mother could've easily stopped me if she wanted to, just by getting the cops involved. But I said, "If you call the cops then you're never going to see me again."

MATT: What drove you away?

MICHAEL: Rock 'n' roll.

MATT: Brilliant. What did you pack?

MICHAEL: Just my ice hockey bag and 150 vinyl records. And I said to my classmates, "I'm out of here. I hope I never see you again. Bye."

ANDREW W.K.—*SINGER-SONGWRITER, PRODUCER, WRITER, MOTIVATIONAL SPEAKER*

MATT: Did you get on with both of your parents growing up?

ANDREW: Yeah. There were intense times at home, and it's only dawning on me now that maybe it was a little more traumatic than I ever realized. But my parents managed to stay together, which I'm quite thankful for.

MATT: Did they argue and fight a lot?

ANDREW: To some extent. But it's difficult to say if it was more or less than any other married couple. I think my dad is quite an intense guy, and I relate to him a lot in that way. But his intensity was tempered by my mother's inverted version of intensity, which was incredibly caring and resilient. I think both my brother and I benefited from the balance that they provided—they both have great qualities, even in the intense version of those qualities. But it would be completely unfair of me to say that it was a bad childhood. And even the challenges of it were ultimately rewarding. I was very lucky, and I never doubted, even during the times of the greatest turmoil, that my parents loved and cared about me and my brother. And I think that's the most important thing that you're looking for.

MATT: I think it's a privileged position to be in, and one that should never be taken for granted.

ANDREW: Definitely.

MATT: My parents split up when I was fairly young, and there was a lot of drama and fighting in the lead up to their divorce. But in the same way as you're saying, I never wanted for love, encouragement, or support. And I'm grateful for that because that can fuck people up for life—if they don't get the right nurture or care early on. That kind of stuff stays with you, doesn't it? It haunts you into adult life.

ANDREW: Oh, absolutely. It's very hard to overcome that deficit. That's not to say that it's impossible, and developing an awareness of whatever shortcomings you've been dealt can help you make up for that. But talk about a challenge: it's how you're building your identity and the tools to craft a place for yourself in the world.

MATT: And your relationships with other human beings.

ANDREW: Everything, yeah—everything. It's a heartbreaking feeling when you realize that a lot of folks don't have that as good. And you don't always know exactly what to do about that good fortune that you have, except just to try to acknowledge it and have as much compassion as you can for others who have not gotten that, and put the benefits that you've wound up with to good use. It's an obligation, I think. And it's a good kind of pressure to be under. If it happened the right way to you, it's your duty to put that to good use in the world.

JESSE LEACH—*KILLSWITCH ENGAGE, TIMES OF GRACE, THE WEAPON*

JESSE: I was raised by two parents who constantly took in people who were down on their luck, whether they were homeless, ex–drug addicts trying to recover, or people who'd just gotten out of prison. My childhood is peppered with those types of people, and it's definitely where I get a lot of my compassion, because as much as I harbor a lot of anger toward the ignorance of this world, I also have a deep love for humanity that I just can't shake. And that gives me a sense of purpose and duty to reach out to people that I know are suffering. We all have issues, and we all have problems.

MATT CAUGHTHRAN—*THE BRONX, MARIACHI EL BRONX*

MATT C: I've always been comfortable in any environment. At school, I was friends with the nerds, the weirdos, the musicians, the athletes—

everyone. I can always find the positive in anything. And I like being a well-rounded person; I was never the type to be unwilling to talk to anyone. I've always been pretty outgoing, too.

MATT S: Were you a good student? Did you get good grades?

MATT C: No, I've always been a pretty average student. As with a lot of kids, as you get older and you go through the high school days and discover all the joys of being a teenage asshole, I cared way less about the whole system. I feel pretty solid in my education now, but I wish I could've gone to college for a little bit, just to see what it was like. But at the time, I had no desire at all. I was just like, "Fuck this. I'm out. I'm going to get a job and make some money." And I had no idea what I was going to do. I always wanted to play music, but I didn't ever think it was going to become a serious thing.

MATT S: You didn't actively pursue a career in music, then?

MATT C: Not at all. It's funny, on the last US tour that we did, we played Princeton. It was this Latin heritage student academy thing, which was really cool. And we also played in Boston, right next to Harvard. I was in Chipotle in Boston, this angry student had made me this terrible burrito, and I'm sitting there all filthy, just staring out the window watching all these different versions of life walk past. Sitting next to me were these two young girls. They were probably in their first year of college—I'm assuming that by the way they were talking—and one of them was venting to her friend about what a shitty guidance counselor she had. I remember her saying, "I told my counselor, 'This isn't just some decision; this is my future; this is my career.'"

There I was, scumbag of the year, and this girl was worrying about her future while she's still in school. When I was in school, that was the last thing I cared about. It was pretty funny, man. It's always a trip for me to see people that are the complete opposite of where I was at that age. And that's not a bad thing at all. It's just interesting to see different people's mindsets.

TOM GREEN—*ACTOR, COMEDIAN, RAPPER, TALK SHOW HOST*

TOM: I didn't enjoy the academic side of school. I was a good student until high school, and then I became distracted by extracurricular activities, like making music and doing stand-up comedy.

MATT: You were doing stand-up comedy in high school?

TOM: Yeah. I started performing at Yuk Yuk's comedy club in Ottawa when I was sixteen years old.

MATT: Was it intimidating performing in front of an adult crowd?

TOM: It was pretty terrifying, yeah. I was onstage talking about funny observations, but I didn't really have any life experience. I mean, I started doing stand-up before I'd even had sex. But I was pretty tall—I was six foot three—so it wasn't like some little kid standing up there.

MATT: And you were making music in high school, too?

TOM: Yeah, I used to make rap music in my home recording studio. It was a lot of fun.

MATT: What kind of equipment were you using?

TOM: Keyboards, samplers, and drum machines. I had an Akai S900 sampler, an Akai S950 sampler, a Roland U-20 keyboard, and a TASCAM 4-track with a SMPTE timecode running on it. I'd sync all the electronics together with a timecode click track to an Atari computer, which was basically my sequencer, then I'd record my vocals onto tape.

MATT: That's an impressive set up. What hip-hop were you listening to back then?

TOM: Public Enemy, A Tribe Called Quest, Beastie Boys, and Run-DMC.

MATT: The classics. You obviously worked with Mike Simpson from the Dust Brothers, who produced *Paul's Boutique*. How was it, as a lifelong Beastie Boys fan, getting the chance to work with him?

TOM: It was great. I met Mike filming *Road Trip*, and he wound up doing the soundtrack to *Freddy Got Fingered*. *Paul's Boutique* is my favorite Beastie Boys album. I just love all the samples. That's the same way I made music back then: sampling and looping. I'd go down to my college radio station and raid the jazz, funk, and R&B records, sample everything onto a digital audio tape recorder, then take the DAT recorder back to my house and plug that into my samplers.

MATT: It sounds like a much more creative time. I don't know if it's just me being nostalgic for the past, but I feel like now that we can do anything that we want to do with computers, that old-school problem-solving approach to creativity has vanished.

TOM: I just think it's different now, that's all. I know what you're saying, and to a certain extent I agree with you. But I don't like to think of Pro Tools as the end of music; I refuse to believe that because we can now have an infinite number of digital tracks at our disposal, we're not going to think of anything new. What Pro Tools does do is make things a lot easier to record. And at the end of the day, it's still content over form. That's actually what Mike Simpson from the Dust Brothers told me: it's not about how you record, it's about the idea. Part of the reason I've gone full force back into stand-up comedy is because there are no technical tricks: it's just you and an audience, and there's no gadgetry involved.

MATT: What took off first, the comedy or the music?

TOM: I guess it was the music. I got a record deal when I was nineteen years old. I'd been doing stand-up for three or four years at that point, then I got a record deal in Canada with my rap group, Organized Rhyme. So I quit doing stand-up and went out on tour with the band—and I did that for a couple of years.

MATT: Did you tour with anyone big?

TOM: We mostly played on our own, but we did do a couple of shows with the Barenaked Ladies, who were a huge band in Canada at that time. That was exciting for us because we got to play in a couple of big stadiums. But for the most part we just did our own shows in the local area. We did do a show down in New Jersey with 3rd Bass once, which was pretty cool. We never actually got to meet 3rd Bass, but we went down and opened for them at Rutgers University in New Jersey.

We used to do weird stuff on stage back then: we brought laundry baskets with us, and mid-show we put laundry baskets on our head and started doing this slow, synchronized rotation. This was in front of an all-black audience, and they loved it because we obviously weren't trying to look hardcore. We weren't hardcore. We were just two goofy kids from Ottawa, Canada. And I think they appreciated that we kept it real in that way. Plus, our beats were dope. You know what I'm sayin'?

MATT: What were the influences behind *The Tom Green Show?* I remember it being so fresh and unlike anything else on TV at that time.

TOM: David Letterman was the number one inspiration. I know he wouldn't like to think of himself as traditional because he was such a ground-breaking pioneer of irreverent late-night talk, but he was on NBC, so as far as somebody who was working within the traditional mainstream media, David Letterman was my hero, for sure. But I also got a lot of inspiration from hip-hop music and skateboard videos— they were all equal part inspiration for *The Tom Green Show.* Inspired by all of those things, I wanted to make my own guerrilla TV show that looked like it didn't deserve to be—and shouldn't be—on television.

MATT: Where do you think that motivation and drive came from at such a young age?

TOM: I was just desperate to not get a real job. I had a real fear of having to grow up and go out into the traditional workforce to get a corporate job to support myself. So I was looking for a loophole and a way around that.

MATT: Amen to that.

ADOLESCENCE PLAYLIST

THE BEATLES—"I WANT TO HOLD YOUR HAND"
THE ROLLING STONES—"COME ON"
BOB DYLAN—"SUBTERRANEAN HOMESICK BLUES"
LED ZEPPELIN—"THE ROVER"
PARLIAMENT—"P-FUNK (WANTS TO GET FUNKED UP)"
NICK CAVE & THE BAD SEEDS—"INTO MY ARMS"
MARVIN GAYE—"GOT TO GIVE IT (PT. 1)"
LOU REED—"WALK ON THE WILD SIDE"
KYUSS—"SON OF A BITCH"
SIMPLE MINDS—"DON'T YOU (FORGET ABOUT ME)"
THE DOORS—"THE END"
SUICIDAL TENDENCIES—"INSTITUTIONALIZED"
BEASTIE BOYS—"SHAKE YOUR RUMP"

PUNK ROCK

"Punk rock gave me self-worth"

Y OU'RE PROBABLY WONDERING WHY I've devoted an entire chapter of
the book to one genre of music, and none to any others. There
are three explanations for this. Firstly, punk rock—or punk, if you'd
prefer—is the *best* musical genre. Secondly, punk rock is more than just
a genre: it's an attitude, a lifestyle, and a set of universal beliefs. And
thirdly, punk rock changed my life, whereas heavy metal, hip-hop, and
pop music did not.

Punk rock also changed the lives of nearly every guest in this
book, with the exception of comedian Doug Stanhope, who doesn't
really care about music. Funnily enough, Stanhope does appear in this
chapter, though, as he's good friends with Fat Mike from NOFX. And
NOFX, incidentally, were my introduction to punk rock.

Growing up, I used to see the letters N-O-F-X spray-painted on
the walls at school. I didn't even know what they meant to begin with,
but I was always intrigued by them, and to this day I can't figure out
why. Maybe they just looked aesthetically pleasing? Or maybe it was
destiny at work.

In September 1997, I was sitting in math class minding my own
business when the kid next to me—my soon-to-be-best-friend Sam
Down—started singing these words: *"New boobs, jugs / New boobs, jugs
/ New boobs, jugs / New Boobs, jugs."* To a thirteen-year-old boy with
hormones coming out of his arse, a song about breasts was music to
my ears. I asked Sam what the name of the song was. He said, "New
Boobs." I asked him who it was by. He said, "NOFX."

As dumb as it sounds, that was my eureka moment: so *that's* what N-O-F-X means! They're a band. Of course. Duh!

Math's class for the rest of that year was spent learning about NOFX, and my new friend Sam told me everything that his brother Jake had taught him about the band. It's impossible to overstate the importance of older siblings when it comes to musical education, and in the absence of one of my own, Jake made a more than worthy substitute—even if he was all but unaware of the knowledge he was passing on.

I'll never forget the first time Sam snuck me into Jake's bedroom, either. Needless to say, Jake was out of the house at the time; if he knew we were in there, he would've ripped our fucking heads off. It was a regular Aladdin's cave of punk rock paraphernalia. There was a full-size drum kit in there. There were cigarettes, lighters, and band posters everywhere. There were fist-shaped holes in the walls where Jake had punched through the plastering. There was a mountain of what I would later learn were magic mushrooms laid out on the bed. And sure enough, in permanent marker, in one of the few spaces not occupied by a band poster or a hole in the wall, were the immortal letters N-O-F-X.

Hand on my heart, that was the day I became a punk rocker. I still wasn't quite sure what punk rock meant, of course. But now I had confirmation of how exciting and dangerous it was, and I wanted *in*. So I saved up what little money I had, and I went to the local record store to buy my first NOFX album: *I Heard They Suck Live!!*

I was instantly transfixed by the multifaceted musicality and humor and politics and excitement of the whole thing. Both the songs themselves, and the band's onstage banter in between, challenged almost everything that I knew to be true about life. It was a real Wizard of Oz moment: the world went from black and white to Technicolor, and I found myself a long way from Kansas without any intention of ever going back home.

Twenty-three years later, I'm still on that trip, and I've met the most unbelievable cast of characters along the way—many of whom appear in this book. So I'd like to take this moment to thank Fat Mike & Co. for introducing me to punk rock, which in turn taught me about the importance of autonomy, freedom, individuality, expression, creativity, integrity, friendship, and having fun. Without NOFX, *Life In The Stocks* would not exist, and you wouldn't be reading this book. Cheers, Fatty!

Let's crack on with chapter two. And we begin where punk rock began, in New York City in the 1970s.

CLEM BURKE—*BLONDIE, RAMONES, IGGY POP, JOAN JETT*

CLEM: The economics of New York in the 1970s meant it was a very inexpensive city to live in. My first apartment in the West Village was only $120 a month, and the loft we had in the Bowery where Blondie rehearsed wasn't much money, either. So, it really wasn't that difficult to come up with the money to sustain any kind of existence. Our points of reference were distinctly underground, too, with bands like The Velvet Underground and the New York Dolls. Those bands never really had any commercial success while they were around—although they were always gods to me, and to see them on the street and in the flesh was unbelievable. So it was a very small group of people that were generating this artistic revolution.

As far as what was going on a bit later at CBGB, you had Television, Patti Smith, the Ramones, Talking Heads, and Johnny Thunders and the Heartbreakers, and we were really feeding off all of that. I think Debbie [Harry] still has the handwritten lyrics for "Venus" by Tom Verlaine somewhere. All of that was impacting pop culture at that time, and things were building in that way. Then across the city, you had disco and dance music kicking off, and that was just as subversive, if not even more so, than punk rock. That stuff was taking place in underground gay clubs—talk about a truly alternative lifestyle. And you had the whole hip-hop scene going on in the South Bronx. Chris [Stein] went down there one night and befriended some people, one of whom was the artist Jean-Michel Basquiat, and he and Debbie [Harry] went to go see a rap battle, which we obviously reference in the song "Rapture."

MATT: I saw a documentary recently where RZA from the Wu-Tang Clan said that song was his introduction to hip-hop.

CLEM: I know. How cool is that? All these black kids watching MTV, and the first rap song that they heard was by Blondie. That's pretty phenomenal.

CJ RAMONE—*RAMONES, SOLO ARTIST*

CJ: One thing I've always loved about the New York scene is the art and music scenes are mutually supportive. If you look at photos from the early days of who was there watching the Ramones and Blondie, or Television and the Talking Heads, you'll see some of the greatest artists to ever come out of New York, just sitting right there in the audience. It was almost as if they all recognized that they were mutually giving birth to something that was going to be historic.

I think the creative influence and the back-and-forth from those two scenes really created something unique, and I'm really lucky that I was able to at least catch the tail end of all that. It made for a lot of great memories, and to become part of one of the bands responsible for kicking it all off was just the icing on the cake.

TOMMY VICTOR—*PRONG, DANZIG, MINISTRY*

TOMMY: Hanging out and eventually working at CBGB was a big deal for me.

MATT: How did you get the gig as their sound engineer?

TOMMY: I was going to the Institute of Audio Research. I wasn't even in a band at that point—I'd sort of given up on that. I had an older brother who told me, "If you're in a band and you're not successful by the time you're twenty, then forget it." So I enrolled in an audio engineering program, and that required me to have an internship somewhere. Inevitably, I already knew everyone that worked at CBGB, and it turned out they had an opening. It wasn't even an internship: I went right to work. And without much knowledge of what I was doing, I was suddenly behind the board during the audition nights. Then I moved up to the hardcore matinee shows on Sundays.

MATT: I bet you saw some crazy shit at those shows.

TOMMY: Oh, yeah. Those shows were intense. There were a lot of crappy bands around, but there were some good ones, too. And the kids were just going crazy back then. It was a vibrant scene: it was new and something different. This was all before grunge. Hardcore was the deal back then. That was what was happening. I actually used to make off-the-board tapes, but being the honest person that I am, I never made copies of them. If I did, I'd have an unbelievable collection of bootleg shows that I could've made an absolute fortune off.

MATT: Can you imagine? Those early Beastie Boys shows, for starters.

TOMMY: It's funny you should say that: one of the first bands that I was in was a band called the Radiant Boys, and we played Tompkins Square Park with the Beastie Boys in 1982. They were still a hardcore band back then. They were always really smart. Rick [Rubin] was really smart, too. I remember I used to walk by NYU [New York University], and he used to keep his dorm window open—somewhere around West Fourth Street or University Place. He'd just be hanging out of his bedroom window DJing rap music and early techno.

MATT: Was he always a key player in the New York music scene?

TOMMY: I would say so. He was a great tastemaker and he knew his records. There's a lot of guys like that who are still around now, like Mike Gitter, who's an A&R guy at Century Media. If you really want to learn a lot about records and hardcore, he's the guy to talk to. He knows everything and can just make a tree in his mind of where everything came from.

EUGENE HUTZ—*GOGOL BORDELLO*

MATT: Talk to me about Jesse Malin. I've seen him wear Gogol Bordello T-shirts on many occasions, and I know you two both live in New York. Are you guys friends?

EUGENE: Jesse is like a guardian angel of rapidly extinguishing New York rock 'n' roll and street culture. All the small institutions that he's part of are all committed to giving gigs to the fathers of No Wave, like James Chance and Suicide—and honorary members of that cohort. It's a very important post to hold, and Jesse's doing it with all the knowledge and the passion for it, being such a longstanding member of its community. He's been playing in punk bands in New York since the early 1980s.

MATT: Didn't he play his first gig at CBGB when he was twelve years old?

EUGENE: With the band Heart Attack, that's right.

MATT: How did you two meet?

EUGENE: I don't remember the exact night that we met, but it was probably at Niagara, the bar that Jesse owns. I used to live two blocks down from there when I first moved to New York in 1998–99. It was probably the same night that Joe Strummer & The Mescaleros played Irving Plaza because the afterparty for that show was at Niagara.

I had an address book back in those days, and everybody that I met was written in the book in chronological order. This was before the digits kicked in—or at least I didn't have them back then. And Jesse's number is somewhere in those early years, in the mix with a lot of amazing names who all suddenly became part of my telephone book. It was like being transferred from my bookshelf into living inside one of the books. I'm really glad that I caught the last call of that New York City party, too. I got to go to parties with all the great creators from that time, from Jim Jarmusch to all the great bands that were around then.

MATT: Do you feel like that party's over for New York in a way?

EUGENE: I think the party is pretty much over, yeah. I think it's transforming into something else now. But as a workshop, it's still there. And New York was always primarily a workshop for me. It's a place where suddenly I didn't feel like the farthest fucking outcast possible. I was still an anomaly in New York, but I was part of a jury of anomalies and that was fine by me. I was just like, "Hey, it's New York City, and we're an anomaly from abroad. Let's be friends. This is our kind of rock 'n' roll. It's not so different from your rock 'n' roll. It's just slightly more loose and gnarly." That eventually became a scene of its own, which all these other people ended up coming to, and it became a big alternative family where people came to find warmth and let their souls breathe.

VINNIE CARUANA—*THE MOVIELIFE, I AM THE AVALANCHE, SOLO ARTIST*

MATT: Tell me about growing up on Long Island. What was in the water back then? Because so many bands came out of there in such a short space of time. It seemed like a proper scene was going on.

VINNIE: It was a proper scene. My first taste of it was when I was around twelve years old. I had two older brothers, and one of them was in this kind of flourishing band, so that's how I got started: going to see my brother's band. Those were the only shows I was allowed to go to at that age because my mom knew my brothers would be there to make sure I was taken care of.

There was a group of bands playing around Long Island at that time, which I suppose would've been 1991–92, that a lot of people don't know about because they didn't get out of Long Island as much as they could have. There was a band called Mind Over Matter that was really important to us. They were a really ahead of their time, progressive hardcore band. There was also Vision of Disorder, who are a band that people might know, and they were from my town, too. They were some of my older brother's best friends. Silent Majority were a band that had a huge influence on the scene, too. And you'd have the future members of the next wave of bands in the crowd for all these gigs.

MATT: Who are we talking? People like Daryl from Glassjaw and Adam from Taking Back Sunday?

VINNIE: Yeah. That's how me and Daryl [Palumbo] became friends: I saw him at a few shows, and we were the only twelve-year-old's there. But we didn't meet each other for the first few gigs because we were both awkward kids, and neither of us had the courage to go up to the other one and say, "Hey. What's up? Let's be friends." Then one day, I was fishing at these docks and Daryl pulled up with his uncle. I was wearing an Anthrax shirt, and he said, "You like Anthrax?" I was like, "Yeah. I like *Persistence of Time*. But I don't really listen to anything else by them," because that was the one Anthrax record that my brother had. I said, "You go to shows, right? I think I've seen you." And he said, "Yeah." From that moment on, Daryl and I went to a lot of shows together.

MATT: So you knew Daryl way before he started Glassjaw?

VINNIE: Yeah, and it was really cool watching Glassjaw grow. The first time I saw them, they weren't called Glassjaw, they were called Minority Overall. Daryl was singing and Justin [Beck] was playing drums. Then I watched that band grow from the basements to a worldwide, beloved group.

MATT: Was it obvious even early on that they were going places? Did they always have that special thing about them?

VINNIE: Yeah. A lot of people would go and see them on Long Island, and it really caught fire. One month there was a hundred people at their shows, then maybe a few months later there was five hundred people. Then they put out the *Kiss Kiss Bang Bang* EP and started getting even more steam. Suddenly, we were like, "Who are all these people singing along to our friends?" Then Ross Robinson came down and signed them, which was crazy.

I remember them saying, "We're doing all these demos," and all of our friends were like, "These songs are crazy." They were the songs that ended up being their first full-length record [*Everything You Ever Wanted to Know About Silence*]. We all knew they were special, and once we started hearing those demos, we knew it was more than just a Long Island thing.

MATT: It sounds like a special time.

VINNIE: It was a really exciting time to see our friends really doing it, and really stepping it up to a crazy level. The leap from *Kiss Kiss Bang Bang to Everything You Ever Wanted to Know About Silence* was incredible. I think even Roadrunner [Records] and Ross Robinson didn't quite realize how killer that record was going to be.

TIM McILRATH—*RISE AGAINST*

TIM: I started getting into music in the late 1980s and early 1990s. Hair metal was starting to give way to grunge at that time, and I was starting to get into punk rock around the exact same time through my friends' older brothers. I remember going to camp one summer in seventh grade, and I'd already heard of the band Pegboy out of Chicago at that point. We were talking about them, and this kid was like, "Oh, well then you need to hear this, this, and this." And he made me one of those mixtapes that we all got when we were kids—Minor Threat, Screeching Weasel, Fugazi, Subhumans, and Social Distortion were all on it. And he didn't label the tracks, so I had to try and figure out who they all were by myself.

MATT: That was half the fun of mixtapes back in the day: the joy of discovery. Even when you knew the band's name, there was very little you could do with that information, as there was no internet back then. You just had to go out and buy the records.

TIM: Absolutely. With a band like Jawbreaker, I still have a hard time telling you which of their songs are on what albums because I just listened to them straight off blank tapes. I remember I went into a record store once, and I stole the lyrics—not the record, just the lyrics. I was like, "I need to know what he's saying."

MATT: Were there any bands from Chicago that you were really into?

TIM: As far as local bands go, there weren't a lot of big bands that came out of Chicago around that time, but there were a lot of little bands that were really important to me: bands like Cap'n Jazz, Screeching Weasel, Naked Raygun, Pegboy, and Los Crudos.

MATT: Were you a Smashing Pumpkins fan at all?

TIM: I didn't get into the Pumpkins. At that point in my life, I was very much punker than thou, and if it was on the radio then I wasn't listening to it. That was very much the scene back then: "Dude, that's commercial radio. You can't listen to that. You have to listen to underground bands instead." But at the same time, I was like, "Soundgarden are really good. And Rage Against the Machine are really good." Helmet were awesome, too. And Tool were making great records back then. When all those songs came out, I was definitely playing them, even if all my friends were like, "No, we only listen to this." I've always been a sucker for great melodies.

TROY VAN LEEUWEN—*QUEENS OF THE STONE AGE, A PERFECT CIRCLE, FAILURE*

TROY: I saw Nirvana right before *Nevermind* came out. I think it was at The Roxy. They were playing new stuff and "[Smells Like] Teen Spirit" wasn't even out yet, but they played it and people were going nuts for this song that they'd never even heard. He [Kurt Cobain] was like, "That was so weird. You guys just reacted like you knew this song already, but it's brand new." There was no way that song wasn't going to take them into the stratosphere.

MATT: Who else did you see around that time?

TROY: There was a movement in Los Angeles that spawned bands like Red Hot Chili Peppers and Jane's Addiction, whom I saw a bunch of times. Those early Jane's shows were dangerous, man. Their first two records [*Nothing's Shocking and Rio de lo habitual*] with Eric Avery were staples. They were really representative of LA at that time.

MATT: How did the LA scene respond to the Seattle bands like Nirvana, Soundgarden, and Alice in Chains?

TROY: They changed everything. They gave the LA scene the kick that it needed, and I was glad to be there to see that go down.

MATT: Did you catch any early Guns N' Roses shows?

TROY: I did. They were dangerous, too. They were on fire. I remember seeing them and thinking right away, "Something's going to happen here."

MATT: What about Tool? What was your first impression of them?

TROY: I was always impressed. I loved them. I thought he [Maynard James Keenan] was dynamic and incredible in every way. I just remember watching him and thinking, "Whatever's going on inside that head is gnarly."

JOE CARDAMONE—*THE ICARUS LINE, SOLO ARTIST, PRODUCER*

JOE: My dad made *Star Licks* videos, which were like musical training videos with famous people, and he did one with Flea from Red Hot Chili Peppers.

MATT: What kind of time period are we talking?

JOE: Somewhere around the *Mother's Milk* era. So I'm sitting there all day watching Flea play bass, and I wasn't even a huge fan or whatever, but I was like, "Wow, this is crazy." He had a buddy with him the whole day, too. And his buddy is in some of the scenes with him in this video where he shows you how to play songs.

Since me and his friend were the only ones there that didn't really have anything to do, we ended up in the green room together just hanging out—me, this little kid, and this older dude. He asked me, "Have you ever heard of Black Flag?" Then he started turning me on to all these bands. I was a sponge—just like you are when you're a kid—just taking it all in. Then a week later, the guy dies, and it turns out it was River Phoenix. I didn't realize it at the time because I was just a kid who only knew him from *Stand By Me*, and he was an adult by this point, but then I saw it on the news and I made the connection. And that made me want to investigate the music that he was talking about even more.

So, River Phoenix is the first person that told me about punk. Weird, right? And I didn't spend my life around famous people growing up; that was just some chance occurrence. From there, I started asking my dad about punk and he rented *The Decline of Western Civilization* for me, which was my whole introduction to the LA punk bands. But that's where it all started: in a green room with River Phoenix.

JESSE LEACH—*KILLSWITCH ENGAGE, TIMES OF GRACE, THE WEAPON*

JESSE: GBH was one of the first bands I remember hearing and thinking, "That's what punk should sound like." The chainsaw guitars and that voice with the accent; it was so different to the Ramones and the Dead Boys, and bands that I knew prior to that. UK punk was one of the things, outside of American hardcore, that really drew me in. And with that came the style and the Mohawks—I started wearing a Mohawk when I was young because of UK punk and that whole look.

As I got older, I fell in love with reggae music through bands like The Clash, and on the American side it was the Bad Brains. From there, I got into roots reggae, and then I discovered Steel Pulse, who were a British reggae band. And from the British reggae scene came my love of skinhead culture. But I didn't know it was called skinhead until later on. Growing up in America with the American media, I always thought skinhead was this neo-Nazi racist movement; I never put two and two together and realized that skinhead actually meant British working class people who fell in love with reggae and ska. And as the skinhead movement grew into punk and Oi! and New York hardcore bands like the Cro-Mags and Agnostic Front embraced it, I realized it was a huge part of my DNA.

CHUCK RAGAN—*HOT WATER MUSIC, SOLO ARTIST*

CHUCK: There was a book that used to circulate called *Book Your Own Fucking Life*, which was basically the internet before the internet. It was almost like a phone book of all the venues, promoters, crash pads, restaurants, and safe places for punks. We used to just go through that book and go, "Okay, we need a show in Atlanta." Sometimes it would take about twelve phone calls because not everybody had answering machines back then, and sometimes whoever you'd be calling happened to be on tour for eight weeks themselves.

On some of those first tours that we did, maybe 60 percent of the shows would actually happen. For the other 40 percent, you'd show up and there'd be no one there—the place would be closed. I remember one time, we showed up in Hot Springs, Arkansas and the show was canceled. We were sitting there in the van on the side of the road, eating our peanut butter sandwiches, and this little kid comes skating by. He sees our boards, and he's like, "Hey, man. Are you guys in a band?" He couldn't have been older than seven or eight years old. We were like, "Yeah, but the show's been canceled." He goes, "There's a place down here that my buddy is at. You guys should play there." He was just this tiny kid, and he was like, "I'll go check it out." So he skates across the street, then he comes back and says, "They said you can play there tonight." We were like, "Really? All right." This kid—his name was Bear—then goes back and draws up this flyer, prints a bunch of them out, then skates all around town handing out flyers to promote the show.

MATT: He saved the day.

CHUCK: He saved the day. And we got to play Hot Springs, Arkansas. That's a great memory. It's great to look back on moments like that. There were many times like that, where you'd just meet somebody on the street, and just by the way they looked or the way they carried themselves, you'd realize they were somewhere within the realm of where you were coming from. So you'd end up talking to them, and maybe you'd find a place to stay, or at least end up at a house party somewhere where you could get a bite to eat and a beer.

LAURA JANE GRACE—*AGAINST ME!, SOLO ARTIST, AUTHOR*

MATT: Tell me about your first major run in with the law.

LAURA: I was fourteen years old, and this was maybe two years into me discovering punk rock. At first, I was really into the nihilism of punk rock: the whole live-fast-die-young thing. I wanted to be Sid Vicious. And I really didn't see a future; I didn't think I'd ever escape south Florida; I just thought I'd be dead by the time I was in my early twenties.

I'd already been arrested a month or two prior to this incident for having marijuana seeds and stems in my wallet. And that was on school grounds, which meant it was a felony automatically. So I already had that charge against me.

It was Fourth of July weekend in Naples, Florida. And on the Fourth of July they do the firework celebration at the beach. I was going down there to meet some friends, and I walked up onto the boardwalk and was looking to see if I could spot any of them. There were two police officers there. One cop was like, "Hey, get off the boardwalk!" So I turned around and walked to the end of the boardwalk, back toward the street. The cop comes up to me again, and he's like, "Get off the boardwalk." I said, "I'm off the boardwalk." And I immediately started to argue the point because I was off the boardwalk.

He grabbed me, dragged me over to the cop car, slammed me down on the hood and kicked my legs apart. It's July in Florida, so the sun's been baking on the car all day and it's boiling hot. I tried to push myself up off the car and the cop just slammed my head back down on the hood. I got lippy at that point and started saying whatever, so they handcuffed me and threw me in the back of the car. I spat on the cop at one point as he was yelling at me through the window, and then they took me out of the car and grabbed me by my inner elbows so all the pressure was on my wrists, which were handcuffed behind my back.

More cops had shown up at this point, and they threw me face down onto the pavement, hog tied me, tied my ankles to my wrists, and started carrying me around like a fucking suitcase. Then they threw me back in the car, took me down to jail, and charged me with resisting arrest and violence and battery on an officer, which were both felony charges. And they charged me as an adult.

Now, I was in the wrong when I got arrested for the weed. It was a dumb mistake, but legitimately I had seeds and stems, and I was on school grounds and I got caught. But this to me was different because I hadn't done anything wrong: I was off the boardwalk and I'd complied with the officer. It was blatant harassment, and I could tell that I was being targeted just because of the way that I looked, because I was a young punk kid with spiky hair and a safety pin through my ear. It was an eye-opening experience that really politicized me, and punk rock became more about the politics and social justice issues after that.

JUSTIN SANE—ANTI-FLAG

JUSTIN: I grew up in a scene that was violent, and I think a big part of the violence was that a lot of the people in the scene were just unstable. Punk is so much more mainstream now and you attract a lot more mainstream people, but when we started playing punk it was really fucking underground.

MATT: And if you had tattoos or blue hair back then, you were a fucking outlaw.

JUSTIN: Oh, a total outlaw. Nowadays, your grandma gets a tattoo. But back in the day, you only got a tattoo if you were a criminal.

MATT: A criminal, a sailor, or a punk.

JUSTIN: Exactly. There were only a couple of guys in our scene that had tattoos, and they were super hardcore.

MATT: Do you have any tattoos?

JUSTIN: Not at all. I never had that much interest in them. Back in the day, if I could save up enough money to get a new guitar—which I really cared about and really wanted—or a couple of tattoos, it was a no-brainer for me.

But I think back in the day, the people who were attracted to the scene—myself included—were so on the fringes, and such misfits, that it just attracted people who might be a little on the edge. And it could be violent in that way, too. Thankfully, what happened in our scene—and what we got really lucky with—was there ended up being a core of people who decided that we wanted it to reflect an ideal that we had, and we wanted it to be a scene that was nonviolent. We also wanted it to be a scene that was inclusive of all people, and one of the bands that had the biggest influence on me in that sense was Fugazi.

I probably saw some of Fugazi's first-ever shows, and they went on stage and just took over the venue. They set the tone: there was no slam dancing at Fugazi shows. In some ways, that was kind of a downer. It kind of felt like, "Okay, the punk police are here." But on the other hand, everybody got that they were trying to make it about more than just being reckless; they were trying to build a scene where people looked out for one another. We kind of took that into our scene, and we had this core group of people that wanted to create a scene that really helped lift each other up. We got really lucky because we came into a scene that wanted to be positive, and right around the time that was happening in our scene, it was happening in a lot of other scenes, too. People were just tired of all the horrible fights and riots at shows. There was a lot of really ugly shows in Pittsburgh when I was coming up.

JOEY CAPE—*LAGWAGON, ME FIRST & THE GIMME GIMMES, SOLO ARTIST*

JOEY: I used to see people get stabbed at shows. That happened a lot. There was a place called Fender's Ballroom in Long Beach, and that was the Venice scene with bands like Suicidal Tendencies. The shows there were so violent that I didn't want to go back. I'd just stand on the outside of the pit and watch—I only had the guts to go in there once. The Hollywood Palladium and the Olympic Auditorium were where a lot of the bigger punk shows took place, and those shows were really violent, too. It wasn't uncommon to be standing toward the back of the room and look out at a pit that was nearly the entire floor. They were the biggest pits you've ever seen. Then someone would come up the stairs toward you with blood pouring out of their stomach because they'd just been stabbed. I saw that happen so many times that I just started to go, "Look, another dude got stabbed." It was terrible. I saw a guy get shot at a show once, too.

AL BARR—DROPKICK MURPHYS, THE BRUISERS

AL: I can remember seeing Agnostic Front in 1984 at the YMCA. The McDonald's massacre had just happened, where this guy went into a McDonald's with a gym bag full of guns and started shooting everyone. I think he killed about twenty people. It was awful. And in terms of mass shootings in America, there'd only been the Texas Tower incident at this point, so it was a big deal. I'm walking up the steps of the YMCA to go to this show, and there's this kid sitting on the steps, and he's got a McDonald's uniform on. He's burnt holes in it with a cigar and put fake blood all over himself. I remember thinking to myself, "A little too soon, maybe?" But that was punk rock back then.

DOUG STANHOPE—COMEDIAN, AUTHOR, PODCAST HOST

MATT: I'm not sure if you saw or heard the news—or even if this is the kind of news that you'd be interested in—but I wanted to ask you about it because I know that Fat Mike is a loose friend of yours—

DOUG: I think all of my friends are loose.

MATT: I would hope so.

DOUG: After twenty-eight years of doing this, I have a lot of friends everywhere I go.

MATT: I listened to the podcast that you guys did together, and it was great. NOFX are one of my favorite bands. And I love Mike; I think you two are cut from the same cloth—

DOUG: I think I know where you're going with this.

MATT: He obviously got into some trouble in Las Vegas recently. NOFX were playing a show out there, and he said some stuff about the Las Vegas shooting—something to the effect of, "Hey, at least they were country fans and not punk rock fans that got shot." Off the back of that, the band have been removed from various festival bills, and they got dropped by the beer sponsor that they were doing their own festival with. I wanted to get your thoughts on all of that, as someone who's obviously an outspoken comedian.

DOUG: NOFX is a whole different league, though. They weren't making any money from that sponsor—they just put out some kind of NOFX brand of beer as a novelty. But it's punk rock. So what if they lose a sponsor? That's like if my podcast loses fucking Shari's Berries or some nonsense that we pitch. It's not the same as a Rosanne [Barr] losing her show.

MATT: True.

DOUG: And Mike loves it. I hadn't even heard about it until he texted me. And he was laughing about it. By the way, I might have to get up and shit several times during the course of this interview.

CHUCK ROBERTSON—*MAD CADDIES*

CHUCK: The only people who should have been offended by what [Fat] Mike said are people from Las Vegas who were affected by that tragedy. And my heart goes out to them. It was a fucked-up thing for them [NOFX] to say. But people make mistakes like that all the time. They're a comedic band whose humor is super dark—we know that. And they made a mistake, which happens all the time. But I found all the fake outrage far more offensive than anything they said.

[At this point, Todd Rosenberg, drummer from the Mad Caddies, steps out of the shower and into the dressing room, and joins the conversation.]

TODD: NOFX has been doing that kind of humor forever, and they've said way darker stuff than that.

CHUCK: Way worse.

TODD: It was just the perfect storm of the wrong time and the absolute worst thing you could say to that particular audience. And with everything else going on, people are very sensitive to anything gun-related right now. But the people who were making the biggest deal out of it probably aren't aware that NOFX have been doing that since the 1980s. It became way bigger than it ever needed to become. Anyway, see you guys later. Have fun.

MATT: Thanks for the strip show, Todd. I've lost my train of thought now... Oh, yeah. I was going to say that I found the response from the punk community very interesting, too. A lot of supposed NOFX fans were like, "Mike's a piece of shit for saying that. He's gone too far this time." But it's like Todd said: that's what NOFX do. It's what they've always done.

CHUCK: Right. Half the people said that, and the other half said, "Fuck no, dude. This is punk rock. This is what it is: it's about being able to make light of a fucking dark situation."

DANKO JONES—*SOLO ARTIST, AUTHOR, PODCAST HOST*

DANKO: Punk rock is a contrarian type of music. It attracts natural contrarians who are likely going to say things that piss people off.

JESSE MALIN—*HEART ATTACK, D GENERATION, SOLO ARTIST*

MATT: What do you make of what happened to The Dickies out on the Warped Tour? Do you think the controversy surrounding their onstage outburst was justified, or misplaced?

JESSE: I've known The Dickies since I was sixteen years old. Back in the day, D Generation toured with them a lot. And I'm a big fan. I think they're a super talented, incredibly underrated band. They're also a fun band, and it's a goof. Leonard [Graves Phillips] has a great sense of humor, and he's highly intelligent. He does a bit where he comes out and says, "We're The Dickies, and we love you so much, we'd like to go down on each and every one of you. But we're sorry, we just don't have the time." It's all just a shtick that he does.

I heard that he was setup; that someone had seen the show previously and was offended by something Leonard had said, and then came back to a different show with protest signs. The clip that you see, from what I understand—and having reached out to Leonard as a friend—was kind of a set up, and you only see him going off. And it is pretty intense. If you only see *that*, I get it. I don't want women being degraded with the C word either. But like Leonard says, "My mistake was that I said the wrong word. If I'd have said asshole, it wouldn't have been this whole sexist thing."

MATT: Do you think their style of comedy is perhaps out of step with the present-day Warped Tour demographic?

JESSE: It shouldn't be; it's complete comedy. The band are called The Dickies, and he has a puppet that's a penis with balls named Stewart. Their whole act has always been very funny, and very smart, and designed to be a little bit provocative and offensive—like Lenny Bruce, or the Sex Pistols. So I think he got a bad rap. He got upset and he overreacted. And maybe they are the wrong kind of band for Warped Tour nowadays. But the Warped Tour is supposed to be about punk rock, and I think they've broken a lot of great bands and people have had a lot of fun there over the years. And I like Kevin [Lyman] a lot. He probably booked The Dickies because he believes in the legacy of that band.

You have to remember that punk rock isn't just some neat thing that fits into a hole at some summer camp or theme park at Disneyland. People should know, if they're taking their kids to a punk show, that it isn't all going to be clean, emocore-type stuff. And maybe Leonard did fly off the handle a bit. But I've lived on many buses and been on many tours with that man, and he's an honorable, great guy. He's also very respectful of women, and he's very open-minded. He's not this sexist creep that they made him out to be.

MATT: What do you think the backlash against them says about the current state of punk rock in this age of political correctness?

JESSE: I look at the punk rock community as a place where we have to stick together; it's us against them; we're outside of society; we're people who've come together through our passion for music because we don't fit into the mainstream cookie-cutter culture. We've dug deeper and found obscure records that have changed our lives, and the message on those records is one of freedom, individuality, and expression. And sometimes there are jokes that are meant to shake people up and move them in a certain way. But I know that Leonard's point wasn't to degrade women or make anybody feel bad. I think if you go too far into all that stuff, you're going to have censorship like they tried to do with the PMRC [Parents Music Resource Center] in the 1980s. They came after Jello Biafra from the Dead Kennedys for putting a H. R. Giger poster on the original cover of the *Frankenchrist* album. Frank Zappa—God rest his soul—spoke out a lot about that stuff.

I get that at a certain age, maybe a kid isn't ready to hear really graphic, crazy stuff—there comes a time when you grow into that. But if you're going to a punk rock show, you have to be prepared to hear some offensive words. And words really shouldn't be able to hurt people like that. They're just words. It all depends on how they're used, I guess. But you have to be able to have a sense of humor about it; you have to be able to laugh at it and spit it back.

MATT: You're right. I think we have to be careful that censorship doesn't go too far. Otherwise, where does it end?

JESSE: Right. I got into anarchy and punk and peace in the mid-eighties, and I read so much about it that I started to judge everybody else. I became the hierarchy that I was fighting against. I'd tell my friends, "You have pornography in your house. How can you call yourself an anarchist? Throw it out!" I also had a friend that was in my anarchist collective come up to me one day and say, "Jesse, you know you love all those old rock bands from the seventies? Aerosmith and Led Zeppelin—all that stuff. Well, they're sexist. You've got to get rid of those records because they're degrading to women." So I sold all my Zeppelin and Aerosmith records on the street down at St. Mark's Place.

We went to get a vegetarian curry or whatever that night, and this same friend said to me, "Jesse, you've got to get rid of the Dead Boys. "I Need Lunch" is degrading toward women." So I sold that record, too. Then he said, "Iggy Pop is really not nice to women with the way that he sings about them either, Jesse." I was like, "No! Not the Iggy!" But I sold my Iggy records, too. Years later, I bought all these records back, of course, because you have to able to see through these things. Obviously, you don't want to support people that want bad for the world, but sometimes you just have to separate the art from the artist.

I love The Rolling Stones, and they've definitely walked the line more than anybody else. They love black people. And they love black music—they've embraced it more than anything. But some of the lyrics that they've had in their songs and gotten away with in the past, if they came out now then forget it—just read the words to "Brown Sugar" or "Sweet Black Angel." But it's important to remember that they're coming from a place of affection, and it was a different time back then. In "Walk on the Wild Side," Lou Reed sings, *And the colored girls go, doo do doo do doo do do doo..."* And the black people loved that song when it came out. They got it, and they knew he wasn't making fun of them. But if that song came out today, then people would be like, "What is that part there? Is this mocking black people?" So, things aren't always so cut and dry.

TIM McILRATH

MATT: What was the name of the first band you were in?

TIM: My first real band was a band called Baxter with Neil Hennessey, who now plays drums in The Lawrence Arms. He's still one of my best friends to this day. We mostly played in our basement, though. I was such a fan of the Chicago scene that I put all those bands on a pedestal. I was like, "Our thing is just this little kid thing that we do in our basement and no one will ever know about it. Then we go see live shows, and those are the real bands." I never considered Baxter a real band.

Eventually, we started playing shows, though. Then we recorded something and the demos got out, and we ended up being the staple local opener. There was a point in time where if a national punk band came through Chicago and played the Fireside Bowl, we were the opening band for a lot of those shows. We opened for bands like Snapcase, Avail, Hot Water Music, Good Riddance, and BoySetsFire. And what's cool is I've gone on to meet, tour, and become friends with a lot of those guys.

MATT: Do any of them remember Baxter?

TIM: You know what? Chuck Ragan did. And I knew Chuck for years before I even mentioned it to him. But we were at a party once, and I was like, "I never told you this before, but my high school band opened for Hot Water Music at the Fireside Bowl. I'm sure you guys were probably playing every single night back then, and you don't remember who all the local openers were, but I just thought that was a cool full-circle moment." Chuck was like, "Wait, what was the band called?" I said, "Baxter." He said, "You had a 7-inch, right?" I was like, "Chuck, you don't need to humor me here. I know you don't remember." He said, "I do. You had a manila 7-inch with a red stripe on it," and he described the thing to a T. He was like, "I saw you guys, I loved you guys, and I bought your 7-inch."

MATT: He even bought your record? How cool is that?

TIM: I know. He even said he'd downsized his collection of 7-inches over the years—because he had too many—but that the Baxter one always made the cut. I was almost in tears.

CHUCK RAGAN

CHUCK: I found skateboarding at a young age, and all the music that came along with it. Back then—and we're talking late 1980s here—it was just a big melting pot of Beastie Boys, Bad Brains, Megadeth, Metallica, and Minor Threat. It all registered with me. And it all made sense. That was really what pulled me into wanting to play music.

I realized that there was expression in the rebellion. I found unity in it: I found like-minded people that felt the same way.

I feel lucky to have met people who showed me—and taught me—that being in a band and playing this music means so much more than just making money or meeting girls—or whatever other reasons people I was around up until that point had been in bands for. These people taught me that music is about therapy. All of a sudden, everything turned to where my mind wasn't just set on rebellion: it was set on becoming a better person.

I'll be the first person to admit that I've made a boatload of mistakes throughout my life. But I look back on it all and I don't have any regrets whatsoever. I feel a lot of joy for where I'm at right now. I have a beautiful wife and a wonderful son. I love my life. I love my friends. And I love the music and the community that I'm a part of. When I found that making music could be a way to overcome my own battles, and my own obstacles, it opened up a whole new world to me. And it changed my life forever. I feel very grateful to be part of a community that's caring and understanding, and believes in a better tomorrow, and is willing to sacrifice everything for it. I've always felt pretty damn lucky that I ended up here—and not somewhere else.

MATT CAUGHTHRAN—*THE BRONX, MARIACHI EL BRONX*

MATT C: Punk rock gave me self-worth, which is a big deal because that's what I was really struggling with growing up. I'm an old-soul type of person, and not having a purpose in life sends me to the graveyard. So getting that self-worth and purpose out of music was the greatest thing ever. I was never going to find it on my own. It was just something that had to happen. And listening to punk music was what led me to it. I've always subscribed to the idea of being your own person, too—work hard, do what you want to do, don't take any shit from people, just go for it. That's what punk rock means to me.

PUNK ROCK PLAYLIST

BLONDIE—"RAPTURE"

RAMONES—"JUDY IS A PUNK"

BEASTIE BOYS—"EGG RAID ON MOJO"

HEART ATTACK—"GOD IS DEAD"

GOGOL BORDELLO—"START WEARING PURPLE"

GLASSJAW—"PRETTY LUSH"

PEGBOY—"STRONG REACTION"

NIRVANA—"SMELLS LIKE TEEN SPIRIT"

BLACK FLAG—"RISE ABOVE"

GBH—"SICK BOY"

AGAINST ME!—"I WAS A TEENAGE ANARCHIST"

FUGAZI—"SONG 1"

AGNOSTIC FRONT—"GOTTA GO"

NOFX—"IT'S MY JOB TO KEEP PUNK ROCK ELITE"

THE DICKIES—"BANANA SPLITS"

DEAD KENNEDYS—"M.T.V. - GET OFF THE AIR"

RISE AGAINST—"SAVIOR"

CHUCK RAGAN—"SOMETHING MAY CATCH FIRE"

THE BRONX—"KNIFEMAN"

SUCCESS

"We were living the dream."

SUCCESS MEANS DIFFERENT THINGS to different people. If you're Gene Simmons, for instance, success means selling millions of records and making millions of dollars. If you don't do that, in the eyes of Gene Simmons, then you're not a success.

When I had Gene on *Life In The Stocks* in 2018, he said the Ramones weren't successful because they barely sold any albums and they couldn't sell out arenas. The Ramones. The band that single-handedly invented punk rock. Weren't successful. Okay, Gene.

But in many ways, he was right. The Ramones didn't enjoy anything the like level of success that their musical legacy warranted: their debut album only went gold in 2014, thirty-eight years after it was released, and it remains their only gold record to date. The band also never played arenas; they were slogging it out in the van, performing in clubs to small scale crowds, right up until the end. And it wasn't until long after the band broke up that people started sporting the Ramones logo on T-shirts all over the world. Plus, I doubt any of the original members reaped the rewards from those sales.

Yet, the Ramones changed music and culture forever. They're one of the most important rock 'n' roll bands of all time. So, what makes a band, or indeed an individual, a success?

What I've learned, from countless conversations with creative people from all walks of life, is if you get to do what you love for a living, and you enjoy some modicum of control over it, then you're a successful human being. If you live a rich, full, and happy life, while holding on to your independence and integrity, then you, my friend, have made it. Congratulations: you're a success. Unless you can't pay your rent. In that case, you're a failure—at least according to Gene Simmons.

But again, Gene does kind of have a point. You may think you're the most incredible artist in the world, but if you host an art exhibition and no one buys any of your paintings, can you really call yourself an artist? It might be time to get a real job if that is the case. Keep the painting as a hobby.

Ultimately, in the creative industries, it's the public who decide whether or not you prosper. If they dig what you do, they'll support you. If they don't, then they won't. It's as simple as that. But you don't need to make millions to be happy. I've actually found having low expectations helps; then you're just stoked with what you've got. Be grateful. Stay humble. Keep the faith. That's my advice.

In this chapter, you'll get a sneak peek into the inner workings of world-famous bands like Queens of the Stone Age and Tenacious D, learn why *Beavis and Butt-Head* were the tastemakers of the MTV era, hear how one musician went from being in jail to playing in his favorite band in the space of two months, and find out how getting your song in a Martin Scorsese movie can change the course of your entire career. And that's just for starters.

Hey! Ho! Let's go!

ROGER LIMA—*LESS THAN JAKE, REHASHER*

MATT: What's the secret to Less Than Jake's longevity?

ROGER: I think part of it is being completely honest with yourself early on in your career. I feel like a lot of bands wrote songs early in their career to go along with whatever was popular at the time, but we always just wrote songs that we really wanted to play. I know there's guys out there now playing songs that are paying their bills, but they don't necessarily love those songs because they wrote them at a different time in their life. We got lucky—to still love songs that you wrote twenty years ago is a huge plus. Whenever I play "Johnny Quest Thinks We're Sellouts" for the three thousandth time, I still feel that same energy as when we first wrote it back in 1995.

MATT: Less Than Jake were never a one-hit wonder, either. You've got lots of songs from different chapters of the band that different people like for different reasons.

ROGER: It was never like that for us. We never had the one massive radio song that catapulted us to the level of limousines and shit like that. That never really happened. We just consistently put out records and tried to write good songs. It never took a giant leap overnight: we don't have the one big Yellowcard song that's on the radio all the time. We've just got a solid bunch of songs that our fans really embrace. There's a real community with Less Than Jake's die-hard fans, too. They're awesome people: they're smart, they're supportive, and they're the kind of people I'm happy to call friends. It's a really cool feeling being able to look out into the crowd and see the face of someone that I know has been to like a hundred or even two hundred shows, and they're still out there supporting us after all these years. That's a really trippy feeling.

BRIAN FALLON—*THE GASLIGHT ANTHEM, THE HORRIBLE CROWES, SOLO ARTIST*

MATT: I heard that *Kerrang!* magazine put The Gaslight Anthem on the cover before ever writing anything about the band. Is that true?

BRIAN: Yeah, that happened for sure.

MATT: How did you wrangle that?

BRIAN: I don't know, man. I think they were just fans of the record, and were like, "We're going to put you on the cover." It had a bit to do with them, but I also think it had a lot to do with Emma Van Duyts, who was doing our press at the time. She was in it, and she knew how to do it, and she sold us as the Second Coming. She was good at it, man. So the combination of *Kerrang!*'s enthusiasm and Emma's enthusiasm is what did it. I had absolutely nothing to do with it, to tell you the truth. I didn't do anything; I didn't even know what a cover feature on *Kerrang!* meant at that time. They were like, "We're going to put you on the cover of this magazine in England." And I was like, "Cool." I didn't know what it meant at all.

MATT: Do you think, in hindsight, that the band was pushed a little too hard a little too soon? Did it almost feel like you couldn't live up to the hype of *The '59 Sound?*

BRIAN: Yeah. When you get pushed at such an early stage in your career, all of a sudden everyone turns the spotlight on you. Everyone was saying, "These guys are the new Bruce Springsteen." I was like, "I don't even know what we are yet." *The '59 Sound* was only our second record, and we were on this indie label from California [SideOneDummy]. We hadn't thought about our five-year plan. So it was a little tough. But it also propelled us into this whole new world of people that were checking us out, which was cool.

ANDREW W.K.—*SINGER-SONGWRITER, PRODUCER, WRITER, MOTIVATIONAL SPEAKER*

MATT: Did you ever think "Party Hard" would be such a huge hit? Because it became a real party anthem for an entire generation of people.

ANDREW: For some folks—if they have that feeling about it.

MATT: Did you at least know you had a good tune on your hands?

ANDREW: Well, enough to be motivated to record it and put it out. And I was adamant that it should be the first single off the record [*I Get Wet*]. There was a bit of debate with the record label about that, and they were still very encouraging, but they wanted to do whatever they felt was right.

MATT: What do you think it was that made Island Records want to sign you? There really hadn't been anything like you before—or since, for that matter.

ANDREW: The main A&R gentleman who signed me to the contract was a man named Lewis Largent. To be honest, I don't know what he saw. I don't know if there was a lot of common sense or rational thought in his decision making. Plenty of people thought he was crazy for signing me. Maybe he was.

FRANK IERO—*MY CHEMICAL ROMANCE, LEATHERMOUTH, SOLO ARTIST*

MATT: After *The Black Parade* came out, My Chemical Romance became such a huge, era-defining band. What was it like inside the eye of that storm?

FRANK: It's hard to fathom. When I think of the bands that have done that for my generation, to even be mentioned in the same way as that is kind of weird. It's a bit daunting, you know what I mean? And I think when *The Black Parade* did come out, we were so far inside the bubble that we didn't really understand the full scale of it. We knew that the band was popular, and that people were paying attention because there was a lot of craziness going on around us, but I don't think we really knew to what extent.

TROY VAN LEEUWEN—*QUEENS OF THE STONE AGE, A PERFECT CIRCLE, FAILURE*

TROY: A Perfect Circle kicked off in a way that I had no idea it would ever do. I knew that Maynard [James Keenan] was not only a savvy singer and lyricist, but also a savvy businessman, too. So I suppose the intention was always to have A Perfect Circle be its own thing. I doubt he ever wanted to treat it like a side project.

MATT: You get that sense with every project he's involved in.

TROY: Yeah, he's really immersed in everything that he does. And playing in that band was a great experience.

MATT: You got to tour with Nine Inch Nails at the peak of their powers, too.

TROY: That's right. *The Fragile* had just come out, and I was a huge fan of that record. That tour was really special.

MATT: How was working with David Fincher on the "Judith" music video?

TROY: It was exceptional—it really was. He'd put out *Seven*, *The Game*, and *Fight Club* in the [previous] few years, and I was such a huge fan of his work. I still am. People might not know this about that video, but it cost a lot of fucking money to make. It was a seven-day shoot. And I don't remember his name [Allen Daviau], but the DP [Director of Photography] on the video shot *E.T.*

MATT: Fucking hell.

TROY: Yeah. I remember he was shooting me stepping on a pedal, and the level of detail that went into lighting my shoe as it was hitting the pedal was so intense. There was one spot in particular where he wanted to get the right shine, and I think we did about seven or eight takes in the end. It was heavy detail. It was all shot on film, too. This was all before digital. He [Fincher] did all those treatments where you drag the film behind the car and scratch it up—all those effects are real. It was an incredible experience, and I really learned a lot from it.

MATT: How did you land the gig in Queens of the Stone Age?

TROY: Well, on the Perfect Circle tour in 2000–2001, we were listening to *Rated R* a lot. Of course, I already loved the first record [*Queens of the Stone Age*]. I'd heard the demos for that one before it even came out because the guy who did sound for Failure [Patrick Hutchinson] also did sound for Kyuss, and everywhere Josh [Homme] went, Hutch would follow. We had to share Hutch with Mark Lanegan and people like that. On one of the Failure tours, around 1996, there was a tape in the van that said "Joshua Homme Demo." "If Only," "Avon," and all those songs were on there. So Josh and I got to know each other in that setting. And the great thing about A Perfect Circle was it kind of got Tool back to work. They were like, "We can't just let Maynard be in that band." So *Lateralus* was spawned from that time, and in the middle of Maynard being on tour for *Lateralus*, I got the call to go out with my favorite band: Queens of the Stone Age. This was before the release of *Songs for the Deaf*, but I'd heard all about this record they'd been making, and I'd heard that [Dave] Grohl was playing drums on it, too.

MATT: I think *Songs for the Deaf* was one of the last, if not the last, genuinely dangerous, commercially successful rock 'n' roll record. They really captured the magic on that one.

TROY: I can say there's magic there, for sure. I heard the record and I knew it right away. I was like, "This is going be the one that takes this band to where it needs to be." I literally had one week to prepare—and I'd never even played lap steel before. I'd played a little bit of piano here and there, but that was about it. And they were like, "Here's forty songs, and three instruments. We start touring in a week." It was pretty gnarly.

MATT: Who was out on that tour with you? Josh Homme, Nick Oliveri, Dave Grohl, and Mark Lanegan?

TROY: Yeah.

MATT: Holy shit. That's an all-time super group right there.

TROY: It was. And I felt like the new kid. It was such an awesome force to be a part of; I couldn't believe it. It was so special.

KYLE GASS—*TENACIOUS D, THE KYLE GASS BAND, ACTOR, CO-MEDIAN*

MATT: What do you remember from the early Tenacious D shows around Hollywood?

KYLE: I remember celebrities would show up when we were far from being celebrities ourselves. David Schwimmer would show up to gigs. And we heard that Ben Stiller liked us. At one point, we were doing a Month of Sundays residency at The Viper Room, and before the third show Dave Grohl came and peeked his head through the curtain. He was like, "Hey, guys! I just came down to check out the show. Have a great gig." It was such an exciting time.

MATT: How did the record deal with Sony come about?

KYLE: There was conflict between me and Jack—which a lot of bands go through—in regard to whether we should sign with a major or an independent label. Jack was much more on the independent side. But even though I knew the major label was going to screw us—because that's how they operate—I also knew they could make us huge and get us around the world because back then that's how it worked. Whereas, I knew if we went with an indie, we might not get the same kind of exposure. Jack and I went back and forth a lot about that.

MATT: You must've enjoyed some decent meals around that time.

KYLE: Oh, the best part about all of it was the wooing process: we got wined and dined. We went to Jimmy Iovine's house one night. He was playing his latest TV show on this big screen. It was so loud—he'd obviously blown out his ears. Then all of a sudden, he takes a call from Axl Rose. I was like, "Are you seriously on the phone with Axl fucking Rose right now?" And John Lennon's piano was in his fucking bathroom or some shit. It was crazy shit, man. And that's just one example. Every major label at that time was courting us. We were given courtside seats to the Lakers and all kinds of shit. Eventually, an A&R guy called Matt Marshall just relentlessly pursued us, and we signed with Sony. Then we got some proper management with John Silva, who managed Foo Fighters and Beck, and all of a sudden the Dust Brothers were in the mix to produce. Getting Dave Grohl to drum on the record was huge as well.

TIM McILRATH—*RISE AGAINST*

MATT: I think almost every modern-day American punk band worth listening to has released at least one album on Fat Wreck Chords. How did Rise Against end up on that label?

TIM: Joe [Principe] played in a band called 88 Fingers Louie, and 88 were probably Chicago's biggest punk band at the time. They already had a 7-inch out on Fat Wreck Chords. So when Rise Against put a demo together, Joe naturally sent it to [Fat] Mike—and Epitaph, Hopeless Records, Victory Records, and Nitro.

MATT: All the classic labels back then.

TIM: The classics. And we thought hopefully one of them would call us back. Apparently, the story goes that Mike called up Joe and said, "I like it. But I don't love it. Maybe I'll do a 7-inch. But I'm not doing a full-length record." And we were like, "All right. That's still pretty awesome." Then Hopeless and Nitro were both on board and we were thinking about going with one of them. But we were taking our time to decide because we didn't even have a drummer at that point: we'd made the demo, but then our drummer quit the band. As we were getting closer to making a decision, Mike called back and was like, "Hey, wait. Have you signed to anybody yet? Don't sign to anybody. I've been listening to the demo more, and I like it. I've been trying to figure out who your singer sounds like, but I can't figure it out, and I like that I can't figure it out." Then he signed the band—before we'd even played a show, by the way.

MATT: How old were you at this point?

TIM: Twenty-two. When I first met Mike, he just looked at me, like, "Who is this kid?" He saw me in all my twenty-two years of naivete and asked, "Have you even toured before? Are you sure you're ready for this? Are you going to be able to handle it?" And I was like, "I didn't really think about it until you just asked." We didn't even have a name at this point; we didn't have a name, and we hadn't played a show.

MATT: Did Mike suggest any names for you?

TIM: Yeah, he had a notepad and he suggested some dreadful names.

MATT: Like what?

TIM: Like Chicago Tar. And Jimmy Crack Corn and the I Don't Cares. I was like, "Holy shit, dude. If we're Jimmy Crack Corn and the I Don't Cares, that makes me Jimmy Crack Corn."

MATT: I think you made the right move going with Rise Against. It's the perfect name for your band.

TIM: Yeah, in a lot of ways it was a great high bar to set. None of us can even remember who came up with the name, but we were like, "How is there not already a band called Rise Against? Shouldn't there already be a band called Rise Against?"

MATT: It's the same with Anti-Flag. How did nobody claim that name before them?

TIM: Exactly. We almost took the name for that reason alone. The band itself didn't have much of an identity yet; we were still kind of groping around in the dark. Rise Against became this bold statement of a name that we then had to live up to, which was cool. And I think we eventually grew into it.

MATT: Were you invited into the Fat Wreck Chords family? Did you go out on tour with a lot of those bands back in the day?

TIM: Absolutely, and that was huge for us. To be a part of the Fat family is something that can't be underestimated, and it's something that we don't take for granted—even to this day. That's why Pears are out on tour with us now: because fifteen years ago, Sick of It All, Strung Out, and Mad Caddies were taking us out. Doing stuff like that taught us how to be a band and play on different tours, and either be loved or be hated.

MATT: As a band, you've always kind of straddled the full musical spectrum, from pop-punk to emo to arena rock. That's evident in the bills that you put together, too. Not a lot of bands can pull that off.

TIM: I'm glad that you realized that because that's something we've always been very conscious of doing—trying to never totally pigeonhole ourselves into one genre, and recognizing that our band has a lot of different sides to our music. Even when we first started out, I was so grateful to be on Fat Wreck Chords, but I didn't want to be just another Fat band. It was always really important to me to be taken seriously as a band, and not just part of a label or roster. To this day, it's something that we're very conscious of—let's always have our feet in the ground of our roots and tour with bands like Pennywise, Rancid, and Bad Religion, but also keep pushing it forward with newer bands like Swimmers and Sleeping with Sirens. I'm glad that doesn't go unnoticed.

ROBB FLYNN—*MACHINE HEAD, PODCAST HOST*

MATT: Who was the first band to take Machine Head under their wing and show you the ropes when it came to touring?

ROBB: Slayer. *Burn My Eyes* had just come out and done nothing in America: it did like one thousand copies in its first week, which for a new band is pretty solid, but not that great. In the UK, though, it went crazy: it charted at number twenty-four. So they brought me on MTV over here, and I guess all the people up there liked me because they kept playing the "Davidian" video. That really took off over here, and in Europe in general, where they still had the *Headbangers Ball*. So it was kind of a no-brainer for Slayer to bring us out. They were going back out on tour for the first time in a while, and we were this hot new band. For me, though, it was like a dream come true. I'd seen Slayer live more than any other band leading up to that point. I used to drive from the Bay Area to LA and Sacramento to see them play. And I was still dealing drugs back then, so that shit was the jackpot: everyone wanted to buy speed at Slayer shows. I'd go there and make hella money. But they were always just a very important band to me.

MATT: What were the crowds like on that tour?

ROBB: This was back when support bands would famously get Slayered off the stage, and they really did get *Slayered* the fuck off the stage. There were a couple of times when that happened to us, but for the most part we held our own. It was like trial by fire, man. I remember walking out on stage in Chicago, Illinois, and every single person in the front row was flipping us off and shouting, "SLAYER!" I was like, "Holy shit! All right, let's do this." In a weird way, there was so much anger and so much intensity, if you could turn it around, somehow you could win them over. It was so fucking extreme.

MATT: And how were Slayer? As if I need to ask.

ROBB: Slayer were awesome. It was amazing to watch a show of that level right off the bat and see how they did it. I learned so much by looking at the light show, and the production, and how they ran their operation. I have to give Kerry King all the credit in the world for bro'ing down with us and taking care of us, too. They took us out in America afterward, and we did five months right off the bat with Slayer.

MATT: How was that?

ROBB: It was brutal, just because the Slayer crowds are super brutal. You either sink or you swim, and if you didn't cut it as a live band, you would get fucking mauled off the stage. But you learn from that how to perform and command a stage. I was probably a below-average front man at that point, and those tours forced me to learn how to communicate better with an audience.

MINA CAPUTO—*LIFE OF AGONY, SOLO ARTIST*

MATT: You were twenty when Life of Agony released *River Runs Red*, which was one of the first albums to put Roadrunner Records on the map. What do you remember from that time?

MINA: We were headlining festivals with 150,000 people showing up. It was insane. It's dwindled down to about eight thousand now, but it's a totally different ball game these days. Radio is formatted and contrived—just like everything else—and the music industry has changed radically. It's very difficult to make money now. Just yesterday, I heard the Pixies song "Where Is My Mind?" on a chocolate commercial. You know the music industry has gone to shit when the Pixies sold their rights to a fucking whack-ass commercial for chocolate. Everyone is getting hit hard. After Life of Agony's new album [*A Place Where There's No More Pain*] came out, it was streamed seventeen million times in the first three months—and that was in Europe alone. But no one's buying it. So what the fuck am I doing this for? For the sheer sake of creating, of course. But mommy needs to live. And if you're not Taylor Swift, Nicki Minaj, or Beyoncé, then you're quite limited.

MATT: The industry definitely isn't what it used to be, is it?

MINA: Absolutely not. And they axe motherfuckers like me. I'm a killer artist, with or without Life of Agony, but I feel like I'm very underrated. I'm so not on the radar, and I often wonder whether I even want to do this anymore.

MATT: Is that where you're at?

MINA: Kind of. I'm on the fence. Some days, I feel like I just can't live without it. Other days, I don't even want to leave my apartment: I just want to be the professional introvert that I am, read voraciously, and be left alone by the outside world. But then there's that part of me that also wants to rendezvous with all different kinds of people like yourself. So, there's heads and there's tails.

DOUG STANHOPE—*COMEDIAN, AUTHOR, PODCAST HOST*

MATT: Weren't you the first comedy act to sign to Roadrunner Records?

DOUG: I forgot that was Roadrunner. I just remember signing to some label that had all these hardcore bands on their roster. But I don't know any bands—I only know *of* them. People would ask me, "What's it like being on Roadrunner Records?" But those days are over. It's not like the 1970s—

MATT: Where you're on Atlantic Records with Led Zeppelin...

DOUG: Yeah. Who fucking looks at a label anymore? All those bands on Roadrunner might have hardcore fans, but I doubt they're going to see me and go, "Oh, look. There's a comic on Roadrunner. Let's listen to a comedy record now." It doesn't fucking work like that.

MATT: You didn't find yourself picking up any new fans from that deal, then?

DOUG: No.

MATT: What a waste of time.

DOUG: Well, they still paid me. So it worked out in that sense.

TOMMY VICTOR—*PRONG, DANZIG, MINISTRY*

MATT: How did Prong end up on Epic Records?

TOMMY: We were trying to get exposure by chasing shows around New York at larger venues like the Rock Hotel, as opposed to just bumming around at CBGB. And it only took one show: our first gig there with the Cro-Mags and Destruction. There was an A&R guy from Epic Records in the crowd that night, and he saw us and he liked us. He came backstage after the gig, and he said, "I want to sign you guys." It really was as simple as that. We did have two independent records out before that, though, so we were working hard and definitely doing all the right things in order to get into that situation. But nothing really changed for us during the first two Epic releases [*Beg to Differ* and *Prove You Wrong*]. We were just traveling around in a van, hitting shows, much like we're still doing now. And no one really cared too much. It wasn't until *Beavis and Butt-head* picked up on "Snap Your Fingers, Snap Your Neck" that anyone outside of our core audience cared about Prong. We were very lucky to have that song; if it wasn't for that song taking off in the way that it did, I definitely wouldn't have a career in music today.

MATT: *Beavis and Butt-head* were like the heavy metal tastemakers back then, weren't they?

TOMMY: Absolutely. If your video was on that show, it would help break your band.

MATT: Wasn't one of your songs used as the theme tune for *Headbangers Ball* as well?

TOMMY: Yeah, they used the riff from "Lost and Found" as the theme song. But it didn't really appear in the credits, so no one knew who it was.

MATT: I guess back then you couldn't just go online and look it up, either.

TOMMY: Exactly. So that didn't really help us all that much.

MATT: That 1994 arena tour with Pantera and Sepultura must've been huge exposure for you, though? What a legendary tour to be a part of as well.

TOMMY: It was monumental. Even to this day, whenever I go to the merch booth at shows across America, I get people coming up to me saying, "I saw you guys with Pantera and Sepultura back in the day." Back then, it was unheard of for hard bands to be playing huge arenas and hockey rinks. That was the first tour in that genre to start hitting like that. It was the new breed of big bands that were coming through, and it was a very exciting time. But with the advent of grunge, it didn't last long.

MATT: How so?

TOMMY: After grunge hit, the record labels had no interest in trying to market metal bands to the masses, so they either diluted or dropped the bands that they had, and focused instead on the Pearl Jams and the countless other copycat bands that were continually being pushed on the radio back then. But that's just the way it goes. I'm not bitter about that. Prong also managed to stay on Epic throughout those years, which we found quite alarming, to be honest—we couldn't believe it ourselves. I remember we were here in London when we finally got the call to say that we'd been dropped. I was like, "Thank God, it's finally over. I don't have to try and fit into this mold of a major label band anymore." Because that comes with a lot of pressure. Back in the day, there was a lot of stigma attached to signing with a major label, too. We lost a lot of fans back then. They called us sellouts and all the rest of it. And we were really affected by that. A larger British grindcore band—who I refuse to mention—severely snubbed us. And right after we got signed, we played at an early Rock Hard Festival [1992], and all the bands on the bill refused to speak to us. We had a lot of problems back then.

LAURA JANE GRACE—*AGAINST ME!, SOLO ARTIST, AUTHOR*

LAURA: I remember this one show in Brooklyn that we played, which was a free show—a free show, I might add—and there was an altercation outside over us being sellouts. I looked over and there was a punk kid who'd picked up a brick, and I had this moment of realization where I was like, "This kid will potentially bash my brains in with a brick because he doesn't like that we're putting out an album on Fat Wreck Chords. We haven't even put the record out yet, but he doesn't like it, and he might potentially kill us. So what the fuck does the punk scene really mean? What does anarchy really mean? Fuck this." I never looked back after that moment. I was done. After years of playing benefit shows and being part of an activist scene and movement, for it to all boil down to that went against everything that the punk scene had taught me: to think for yourself. And to see that kind of hypocrisy in the punk scene was really eye-opening. I saw it all for what it was.

TIM McILRATH

TIM: I grew up in the Chicago scene where I was a traitor the second we signed to Fat Wreck Chords.

MATT: Laura Jane Grace told me the same thing. She said the second Against Me! signed to Fat Wreck Chords, everyone called them sellouts.

TIM: Exactly that. Luckily, I don't judge people who judge me. And what I mean by that is that I was that kid: when Bad Religion went to a major label, I was like, "Fuck Bad Religion." But everyone is on their own journey, and I can't change that. If that's how you feel, then bless your heart. All I can do is take one step at a time to prove to you who I am, and what this band is going to do—because what we do is real and I stand by it. That's what we did with *Siren Song of the Counter Culture*. It came out on a major label, but it's still a Rise Against record.

We sat there and we bit our tongue whilst everyone said, "Major label? Fuck those guys!" Then we put out the record, and everyone was like, "Okay, they're still Rise Against." And there was never any external pressure to be anything other than Rise Against. We just looked at it like this: we're releasing a record on a major label, it probably won't be successful, and we'll probably get dropped, then we'll beg Fat Mike to take us back. That was basically our plan. So, we went with our budget to an all-star producer like Garth Richardson, and I don't think he knew quite what to do with us. He didn't really know what kind of a band we were, because we weren't part of the nu-metal stuff that he was doing, and we weren't a poppy rock band, either. I don't think he could quite put his finger on what Rise Against was.

MATT: The early 2000s was a weird time for music as well. Everything was changing, and a whole new batch of bands were coming through.

TIM: Yeah, bands like Thrice, Thursday, and Taking Back Sunday were kind of taking over the airwaves around that time—a lot of that post-emo, poster child stuff was happening. Bands like Alkaline Trio, My Chemical Romance, and Avenged Sevenfold were all getting really big as well. And they were our peers, and bands that we toured and played shows with. But it made sense to me that those bands would get big, they were charismatic bands with amazing front men. I always looked at Rise Against's success as unlikely. We didn't have that thing, or that look, or any of that stuff. But we made that record with Garth, and lo and behold people dug it.

MATT: Was *Siren Song of the Counter Culture* the album that launched your career?

TIM: Absolutely. And what's interesting about that album is it was our major label debut, but the two singles off that record—that for all intents and purposes launched Rise Against's career—were two previously released songs. "Give It All" had come out on a *Rock Against*

Bush [Vol. 1] compilation via Fat Wreck Chords almost a year prior, and "Swing Life Away," which was a very unlikely single, was written during *Revolutions per Minute* and recorded for a *Punk Goes Acoustic* compilation for a Fearless Records, which also came out like a year or two prior. Those were songs that were already out there in the ether. And they were good songs that we played live, and people dug them. But they didn't change our lives by any means. Then we rerecorded them and put them on *Siren Song of the Counter Culture*, and all of a sudden lots of people heard them, and that kind of launched Rise Against.

MATT: That just goes to show that if you sign to the *right* major label, you have the chance to get your music heard by a lot more people, and that can set you up for the rest of your career.

TIM: Trust me, as a kid who grew up listening to Steve Albini and Fugazi, even I found myself in a moment where I became a believer in the power of a major label. It was as clear as day to me: if you put the music in the hands of the right people, they will find your audience. We signed a five-record deal with Geffen, and we did all five records with them.

CLEM BURKE—*BLONDIE, RAMONES, IGGY POP, JOAN JETT*

CLEM: Everyone always used to say that we [Blondie] sold out with "Heart of Glass," like we knew it was going to be this huge success. But back in the day, bands used to put their most appealing songs on the first, second, or third track on Side A of the record. That was because the radio programmers would only listen to each song for about ten seconds, and if they didn't like it by the third track then they'd throw the record right out the window. Well, "Heart of Glass" was on Side B of the record [*Parallel Lines*]. It was track number ten. So how do you explain that? We were just experimenting with that song—inspired by Kraftwerk, who we loved.

I ended up doing the first Eurythmics album soon after that: a record called *In the Garden*, which we recorded in Germany with Conny Plank, who produced Kraftwerk. And the first thing Conny said to me was that he loved "Heart of Glass." He said he saw the whole connection with Kraftwerk, and I was like, "Finally, someone gets it," because most people were saying it was just some crappy disco song.

MATT: It was definitely out of step with the rest of the songs on *Parallel Lines*.

CLEM: Perhaps. But I think all four of our big singles in the States were real one-offs: "Heart of Glass," "Call Me," "Rapture," and "The Tide Is High." So I've got no idea what most people think of when they think about Blondie. Is it a woman? Is it a solo artist? Is it a pop band? Is it a punk band? Is it a disco band? I think we blur all those lines, and I think that's been a big part of our success.

MATT: I'd never thought about it like that, but now you come to mention it, Blondie is a hard band to define.

CLEM: Right. And the Ramones were great, but they really only had one sound. And punk rock was great, but it really only meant one thing at the end of the day. Of course, now it's more about an attitude and a lifestyle, but when we were coming up, it was really just a specific sound. And Blondie assimilated many different sounds. It's interesting: we're almost still a cult band in the States, even though we've had four Number One records.

ROGER LIMA

ROGER: For our album *Anthem*, we had Green Day's producer [Rob Cavallo] working with us, and we recorded it at the *Morning View* mansion where Incubus recorded their massive record. Getting to experience that level of a recording situation was crazy. We had a personal chef, man. We were living the dream. There was money to be spent and we were spending it. It was amazing. And the album did well, but I think the label [Warner] had greater expectations in terms of sales figures.

For *In with the Out Crowd*, we went back to another producer that we'd used before [Howard Benson]. But somewhere along the way, things got a little off track in regards to what a Less Than Jake record should sound like. And I don't think that derailed us off Warner Bros. Records, as such. But it definitely didn't help keep the *Anthem* momentum going, and it definitely slowed us down a little bit. After that, it just made sense to take back control and go back to doing things on our own. So, we put out the next album [*GNV FLA*] on our own label. There was literally no one involved in that one, aside from us and the producer [Matt Allison]. You really learn a lot making records.

MATT CAUGHTHRAN—*THE BRONX, MARIACHI EL BRONX*

MATT C: The recording of the second Bronx album [*The Bronx II*] was insane. It was a dream come true, and then it turned into a nightmare. But looking back on it, it was one of the greatest experiences of my life. If we were to go back and record it again, we definitely wouldn't do it in the same way. But I think the fact that it did happen that way shaped us in a lot of ways, and gave us so many different views on music and how to approach it from different creative standpoints.

MATT S: What do you remember about the making of that record?

MATT C: Well, it was the major label record, and Michael Beinhorn was producing it. He's done everyone: Soundgarden, Red Hot Chili Peppers, Social Distortion, Korn—all these bands that have sold millions and millions of albums. And we recorded it in this giant studio down on Venice Beach—right on the boardwalk—which we had for as long as we needed. We went from the outhouse to the penthouse in one record. And that was the thing that we weren't really sure about. But at the end of the day, we knew if we didn't do it then we'd kick ourselves in the ass later on.

MATT S: I think you have to go for it in those situations. You'd be crazy not to, right?

MATT C: You have to. So we did. And it took on this whole Brian Wilson/Dewey Cox–type mythology, and we were just this little punk band. But the learning process was amazing, and the cool thing about it was we fucking played those songs live in that room, over and over and over again, until we fucking got it right. That's what ruled about that record: it was us just fucking hammering that shit out.

Doing all the vocals was a fucking nightmare for me, though. Beinhorn is notoriously hard on singers, and we'd typically get around to vocals later in the evening, after all the music was done. We did the first song "Small Stone" in two or three takes, and Beinhorn was like, "Boom! We got it. That's good. Let's move on." And that was at the end of the night. Job done. When I came back in the next morning, he was like, "You know, I listened to it again, and we didn't get it." We proceeded to spend the next four months tracking vocals, and it got so bad that we couldn't even be in the same room together. Michael does the whole Marine Corps thing where he breaks you down and builds you back up, and whether or not that's completely necessary is beside the point—it's just what he does. So I was going through that whole process of his, and I was young back then, so I fell right into it. He absolutely smashed me. But I was able to come back from it, and I learned a lot of awesome stuff about myself and about my voice, and that was all because of him. When I listen back to that record, I'm super proud of what we achieved and what it took us to get there. I think my voice and all the instruments sound amazing, too. But making that record was not a lot of fun.

MATT S: Was that tradeoff worth it for the end result?

MATT C: I think so. I don't need my entire life to be fun, you know what I mean? And going through tough times is what shapes us as human beings. It doesn't always need to be cotton candy and all that shit. So, yeah, it was worth it. It was definitely worth it. And that's definitely the last time we'll ever get to do something like that. It was a trip, man. We grew up fast.

MATT S: What about the Mariachi El Bronx? That project must've opened a lot of doors for you guys?

MATT C: One hundred percent. The Bronx actually got signed to Island Def Jam at the same time as The Killers—they're great friends of ours. We literally had our signing dinners together, and we've maintained that friendship to this day. But The Killers aren't ever taking The Bronx out on tour; their fans would fucking shoot themselves. Once the first El Bronx record came out, though, The Killers were like, "Hell yeah. Let's go." We finally got to do [Jay] Leno and [David] Letterman and all that awesome stuff, too. It was a huge thing for us. And it helped out The Bronx *a lot.*

AL BARR—*DROPKICK MURPHYS, THE BRUISERS*

AL: *The Warrior's Code* recently went gold. We played a show out in LA where Brett Gurewitz and Tim Armstrong came down, and we had a ceremony where we got our gold records. It's mind-blowing to think that record sold five hundred thousand copies over the course of ten years. You have to understand this: a record comes out, it sells what it sells, and the ground zero of that then dies. It does what it does and then it's over. But I'm the Rain Man in the band; I'm the numbers guy. I watched that horse, and I told the rest of guys, "It's going to get there eventually." It kept doing four hundred copies a week—every week. Then the new record would come out, and obviously that would do better for a bit, but after a month *The Warrior's Code* would be selling as much if not more than the new record again.

Well, here we are ten years later, and it's now sold five hundred thousand copies. We've got a gold record, and a single that's almost double platinum.

MATT: After Martin Scorsese put "Shipping Up to Boston" in the soundtrack to *The Departed,* did that have a big impact on your album sales?

AL: For sure. We were rightly successful in the punk world by then, but we weren't on anybody else's radar. *The Departed* really blew the doors open. And "Shipping Up to Boston" almost wasn't even on *The Warrior's Code.* Can you believe that? We'd played it live a couple of times and it always went over like a fart in a spacesuit. Then I get this email from our manager: it says, "Martin Scorsese is making a movie about the Irish mafia in Boston, and he's thinking about using one of the songs from *The Warrior's Code*." I remember thinking, "That's amazing, but it will never happen." But it comes to fruition and we get a song in the movie.

At that point, "Kiss Me, I'm Shitfaced" was our most downloaded song. It'd done about ten thousand downloads. Then *The Departed* comes out, and that week I get a call from our manager. She goes, "Are you ready for this? 'Shipping' has just done 1,700 this week." The next week she calls again: "'Shipping' has just done 3,400 this week." I'm like, "What?" Then she calls again the next week: "'Shipping' has just done seventeen thousand." I couldn't believe it. "Seventeen thousand?" "Yeah, Al," she said. The following week she called to say, "'Shipping' has just done thirty-five thousand in this week *alone*. Do you realize you're going to have a gold record?"

We were all at Logan airport getting ready to fly to the UK, and we got a mass text to all our phones saying, "Gentlemen. Congratulations. You have a gold single." I looked at Kenny and went, "Holy shit! Wouldn't it be amazing if it goes platinum?" He goes, "Dude, it's amazing it even went gold. That's never going to happen." Well, check it out: that song is now almost double platinum, and it's been in all sorts of commercials and TV shows. It's even been in *The Simpsons*, which is mind-boggling to me. So it definitely brought us on the radar of a lot of new people.

B-REAL—CYPRESS HILL, PROPHETS OF RAGE

B-REAL: Joe Nicolo [Butcher Bros.] was the first person to see the potential in Cypress Hill. He knew Muggs via The 7A3 album [*Coolin' in Cali*], and he liked Muggs and Muggs's ideas. He thought he was on the path to becoming a great producer, and he was always interested in what Muggs was doing. So when he heard about this new band that Muggs was in called Cypress Hill, he wanted to hear it. The only one other person interested in us at that time was [Dave] Funkenklein—rest in peace. Funkenklein was a big hip-hop figure back in the day, and he was at a label called Hollywood Basic. He had his finger on the pulse. He was also a friend of Muggs and myself, and when he heard what we were doing, he wanted Cypress Hill for Hollywood Basic. But no one else wanted us—just Joe and Funkenklein. Everyone else took a hard pass on Cypress Hill.

MATT: Because you were so different to everything else out there?

B-REAL: Right. And my vocals were so different, too. It was raw and it was different, and they didn't understand all the weed shit, either. We got hard passes from a lot of labels. But those were the two [Ruffhouse Records and Hollywood Basic] that absolutely wanted us. There wasn't necessarily a bidding war because we didn't want to play our friends off against each other. And at first we were leaning to Funkenklein because we were closer to him than we were with Joe. We had a friendship with him and would see him almost every other week, so we hung out all the time. But Joe the Butcher was like, "I want this group. I have to have it."

I think Sen Dog was the ultimate decision maker on where we went in the end. He was like, "I'm done giving these guys [Hollywood Basic] demo after demo. We've given them six or seven demos already, and they can't even make a decision. Joe wants us. Let's go with Joe. And if we're not going with Joe, I'm going back to work." So it was decided: "I guess we're going with Joe then." Sen Dog being the elder in the group, we went where he wanted to go. And it ended up being a great decision. Joe saw our vision and just let us do our thing, and we had a lot of success with our sound, imagery, and live show—because they let us be who we wanted to be.

MATT: "Insane in the Brain" was obviously a huge crossover hit for you. Did you have a good time recording the *Black Sunday* album?

B-REAL: It was great. We got to go to New York and record at Baby Monster Studios, which was a dream of mine as an MC. The birthplace of hip-hop is New York, and if you're going to make a hip-hop album, why not go to the mecca and record there? Muggs rented an apartment in New York for the best part of two years, and the second year was when we started getting rumblings from Sony. They were saying, "We've got to get these guys back in the studio. There's a momentum building." That was due to "How I Could Just Kill a Man" catching heat.

MATT: Was that heat due to its inclusion on the *Juice* soundtrack?

B-REAL: It was two things. Firstly, the mix shows started flipping the record and playing the track, which was on our first double A-side alongside "The Phuncky Feel One," which was when it caught the attention of Chuck D and The Bomb Squad. They were doing the soundtrack to *Juice* at the time, and decided they had to have that song in the movie. We really didn't know how big that movie was going to be. So it was catching momentum on the mix shows. Then the movie came along and propelled the song in a way that we didn't foresee at all—because we knew how aggressive it was, and what the content was about. We thought there was no way that song would ever do anything on radio, or anywhere else for that matter. We just thought it was a great album song, and we definitely didn't see what was coming after that. But before we knew it, we were doing all kinds of shit.

The first record—which started in the charts at the bottom of the Top 200, and then fell off—suddenly popped back on, and for the whole year and a half that we were touring it kept rising up the charts. Slowly but surely, it kept elevating, and we had no idea what was going on. We were just doing the work. Then before we knew it, they pulled us off tour to start working on a follow-up. When we unleashed *Black Sunday*, everything just went crazy. We were in Europe doing our first shows here, and we started getting calls from back home saying, "The album comes out tomorrow, it's only just gone midnight, and there are people wrapped around the block waiting to get your damn record." We were getting that information from back home and we were blown away by it. By the time the album came out, it entered at

Number One on the chart, at which point our debut album [*Cypress Hill*] was also at Number Five. In the same week, our first album was at Number Five and our second album was at Number One. We were the first ever hip-hop group to do that.

MATT: That's wild.

B-REAL: And the decision to put "Kill a Man" in that pivotal scene in *Juice*, right before Tupac's character dies—rest in peace, Tupac [Shakur]—was what propelled the group in such a way that eyeballs and ears were now on us, and we were in demand. Then we followed that up with "Insane in the Brain," and those two songs put us on the map forever.

CJ RAMONE—*RAMONES, SOLO ARTIST*

CJ: I was in jail when I found out I got the gig in the Ramones. I'd auditioned to be in the band whilst I was still in the Marine Corps, and I'd called up to turn myself in because I was a deserter.

MATT: Are you basically on the run until they catch you if you don't turn yourself in?

CJ: Yeah. And they don't come looking for you, but if you get pulled over for anything else then they pick you up and send you straight to military jail—we call it a bench warrant.

On my third night in jail, the guard on duty came in and said, "Hey, Ward. You got a phone call." I thought it was going to be my mother and she was going to be crying her eyes out. I picked up the phone, and a voice said, "Chris, it's Johnny Ramone." I was like, "Johnny, I'm really sorry. I should've told you what was going on." It was a tough situation to be in: I wanted to say something to the guys, but I also wanted to see how far I'd get with the audition process. So Johnny's on the phone, and he asked me, "Well, what did they say?" I said, "I'm probably going to be here for two weeks to a month, and then they're going to discharge me." Johnny said, "All right, well, do your time, and when you come out you've got a job." I was stunned.

I'd always heard all these great stories about famous Black blues musicians from back in the day that were in and out of jail, and how unrecognized their talent went. And not to compare myself to them in any way, but it was really interesting: I went from being in jail to playing with the Ramones in a seven-week time period. I literally went from the lowest point in my life to the highest point in my life in less than two months.

MATT: Do you remember your first show with the Ramones?

CJ: Yeah, it was actually in the UK, on September 30, 1989—in Leicester, England.

MATT: How was it?

CJ: It was my introduction to what being in the Ramones was going to be like. It was really a trial by fire: I had five weeks to learn forty-five songs. And I had two days off between when I got out of jail and when we started rehearsing. So it was a huge change in lifestyle. Luckily, I was right out of the Marine Corps, and I was very mission orientated. So that's the mindset that I went into it with.

When the lights came on and we started playing, I started getting spat on immediately. I was getting pummeled with coins and shoes and bottles—just about anything you could imagine. But I totally understood and related to where those kids were coming from. When I heard that Dee Dee [Ramone] had quit the band, I turned to my friend who was driving at the time, and I said, "I'll never go to another Ramones show again. It ain't the Ramones without Dee Dee." But I knew if I just stood up there on stage and let them pummel me, and I didn't do something about it, it was only going to make it worse. So I went right out to the front of the stage and shouted, "Fuck you!" I really let them have it back, and I made all kinds of nasty comments about the Queen. That's what I went through night after night, city after city, every time I played somewhere for the first time with the Ramones.

The beautiful thing for the most part was this: at the beginning of the night, the crowds always chanted "Dee Dee," but by the end of the night, they mostly chanted "CJ." And I wasn't trying to take Dee Dee's place. I was just a fan who had made it into the band, and that gave me a whole different type of camaraderie with the fans, which Joey, Johnny, Dee Dee, Tommy, Marky, and even Richie never had.

After the shows were over, the first thing I did was go out and find local kids, and ask them to take me out to the pub where they went drinking. That's what I did everywhere I went. And I ended up making so many friends that even now, people come out to my shows and we go out for a couple of pints after the gig, just like we did when they were eighteen years old, and I was twenty-two. It was tough to get to that point, but when all's said and done, I hold a completely different space in the Ramones legacy to the rest of the guys in that band. And I'm not saying it's a better or more meaningful space. But I really do have my own spot in the Ramones legacy that I'm one hundred percent proud of.

TOM GREEN—*ACTOR, COMEDIAN, RAPPER, TALK SHOW HOST*

TOM: I feel like I have more control over my career now than I ever did before. I'm able to perform all around the world, I don't have a network that can cancel or take away what I'm doing, and I'm not living under this constant blanket of fear and control. Stand-up comedy is completely independent, and for that reason I feel more in control of my life now than I've ever felt before. I'm not actively out there chasing films anymore. I have a TV show in development, and that's something that's exciting to me, but it's not my main focus or goal. And I mainly want to get it on the air to help build my stand-up comedy—not the other way around. I look at it as a purely promotional mechanism for my stand-up: get a TV show, then more people will come see me do stand-up, which is my first love, and what I love to do the most.

When you do a TV show, and it doesn't matter how edgy the show is, every single moment of that show has been run through executives and writers—it's not just coming from the mind of one person. Stand-up gives me the total freedom to be able to get up on stage, say whatever I want, and talk about things that are completely absurd and ridiculous. And I don't have to run it past anyone for approval. In order to make a great TV show, which is a fun and amazing thing to do, the process is more about building a team of a hundred people who can work well together to execute this collective idea. But when you watch a stand-up comedian, you're watching what's coming out of their mind, and that's what I love about the art form: it's completely unfiltered.

Doing what I'm doing right now is sort of what I've always wanted to do. The reason I started making *The Tom Green Show* in the first place was because I didn't want to have a boss or go to work. That was the most disappointing thing when I ended up on MTV: we had executives there telling us what to do, and what not to do. And that was exactly what I was trying to avoid: authority in my life. With stand-up comedy, there's none of that. You're in business for yourself, and you're completely artistically free.

KYLE GASS

MATT: What's the story behind your role in *Almost Famous*?

KYLE: Cameron Crowe came and saw Tenacious D one night, and he enjoyed the show. It was just another one of those things that happens in Hollywood—if you're lucky. Everybody lives there, and if you do something good then you might get seen by somebody and given the opportunity to do something else.

MATT: When you get sent the script for a film like that, do you know it's going to be a classic right away?

KYLE: With that one, we weren't allowed to read the whole script. Cameron Crowe was really hot at that time, and when you're really hot—like a Tarantino—then you might get sent a couple of pages, or you'll receive a watermarked script and you'll have a guard watch over you as you read it. Cameron actually called me up about that role, though. There wasn't even an audition. I just came in and we sort of talked about it for a while, and we work-shopped the part together. It was such a special movie to be involved with. It was obviously his love letter to rock 'n' roll, and his formative years as a music reporter. So you knew you were in for something special. But what a disappointment it was when I was cut from the theatrical release. I actually found a preview screening of the film in Pasadena, and I went in to watch it. When it got to the scene that I was supposed to be in, I'd been cut out. But that's just Hollywood: it's an up and down industry.

MATT: What's your favorite film that you've worked on?

KYLE: *Elf,* without a doubt. Growing up, I had a fantasy about being in one of those Christmas films that's an annual thing, and as luck would have it somebody dropped out of the movie, so I flew up to Vancouver the next day. It was directed by Jon Favreau, who I'd worked with on *Freaks and Geeks*, and I stepped in for this other guy last minute. It was just the greatest experience. You could feel the magic on the set. Will [Ferrell] was hilarious as always, and I got to do a scene with Peter Dinklage before he blew up. He was a really nice guy. It was just a really fun movie to work on. I got to meet James Caan, too. He was a trip, just endlessly telling stories from the old days. Every story he told ended with him beating someone up. I'm old, and I've never been in a fight in my life, but every one of James Caan's stories had a fight in them. I'm amazed he's never been drawn up on assault charges. What a guy!

SUCCESS PLAYLIST

LESS THAN JAKE—"JOHNNY QUEST THINKS WE'RE SELLOUTS"

THE GASLIGHT ANTHEM—"THE '59 SOUND"

ANDREW W.K.—"PARTY HARD"

MY CHEMICAL ROMANCE—"WELCOME TO THE BLACK PARADE"

A PERFECT CIRCLE—"JUDITH"

QUEENS OF THE STONE AGE—"NO ONE KNOWS"

TENACIOUS D—"TRIBUTE"

MACHINE HEAD—"DAVIDIAN"

LIFE OF AGONY—"THROUGH AND THROUGH"

PRONG—"SNAP YOUR FINGERS, SNAP YOUR NECK"

AGAINST ME!—"PINTS OF GUINESS MAKE YOU STRONG"

RISE AGAINST—"GIVE IT ALL"

BLONDIE—"HEART OF GLASS"

THE BRONX—"WHITE GUILT"

DROPKICK MURPHYS—"I'M SHIPPING UP TO BOSTON"

CYPRESS HILL—"HOW I COULD JUST KILL A MAN"

RAMONES—"I DON'T WANNA GROW UP"

EMINEM—"THE REAL SLIM SHADY"

ELTON JOHN—"TINY DANCER"

BOOZE & DRUGS

"It's fun until it isn't fun."

THE FIRST TIME I GOT drunk I was ten. I was in Wales visiting my grandparents with my mum, my three-year-old sister, and my then-girlfriend Alana, who was also ten. That might sound strange to some people, going on holiday with your girlfriend when you're only ten years old, but I guess I was an early bloomer in more ways than one. It was also perfectly innocent: we slept in separate bedrooms, and it was a lovely, family-friendly holiday. Until I spoilt it by getting pissed.

It was 1996, and the alcopop Hooch had just come on the beverage market. I'm sure I don't need to explain to you what alcopops were/ are (are they still a thing?), but in case you don't know, they're alcoholic fizzy drinks. They were pretty controversial in the late nineties, as people were afraid—due to the sweet taste and cartoon packaging— that they'd encourage young children to get drunk. I guess I was the poster boy for that whole anti-alcopop campaign.

We were out at a country pub one afternoon, and I told my mum there was a new brand of lemonade called Hooch that I'd like to try. To my amazement, she bought the lie and ordered me a bottle. Then she ordered me another bottle. And then another. She genuinely didn't know it was alcoholic, though. I can't stress that enough. My mum is the most protective and caring parent alive, and she'd be mortified if anyone ever thought anything to contrary. So please don't pass judgment on her. Her only fault was being too trusting, and having a devious little drunk for a son.

Needless to say, by the time I finished necking back that third bottle of Hooch, I was completely shitfaced. The jig was up. And my mum was devastated: she'd let her ten-year-old son get drunk right in front of her. Alana was devastated, too. She was on holiday with her boyfriend and his family, and he turned out to be a juvenile alcoholic. Incidentally, we broke up as soon as we got back to Birmingham, and I don't think we ever spoke to each other again. My life-long love affair with alcohol, on the other hand, had only just begun.

Drugs didn't come into play until much later on. I had a year-long fling with marijuana when I was sixteen, but that came to an end when I was arrested for possession of a controlled substance, and mum sent me to live with my dad. I quit smoking weed after that. And I didn't get into hard drugs until several years later.

My family were always very anti-drugs. Like most kids, I was spoon-fed anti-drug propaganda at home, in school, and in the media. But having now tried most legal and illegal substances, I can safely say that alcohol is by far the deadliest. He writes as he takes a swig of beer.

But it's true. Every dumb, dangerous, disgraceful, shameful, regrettable, criminal deed I've ever done has been a direct result of alcohol. And I'd advise any budding booze enthusiasts out there to tread with caution. The same goes for all you aspiring drug addicts. These are powerful, potentially life-threatening forces. Experiment, sure. But fuck around with them at your peril.

Thankfully, during my twenty-year party career, the good times have far outweighed the bad, and most of my favorite memories have been sponsored by one mind-altering substance or another. I guess I just love getting wasted. I always have. Maybe I'll go straight edge when I turn forty, though. Time will tell.

Right now, it's time to kick back, relax, pour yourself a drink, roll yourself a joint—do whatever you need to do—and enjoy some first-rate tales of excess, rehab, ecstasy, speed freaks, magic mushrooms, getting stoned with Bruce Willis, getting drunk with Johnny Depp, and the craziest Jimi Hendrix story you've ever heard in your life. Welcome to the good, the bad, and the ugly side of booze and drugs.

DOUG STANHOPE—*COMEDIAN, AUTHOR, PODCAST HOST*

DOUG: I've done tons of fucking drugs on stage.

MATT: Are there any drugs that don't go well with stand-up comedy?

DOUG: Hallucinogens. The only time I got away with doing them was right before I went on stage. At the forty-five-minute mark, it started kicking in, and I was telling people, "All right, at some point you're going to see my head go a little bit sideways. And that's when I'll know I better wrap to a closer."

Cocaine is good medicinally, but you don't want to go on a crazy fucking jag—you want your tongue to be able to keep up with your thoughts. But when I used to have to do three shows on a Saturday night, back in the comedy club days, a medicinal bump before that third show might be all that gets you through.

I've done ecstasy on stage a few times, too. And that's fun because I have such an awful, angry delivery, so to do that with a permanent smile plastered across my face, whilst I'm talking about dead kids or something, is hilarious.

MATT: What's your favorite drug?

DOUG: I almost never do drugs anymore, but I think ecstasy would be the one, even though the comedown is so hard.

MATT: It's brutal. But the high is so good.

DOUG: It is if you get clean stuff. But that's the problem: you can't count on it. And mushrooms are the opposite: they're the hardest come on. You're like, "Ah, fuck. I don't want to puke."

MATT: It feels like you're on a fairground ride when you're coming up on mushrooms.

DOUG: Yeah, your legs start going weak, you don't know how hard it's going to kick, and you don't know if you're going to vomit. But it ends in totally the opposite way to a drunken bender, where you say to yourself, "I'm never doing that again." When you do mushrooms, you say, "Why don't I do these all the time?"

MATT: I feel like that. My friend and I tripped about two months ago—there was some freak weather in London, and it snowed, and we went out to a place called the Epping Forest, which is where Henry VIII used to go hunting. It's this magical, beautiful, famous forest. And it was covered in snow, so it felt like being in fucking Narnia. We went out there, took a heroic dose, and spent the day out in the forest losing our minds. It was one of the best days I've ever had.

DOUG: That sounds horrible to me.

MATT: Really?

DOUG: Yeah. First of all, I want to be in a hotel room—perfectly clean, with thick comforters. I get cold easily anyway, so on mushrooms I'd be freezing. I want to be wrapped up warm in a comforter. Fucking snow? No.

MATT: But when you're in nature on mushrooms, that's the ultimate hit.

DOUG: I feel like that just going out into my backyard. All of a sudden, it's a brand new nature. I'll stare at a fucking branch, or watch a bug crawl across a fucking picker bush, and that feels like National Geographic to me. And the comforter is inside just a few feet away.

B-REAL—*CYPRESS HILL, PROPHETS OF RAGE*

B-REAL: Cypress Hill and House of Pain played a show together once in Humboldt County, which was a big place in California at that time for marijuana and cannabis cultivation. Everybody was always reeling about Humboldt County weed, and we had the chance to play a show out there at the university, so we took it. After the concert, both bands were in a hotel room together, and all our crew had one floor. It was Cypress Hill and House of Pain taking up an entire floor in this hotel, where there might have been about six or seven other guests in the whole building, as it's a very small town. And we all took magic mushrooms that night.

This was the day before the LA riots, and we were still high on mushrooms when we were driving back into Southern California. We saw all this black smoke in the sky as we were driving into the city, and we were like, "Fuck. This looks like the apocalypse." Obviously, the verdict for the officers who were on trial for the abuse of Rodney King was a "not guilty," and the city just went crazy. But we were coming back from a crazy night in Humboldt County and we had no idea. The city was burning, and we were still semi-high on mushrooms, and we totally freaked out. Talk about a snap back to reality.

VINNIE CARUANA—*THE MOVIELIFE, I AM THE AVALANCHE, SOLO ARTIST*

VINNIE: There's been times when I've nibbled on mushrooms and gone out to a pub, and been like, "Nope."

MATT: It can be too much, right? You've got to be secluded in nature, or at least in a safe space.

VINNIE: Yeah, maybe a nice fire right there. A few close friends—

MATT: Chosen companions. No strangers.

VINNIE: Exactly. I enjoy taking mushrooms every once in a while, but I actually took a very long break from them for about eight years.

MATT: How come?

VINNIE: I was in Brooklyn one day with some really close friends, and we took mushrooms. Then my friends were like, "Let's go here." We were just hanging out listening to music and my friend had a roof deck looking out over the city. It was perfect. I was like, "Why are we going anywhere?" We ended up in a park, he bumps into some other friends, and the next thing I know there's twenty people around the circle and half of them aren't on mushrooms. I was like, "I don't know these fools."

MATT: So you started spinning out?

VINNIE: Yeah, and there were ambulances flying by and all sorts of shit. Then they were like, "Let's go here." And I was like, "How are we going to get there?" "Let's take the train," they said. I couldn't believe it: "Yeah, that sounds like a good idea. Let's get on the subway. I'm uncomfortable on the subway every day. That's the last place I want to be right now, whilst I'm high on mushrooms." So I took a little break after that. I figured I needed to choose the right time and place to do them.

MATT: They're the make-or-break factors of a good trip right there.

VINNIE: Absolutely. Nowadays, as in every once in a blue moon, I'll take a cap and a stem. But I don't want to trip on mushrooms anymore. I like taking a cap and a stem, being in nature like you said, then having it wind down, and me say, "Well, that was nice. Now I'm off to bed." As opposed to lying there in bed going, "Please fucking wear off." Those days are well behind me.

MINA CAPUTO—*LIFE OF AGONY, SOLO ARTIST*

MINA: You don't get addicted to mushrooms. The last mushroom trip I had was twenty-five years ago.

MATT: I say this on the podcast quite a lot, and it's not because I want to encourage drug taking in any way—

MINA: But listen, let me correct you: marijuana, psilocybin, and DMT *aren't* drugs. "Drugs" is a corrupt word. It's bullshit. Why do you think psychedelics are on Schedule 1 drug lists in the first place? Because they break down the fucking barriers, man. They show you what it is to really understand, and think, and feel.

MATT: I was going to say, I think mushrooms are great. I've had nothing but positive experiences on them.

MINA: You know what? I'm fucking dying to trip on a heroic dose. Maybe six fucking grams—Terence McKenna style.

MATT: Can we trip together some day?

MINA: We can. But we might have sex.

MATT: It is what it is, Mina. It is what it is.

MINA: You're entering a zone when you take mushrooms: you're entering God's vagina. And they put alcohol, tobacco, and cocaine below that? These belligerent, fucking disease-ridden, toxic substances that people take, which poison their bodies and their minds. Milk that people drink is more poisonous than a proper 'shroom that you pick from cow dung. And you'll learn more in an hour tripping on magic mushrooms—about loving yourself and loving your neighbor—than mankind has learned in a hundred thousand years.

JOEY CAPE—*LAGWAGON, ME FIRST & THE GIMME GIMMES, SOLO ARTIST*

JOEY: Willie Nelson said the only way he could get off whiskey—because once you're on that road, it's the road you're going to be on for the rest of your life, and if you don't stop drinking it then you're going to die real young—was by switching to marijuana. And there are similarities in the effect: whiskey has a little bit of a skunky high. I guess it all depends on who you are, though. Some people want to fight when they drink whiskey; I just want to kiss everyone. Whiskey's a funny one.

MATT: Are you partial to a wee dram?

JOEY: Well, last year sometime, Lagwagon was in the UK touring with NOFX and Alkaline Trio, and I was drinking way too much. We were in Luxembourg, and I just got really sick. Our tour manager—a great guy from Canterbury called Ben Davis—kept saying, "You need to go to the hospital." He knows me really well, and he said, "This isn't just a hangover. This is different." So he took me to the hospital, and the woman said, "You feed your liver too much." And then she held out her hands like she was holding a football. She told me, "You have to stop feeding it." So I quit drinking there and then.

Over time, I slowly started drinking again—things like Campari and soda, which is so disgusting, but I've grown to love its bitterness. I have like three drinks of that and I'm good. So that's sort of where I'm at now. But last night, I took a holiday from my new lifestyle, and the whiskey came out.

MATT: We've all been there.

DR. AMIE HARWICK—*THERAPIST, WRITER, MODEL*

MATT: Is there a reason why you gave up alcohol?

AMIE: Yeah. I wasn't an alcoholic, but there were definitely times when I drank more in quantity, and I got really bad hangovers and I put my foot in my mouth with some of the things that I said—stuff like that. But I actually had an illness that I was born with, and since I was adopted I didn't know until I was about thirty that I had a degenerative issue with my body. When I went to my doctor, they said, "Yeah, if you drink at all, you could kill yourself." So I had to take care of that part of my life for a while, which meant that I had to be on medication for about a year. And if I hadn't been diagnosed and treated, then I would've died. I found out that my body stopped processing alcohol effectively, and at that point I had to quit. So I went through all the medical treatment, which was an extremely traumatic experience, and after going through that I noticed that my friends had changed because I'd stopped going out drinking.

As a result, I no longer wanted to go out and meet people at a dive bar, or hang out late drinking after shows. And the types of people that wanted to hang out with me more, and the types of people that wanted to hang out with me less, really changed for the better. I'd go and catch up with people on hikes instead, or go for coffee during the day. And those little changes made a big impact on the types of people that were around my life. So I thought, "You know what? I think I'm just going to leave that in my past." I'm healthy now, and I *could* drink now, but it's really been a positive change not to have that in my life. And although I was never an alcoholic, I did have experiences that I'm glad I don't have anymore. And I no longer have to worry about hangovers and things like that, which has made a really big difference in my life.

MATT: When was your last drink?

AMIE: I think almost six years ago.

MATT: I give up alcohol for a couple of months every year, and I do find once you get past the one-month mark, you achieve this newfound sense of clarity that you just don't get when you drink alcohol—even if it's only a couple of drinks over the course of the week.

AMIE: Absolutely. What alcohol does, too, as you get older, is it causes depression. It slows you down, and it changes the way you see things. And I don't like putting much in my body that changes anything. I don't even like taking Tylenol when I have a headache—I'm extra cautious at this point in my life.

MATT: Do you drink coffee?

AMIE: That's my only drug. But I've even been trying to pull back on that, and I'm down to one cup a day now.

DANKO JONES—*SOLO ARTIST, AUTHOR, PODCAST HOST*

DANKO: I've never sung about anything that I don't do, and I've never sung about a drunken night out because I don't drink.

MATT: You don't drink at all?

DANKO: I'll have a glass of wine with a nice meal to enhance the meal, but I won't even finish the glass. And when I do get drunk— once every two years or so—everybody takes out their phones and watches in amusement, and I feel like a dancing monkey. Over the course of twenty-two years of touring, there has been times where that's happened. But I've never painted myself into a corner to where I can't look at myself in the mirror and go, "That wasn't you." And I can honestly say, I'm completely cool with 95 percent of everything that I've done over the last twenty-two years in the music industry. And there's always 5 percent shrapnel as you go through this life.

DAVE HAUSE—*THE LOVED ONES, SOLO ARTIST*

DAVE: There's the fun aspect of drinking, and then there's the addiction aspect, and the thing that can lead your life into sketchy territory. It's fun until it isn't fun.

MATT: When did you start drinking?

DAVE: I started drinking when I was around twelve or thirteen. And I've had times when there was a lot of drinking, and other times where I'd take a break. But from my mid-twenties on, it was pretty much straight hard partying for many years.

MATT: Do you think that was down to the lifestyle that comes with touring, or an innate alcohol dependency within you?

DAVE: I think it was probably a mixture of the two. I don't really know; I still have to work it all out in therapy.

MATT: Did you do the whole rehab thing?

DAVE: I didn't go through rehab, and I'm not sure that was the wisest idea—to not go. I think everyone has their methods, and there's lots of ways to get the job done, but cold turkey was a little bit sketchy and it took me down some really weird paths. It's still a work in progress as well, and I don't know if it will be forever. But it probably should be. You don't want to wake up on the front porch of the place that you're staying in your thirties, and that's definitely happened to me.

MATT: I guess, at a certain age, you'd like to think you're old enough to know better.

DAVE: I don't know. When you study addiction and you bring in the psychology of it, "old enough to know better" is tough because when you have that propensity you might well know better, but not have a whole lot of control over it. And I think, just like anything in life, the older you get the less you know. For me, I just didn't want to go back down a few of the paths that I'd been down.

MATT: Did drinking take its toll on your relationships?

DAVE: I had a friend of mine say, "What do you mean, you're stopping drinking? You always have your shit together." And it may have presented itself that way to him. But I had a marriage, two houses and a construction business, a fairly on-their-way-up band in The Loved Ones, and all of that was gone. You could maybe count some of that as wreckage in the ravine, so to speak. But at least some of it had to be attributed to drinking. And he was like, "I guess I never thought about it that way because you always seemed to be landing on your feet"—as by this point I'd already gone solo and had a couple of records out.

I really think it's just a personal thing: you have to figure out what you want out of life. Aging with any kind of grace is difficult, especially in rock 'n' roll, but it's working out for me so far. And I don't think I could manage everything that's on my plate right now if I added heavy partying into the mix.

MATT: Are you not the kind of person that can just enjoy one or two beers, then? If you start drinking, does it tend to get out of control pretty fast?

DAVE: If we were to have a beer together in Birmingham tonight, I very much doubt it would go that way. But it would accumulate pretty fast, I think. By summertime you'd be seeing a very different version of me. And I don't know about that guy; I don't trust that guy as much.

MATT: Did you find when you stopped drinking that certain friendships changed, and you started seeing certain people less often?

DAVE: I guess I'm finding that out over time. The thing that brings everybody together is music, though. I still get to spend that time with people, it's just that the focus is a little different, and I'm gone before it starts getting crazy. I'm learning a different tempo, I suppose, of what the night will bring. Some relationships do change, though. And that's got its own baggage and sadness. But when you get into your thirties, you start to see people go down some really dark paths. Your body starts to give out—I've seen it with friends—and you start to lose people; people start to die. So I'm also trying to stay ahead of that. I don't want to be that causality. I don't want to be pissing out of a fifth floor window in Germany, and fall out and die. That's what it can get to. And coming to terms with the fact that I'm not invincible, and being willing to admit that, has had a really positive effect on me.

I've had a lot of people reaching out to me as well, whether it's Jonny 2 Bags [Wickersham] from Social Distortion, or Jay Bentley from Bad Religion—various people that have gone ahead, and continued to play music for many years longer than me with the elimination of booze and drugs. They've reached out to me and said, "There is a way to do this. I know it probably seems weird now"—and it does, it feels really strange at first—"but give it a little time, see if you can hold out, and then it starts to get a little easier." And that's been true so far.

MATT: I find myself notably more present in the moment and susceptible to emotions—both good and bad—after not drinking for a while. Do you find that as well?

DAVE: Yeah, I think that's true. There is some weird thing about the hangover that softens you up, though. For me, lots of creative stuff would happen the morning after drinking. Maybe you're still kind of drunk and your guard is down, and you feel a little more vulnerable and exposed. I do miss that a little bit. There's weird things about it that I miss, actually. But I think you get nostalgic for all kinds of strange things that you don't necessarily want in your life anymore, like your old town—you miss it, but you're not necessarily going to go back and live there. And I want to look forward, not backyard. That's what I'm trying to chase now—on to the next thing—because you can't Peter Pan it forever.

STEVE-O—*JACKASS, STUNT PERFORMER, ENTERTAINER, COMEDIAN*

MATT: At what point did the drinking and the drug-taking stop being fun?

STEVE-O: I thought I was having fun right up until the very end.

MATT: Really?

STEVE-O: Well, fun might not be the right word for it. But once the voices started talking to me—once I started hearing voices, and watching people walk around my apartment who had never actually been there—is when I felt connected to the spirit world, and I just wanted to keep that happening. I was peeking behind the curtain of some other dimension spirit shit, and that was a big deal. I still reflect on that and think it's amazing.

Fuck, I just love drugs, man. I'd love to be on drugs right now. But the problem is, it just came to a point where my actions were no longer acceptable—not by me, or anybody else. And it was impossible to get through any given day without me really disrupting someone's life. I became, at times, terribly mean-spirited, and would just think it was a great idea to do really shitty things to people. My food groups became shame, guilt, remorse, and humiliation.

MATT: Repeat.

STEVE-O: Exactly. Every day there was some fucking thing I did that made me feel so guilty because I'd harmed another person, or so fucking humiliated because I'd embarrassed myself so terribly and publicly. I was doing fucking shitty stuff, man. I was humiliated, I was ashamed, I was fucking racked with guilt, and my self-esteem was just so low. And then you're right: repeat.

I was killing myself, man. I was fucking killing myself. And I was burning every bridge in my career. I had good things going for me and I just fucking ruined everything. I went into freefall mode, and there was no way to continue what I was doing. I think it's kind of clichéd and lame to say, "I would've died." But it wouldn't have been fucking surprising. Over the years, I've really fucked over more people than most on the celebrity death pool. I've been the odds-on favorite in the death pool community, and really cost a lot of people a lot of money. It was even a joke at the end of the first *Jackass* movie, where you saw everyone die except for me—because I was guaranteed to be the first person to die.

MATT: You must be grateful to Johnny Knoxville for stepping in and staging that intervention.

STEVE-O: Yeah, that was a big deal, man. It was a big deal. I love that guy. I fucking love him. I refer to him as the captain.

MATT: Was *Jackass 3D* the first movie you did sober? If so, how was that experience, compared to being out of it for the previous two?

STEVE-O: I was participating in a way that I really hadn't done before. In one sense, I was still kind of uncomfortable in my own skin because I hadn't really found my voice or broken out of my shell yet. I was still sort of awkward in my early sobriety, and I think that's kind of evident to look at it. But I was also really motivated and so fucking creative.

On the second *Jackass* movie, I don't think a single idea that I wrote or submitted got filmed. The only thing I contributed creatively to that film—from a standpoint of writing bits—was showing up at Jeff Tremaine's house for a writing session one day, and saying, "For what it's worth, I was looking in the mirror this morning and I found my pubic bush to be really fucking out of control. So I shaved it off with an electric shaver, and there was a huge afro in my hand that I tucked into an empty drug baggy. So I have this empty drug bag filled with pubic hair in my kitchen—for what it's worth." That, of course, was the genesis for what would become the pubic hair beard in the *Terror Taxi* skit from *Jackass Number Two*. But other than that, I really contributed nothing: fucking fuck all. I was just not on point at all. Come *Jackass 3D*, we fucking shot almost everything I came up with. So whenever I hear someone say, "Steve-O was funnier when he was on drugs," it's just not fucking true. Those people are wrong. And they can fuck right off.

KYLE GASS—*TENACIOUS D, THE KYLE GASS BAND, ACTOR, CO-MEDIAN*

KYLE: I had to go to rehab in the middle of recording *The Rize of the Fenix*. "The Ballad of Hollywood Jack and the Rage Cage" is really a true story. That song is dedicated to that whole experience. It was really hard to go through, but I think it helped us out in the end. And Jack really rode to my rescue. I think maybe I was testing him by falling apart. I was like, "Are you going to save me?" And he did. It was a difficult time, but we came through it.

MATT: Do you still struggle with addiction issues now?

KYLE: No. I don't even know if that's what it was in the first place.

MATT: Do you think it was more circumstantial?

KYLE: I think it might have been. I was frightened that it was all sort of going away, and I just kind of fell apart. I felt like I didn't have control of anything anymore: here was this great thing that we'd created, and I thought it was being taken away. Everything just conspired to…who knows? Maybe I'm just insane.

MATT: Maybe we all are. I know I am.

LAURA JANE GRACE—*AGAINST ME!, SOLO ARTIST, AUTHOR*

MATT: How old were you when you first smoked weed?

LAURA: I was thirteen. It was a whirlwind year because I smoked weed for the first time, I did cocaine for the first time, and I tried LSD for the first time. Drugs were just around, and they were really easy to get hold of. The one thing that I left out of my book—and I regret leaving it out, but there was reasoning behind it—is when I'm talking about when that kid comes up behind me and clocks me on the side of the head, and then we get into a fight, and I hit him with a paint can. The truth is I was actually on acid when that happened. I had to fill out a police report whilst I was on acid, too. But the reason that wasn't mentioned in the book was because I hadn't mentioned drugs yet, so it felt weird to introduce them at that point.

MATT: Doing acid as a kid must've been a fucking trip—pun intended.

LAURA: It was kind of terrifying. But I was experimenting in an actual way; while I didn't have the words for dysphoria, or know what being transgender or anything like that was yet, I was experimenting to ultimately find out, "What will this do to the way my brain is working right now?"

I'd smoke weed and recognize that it did something to my dysphoria—even though I didn't know the word dysphoria yet. It would do something to the way I felt; the same with acid; the same with alcohol; the same with cocaine. And that really shaped what I was drawn to. I loved smoking weed because it eased my dysphoria. And I loved doing cocaine and alcohol, but for entirely different reasons— they killed the dysphoria by numbing it.

MATT CAUGHTHRAN—*THE BRONX, MARIACHI EL BRONX*

MATT C: I'd taken a liking to experimenting at school, and when you're young, drugs are a part of that. But I got a little too carried with it. I became a mess; I was high on speed; I became a really bad drug addict, and I was completely out of my mind. I was doing speed in gas station bathrooms, trying to come up with lyrics for the first Bronx record [*The Bronx*] in my car.

I'm glad it wasn't heroin or anything like that, but speed is pretty bad, and I was pretty tweaked on that stuff for a good amount of time. I overdosed at one point; I didn't die and come back; it wasn't some sort of Nikki Sixx situation. But it was enough for me to be like, "Okay. It's time to stop." And I'm very thankful to my mom and my dad for giving me the ability to look at myself from the outside in that way. I have common sense, and a smart enough brain and strong enough willpower to understand when I can't control something and it's time to change. I've been fortunate enough to be able to do that in my life, which is amazing, because a lot of people can't—when something gets a hold of them, it really gets a hold of them.

MATT S: It sounds like you were out of control for a minute there. It's great that you managed to pull it back, though. And it's great that you can talk about it so openly and honestly.

MATT C: It is what it is, man. I can talk about it because I'm not ashamed of it; it's all part of my life, and it's all part of the path that brought me here today. And it's all good. People go through fucking crazy shit in their lives. I'm just stoked that I'm in a better place now. I still go down my wormholes every now and then, as we all do. But I'm stoked with how I came out, and The Bronx are still going strong after all these years.

ROBB FLYNN—*MACHINE HEAD, PODCAST HOST*

ROBB: I was really addicted to speed at one time. I was *really* addicted. I'd lost like fifty pounds, and I was completely emaciated. But I decided if I sold speed, it would force me to stop doing speed because I wouldn't get high on my own supply. And somehow that ridiculous twenty-two-year-old logic worked: I stopped doing speed and I became a speed dealer.

MATT: The Robb Flynn rehab method. I've never heard of that one before.

ROBB: Don't ever try it. I don't even know how it worked, but somehow it did. And I started making some money—good money, in fact. I guess they kind of saw me as a rising star in this thing. But all I was trying to do was make ends meet and have fun; I was single and dating strippers, and doing all that stuff. But pretty soon it got crazy, and there were a couple of moments where I got offered a lot of drugs up front—it was a lot of money's worth. When that big amount of money came my way, it freaked me out. I realized that if I carried on doing what I was doing, then I'd never get out of it. And I just wanted to play music—that's all I ever wanted to do. So if anything, it became this huge inspiration to make Machine Head successful because I wanted to get as far away from dealing drugs as I could.

MATT: I bet you were dealing with all kinds of shady characters, too.

ROBB: I was dealing methamphetamine, so I was dealing with rough, violent, paranoid people who'd been awake for seven days. And I had a dealer who was freaking out because he kept getting busted all the time, so every time someone came over to buy drugs, he'd make you suck the glass dick, which meant you had to take the glass pipe and do a giant hit of speed. When you blew it out, this huge cloud of smoke came out of your mouth, which he called the dragon's breath. I'd be there just to score a bit of speed to sell, and the next thing I knew I'd be awake for two days because I had to take a giant hit of speed to prove that I wasn't a cop. It was a crazy two years of my life, and when I finally did get out of it and Machine Head started taking off, it was a huge driving force in making sure the band was successful.

NICK OLIVERI—*QUEENS OF THE STONE AGE, KYUSS, MONDO GENERATOR, DWARVES*

MATT: Were there a lot of drugs in Palm Springs when you were growing up?

NICK: There was a lot of meth, especially in the desert. It was a big open space with lots of wind, so there were a lot of meth labs out there. I was exposed to all that stuff from a very young age.

MATT: How old were you when you first got high?

NICK: My uncle first gave me speed when I was eleven. That kind of throws me when I look back on it now. I'd never even give an eleven-year-old weed, let alone fucking speed. I would never do that. I don't have kids myself, but all my friends do, and if anyone tried to give any of them drugs at eleven—or even a few years older—then I would hurt them. I'd lose my fucking mind. He should've known better than to give speed to an eleven-year-old. That's the same as molesting a kid as far as I'm concerned: it's abuse.

MATT: It's certainly a corruption of innocence, that's for sure.

NICK: There you go. That's a better term for it. I don't blame him for it anymore, though. There's been times in the past when I've been like, "That motherfucker." But he's still my uncle. And he was young at the time, too. He was only four years older than me.

MICHAEL MONROE—*HANOI ROCKS, DEMOLITION 32, SOLO ARTIST*

MICHAEL: Stiv Bators accidentally hung himself with his mic cable on stage once. He literally died on stage. He used to climb up on the lighting rig and wrap the mic cable around his neck, and pretend to hang himself. But one time his hands were sweaty, and he was a little out of it, and all of a sudden the roadies noticed he had piss pouring down his leg and he was turning blue. When they took him down, he was actually dead.

He was clinically dead for quite a while. But they managed to revive him. At first, they didn't tell him. But they asked him about a week later, "Do you realize that you died?" He said the only regret that he had was that he hadn't had an out-of-body experience. He was like, "Shit, man. I don't remember anything. I just blacked out."

MATT: Didn't you live with Stiv Bators for a while?

MICHAEL: Yes. When Hanoi Rocks was breaking up after Razzle died, I moved in with Stiv in London in 1985. We lived together for a year before I moved to New York. Johnny Thunders moved in with us as well. He'd been living in Stockholm with his girlfriend, and her family had thrown him out of the apartment. He wound up homeless, so I said he could come and stay in London with me and Stiv.

MATT: You, Stiv Bators, and Johnny Thunders—all living together. That's wild!

MICHAEL: There was definitely never a dull moment. Stiv was on the road a lot, though, so I was mostly just there with Johnny. I really miss both those guys. Stiv Bators is one of the best-kept secrets in rock 'n' roll. I always felt a spiritual connection to him. We stayed up late many nights thanks to artificial enhancers, or what Stiv liked to call subconscious awareness. He would say, "Speeding is subconscious awareness: while our conscious state is asleep, we acknowledge our subconsciousness, which reveals to us things that we shelter from ourselves in our self-conscious cocoon. Write this down, Michael." As I wrote it down, I said, "I think we're in trouble, Stiv. We just came up with the perfect excuse to stay up for weeks on end."

MATT: How do you feel about the idea that taking drugs removes your inhibitions and actually helps people express and reveal their true selves?

MICHAEL: I think we're all here for experimentation—as long as you move on, and don't get stuck or hooked on a drug because then you're screwed. You might as well be a slave to the system if you do that. It doesn't accomplish anything. I think we're all here to learn and evolve. And I think with Stiv—because we were such good friends—we could let our guard down, and we didn't have to worry about embarrassing ourselves or anything like that. We'd have all sorts of moments of clarity and epiphanies together, and you can really do that with your best friend.

I stayed up so many nights with Stiv. Sometimes the door would slam shut, and I'd say, "There's a draft. The window must be open." But it never was. I think there was actually other dimension stuff going on. And Stiv used to tell me stories, which I'd call deadtime stories—because they were like bedtime stories, but we were the living dead. That's what the Demolition 23 song "Deadtime Stories" is all about; there's about fifteen Stiv Bators song titles in the lyrics.

I wouldn't personally recommend doing drugs to anybody, though. People can flip out, and they can be pretty dangerous. It's really just an individual thing. It's like Lemmy used to say, "You don't have to go to the moon." That was his secret to surviving all those years—moderation. He knew exactly how much to take, and how much not to take.

NICK OLIVERI

NICK: My first gig back with Kyuss after leaving for the first time was in September 1990. It was also Ginger Baker's first show playing drums with Masters of Reality. He'd played drums on the *Sunrise on the Sufferbus* album, and he toured with them for a little bit after that.

Chris Goss told me that Ginger Baker said to him, "Jimi Hendrix didn't die because of the drugs. He died because of the *lack* of drugs." According to Ginger Baker, Jimi Hendrix wouldn't have gone to sleep and choked on his own vomit if he'd have shown up on time with the liquid cocaine that he was supposed to arrive with. They had liquid cocaine and a bunch of syringes, and they were going to shoot liquid cocaine all night. But Ginger didn't make it to Hendrix's place on time, so Hendrix got drunk, passed out, and choked on his own puke. That's what Ginger Baker told Chris Goss.

MATT: Fucking hell.

B-REAL

B-REAL: People often ask me, "Who have you smoked with that surprised you the most?" There are two. The first was Oliver Stone, and that was in Damian Marley's studio session some years back. There was a bunch of people there, including Joss Stone, who was working on something with Damian [SuperHeavy], which sounded incredible. There were a couple of other people there, too. And then Oliver Stone showed up.

I saw Oliver smoking some of Damian's weed, and no disrespect to Damian, but my weed was much better. So I offered Oliver some of my weed. He didn't know who the hell I was. But his young girlfriend at the time—or whatever she was to him—said, "I'll tell him later." And he got so stoned after smoking some of our high-grade that he lost his keys. He completely lost it. Some of those older guys may have been smoking weed a long time, but they haven't smoked the weed that we smoke because it wasn't available back then.

The other guy who was really surprising, and really cool, was Bruce Willis. I was at this club one night, and Mark Wahlberg—who's a friend of mine from the Marky Mark days—hits me up, and says, "Yo, B! One of my friends wants to know if he can partake?" I said, "Yeah, whatever. Bring them over." I didn't know that this friend was Bruce Willis. So he comes over, and we start smoking out with fucking Bruce Willis. It was the coolest shit ever.

MATT: Was he cool?

B-REAL: Oh, yeah. He was very mellow.

DOUG STANHOPE

MATT: Who's the biggest hellraiser you've ever partied with?

DOUG: Fucking Dylan Moran is the first one that comes to mind. That's one of the most fucked up I've ever been. I don't even know if he would remember that. I was at the Montreal Comedy Festival with Otto and George, who are a puppet act—Otto [Petersen] was the guy, and George was his puppet—and someone had blow. We all ended up back at Dylan's room, and he kept falling asleep with his cigarette in his hand, so I had to keep picking it up and flicking it for him. Then I just remember the sun coming up off his balcony. I only met him that one time, but I imagine he's probably one of those guys who binges and then straightens up to do a movie or something. Ron White is a drinking icon, too. He's constantly there with a cocktail in his hand, and he never slurs or misses a step. He's one of the all-time greats—that's still alive.

MATT: What about Johnny Depp? Have you ever cut loose with him?

DOUG: Yeah, and he can hold his own. I'll go and stay at one of his houses from time to time, and at three in the morning I'll be half asleep on the couch, and he'll appear out of nowhere, like, "Hey! Do you wanna do some shots?" He's a fucking vampire.

MATT: Is he a cool guy? He seems like he'd be a cool guy.

DOUG: Oh, yeah. He's exactly what you'd expect. He's that fucking Hunter S. Thompson character through and through.

MATT: He's fully in it?

DOUG: Yeah. He's stuck there. I didn't realize until the other day how old that movie is.

MATT: *Fear and Loathing in Las Vegas?*

DOUG: Yeah. It came out in '98.

MATT: Yeah, it's over twenty years old.

DOUG: How old are you?

MATT: I'm thirty-two.

DOUG: I was going with thirty-one.

MATT: There you go. My friend and I actually met a couple of girls at a bar last night, and they were too young to remember the film *The Beach*. That came out in 2000. We were trying to explain a story that had happened to us in Morocco, where we accidentally found a field full of cannabis plants, and we were like, "Holy fuck. We're in *The Beach*—only it's on a mountain." But neither of them had heard of the film, so the story fell short. They also thought Dr. Dre was just the guy who invented Beats headphones—they had no idea he was a famous rapper and producer. I was like, "Fuck, we're old."

DOUG: Did you read that story in the news yesterday about the beach?

MATT: No, which one?

DOUG: They had to close that beach from the film down because it's become too popular. In the movie, it's this quaint little oasis in Thailand, but now you show up there and it's like fucking Times Square. So they've closed it down and turned it into a nature reserve. I never saw the movie, either, to be honest. I'm glad you're picking up young women, though. It's good to hear someone's getting pussy from a podcast. It's hard enough getting guests, much less laid because of it.

DRUGS & ALCOHOL PLAYLIST

CYPRESS HILL—"I WANNA GET HIGH"
JEFFERSON AIRPLANE—"WHITE RABBIT"
WILLIE NELSON & MERLE HAGGARD—"REASONS TO QUIT"
DESCENDENTS—"COFFEE MUG"
DAVE HAUSE—"LEMON HILL"
ROGER ALAN WADE—"IF YOU'RE GONNA BE DUMB, YOU GOTTA BE TOUGH"
TENACIOUS D—"THE BALLAD OF HOLLYWOOD JACK AND THE RAGE CAGE"
AGAINST ME!—"THRASH UNREAL"
THE BRONX—"STROBE LIFE"
MACHINE HEAD—"I'M YOUR GOD NOW"
QUEENS OF THE STONE AGE—"FEEL GOOD HIT OF THE SUMMER"
DEMOLITION 23—"DEADTIME STORIES"
CREAM—"WHITE ROOM"
CYPRESS HILL—"HITS FROM THE BONG"
BREWER & SHIPLEY—"ONE TOKE OVER THE LINE"

POLITICS & RELIGION

"Good communal energy starts in your own circle."

I FEEL LIKE WE need to atone for our sins after the last chapter, which leads us nicely into this one: Politics & Religion. Or maybe it's the religious leaders and heads of state that need to atone for *their* sins? After all, they're the figureheads of oppressive systems of control, fear, and manipulation. Are they not?

Albert Einstein once said, "Those who believe that politics and religion do not mix understand neither." Mahatma Gandhi said something similar: "Those who say religion has nothing to do with politics do not know what religion is." I'm with those guys. Let's throw economics in the mix, too. For capitalism is the new religion, after all. And the unholy trinity of church, state, and coin is set in place so the rich get richer and the poor get poorer.

We all have our own beliefs, of course. And they're all equally valid. But everyone surely must see that the overriding theme of human history is one of elitist advancement at the expense of the underprivileged. That's not just me on some Marxist rant, comrades. That's the stone-cold truth. It's a rigged game. And it's a game this chapter hopes to explore, with the help of politicized punks like Justin Sane from Anti-Flag; musician, actor, and activist Steven Van Zandt; and self-proclaimed "intergalactic being" Mina Caputo.

I'm not what you would call a political person. I have as many problems with left-wing people as I do with right-wing people, to be honest. There are liars and hypocrites in equal numbers on both sides. But I do pride myself on being socially conscious. And in my mind there is only *one* race: the human race. I'm proud to be a part of it, too. I love people: I love talking to them, I love listening to them, I love meeting them, and I love getting to know them. I try to actively engage with the world around me at all times. And my podcast has been an amazing platform via which to do that.

I also consider myself a deeply spiritual person, and I think about the meaning of life *and* death a lot. Why are we here? What happens after? These are the age-old questions that I ask myself on an almost daily basis. I enjoy asking my guests these questions, too. And whilst I don't personally subscribe to any organized religion—I think there are good and bad elements in all of them—I respect everybody's spiritual viewpoints equally, and I'm always fascinated to hear them, whatever they are. That goes for politics as well.

If you're passionate about *anything*, even if your opinions are unpopular, I want to hear about them. I want to know what you think, and I want to know *why* you think that way. The only people I'm not interested in talking to are the ones who have nothing to say. Luckily, the contributors to this book have plenty to say. So, let's get into it.

JUSTIN SANE—ANTI-FLAG

MATT: It's funny how Russia and America are sworn enemies, yet the two countries have more in common than either would probably like to admit.

JUSTIN: The thing that I find most interesting about Russia and America, as far as attitude and culture goes, is they're the two most closely related countries. There's a level of patriotism in both countries that I would call corrupted patriotism, or nationalism. And it's fascinating how both populations are controlled as a result of that level of nationalism. Another example of their similarities is the wealth inequality in both countries: in the US, we have a historic wealth gap right now, and in Russia it's the same thing. But people just accept it and keep rolling with it, and that wouldn't be possible without the level of corrupted patriotism that exists in both countries.

If you travel around the world, most of the time you won't see the flag of the country that you're in everywhere that you go. But in Russia and America, you see them everywhere you go. I think there's a lot of similarities between those two countries, and the irony is, the people in both of those countries are great. But I find it fascinating that the two countries were considered enemies for so long—and in a lot of ways they're still total adversaries of each other—but they're also really similar in so many ways, too.

MATT: You raise an interesting point there, and the oversimplification that I'll make is this: in England, almost every time you see an English flag dangling from the window of someone's house, you can almost guarantee the person who lives inside that house is a nationalist, and often also a racist as well.

JUSTIN: I think that's the case in most countries.

MATT: And that, of course, relates back to the name of your band: Anti-Flag.

JUSTIN: It's interesting, right, with the whole taking a knee issue in America with the National Football League right now. That protest started because African Americans are being killed at an unprecedented rate by police officers. And there's a lot of African American players in the National Football League that wanted to call attention to this, so they started taking a knee during the national anthem. It's basically their way of saying, "Look, this flag does not represent me. People who look like me are being treated very different. It's being caught on video camera. Nothing is changing. And we have so many examples of this now. Why is this not being addressed by our politicians? Something has to change."

What the politicians then did is they immediately co-opted that issue and turned it into an issue of nationalism, and that immediately turned the public against these players. They'd previously go out and worship these people on a Sunday, but now they hate them. And when this whole issue came around, I realized that we were dead on by challenging this issue of nationalism in America with our band name. I don't think it's totally wrong to be patriotic. The definition of patriotism is a love of the place where you live or come from, and that's a positive thing. I *love* where I grew up. But when it becomes corrupted in the way that it has been, to turn people against their own best interests, then I think we fucking hit the nail on the head with our name.

MATT: What was the original inspiration behind it?

JUSTIN: The reason the name Anti-Flag first came about is I was in high school when the first Gulf War was starting, and it was very clear to me—even then—that the war was going to be about oil, and that was it. Most Americans had never even heard of the Persian Gulf. Maybe a handful of Americans had heard of Iraq, but forget Kuwait. It just wasn't a place that was understood by most Americans. And it certainly wasn't going to make a positive impact on the lives of any Americans. So, why were we going there? I was just a teenager in high school, and I could see that.

In the back of my mind, I was also thinking, "If this thing drags out like Vietnam, and they bring the draft back, myself and a lot of my friends are the perfect age to get drafted." Furthermore, I lived in a city that was basically in a great depression. So guess what most of my older friends did? They joined the military—there was no other option. All of a sudden, my buddies were getting ready to go to Iraq, and most of us had never even heard of Iraq.

To top it all off, when they started talking about invading Iraq, all of a sudden there were flags everywhere. It was overwhelming and unbelievable. And it was amazing—with the news and media, and certain parades and events—how quickly people were convinced that this war was necessary. I was just a teenage kid and I could see that it was bullshit. That was when I decided that I wanted to have a punk band called Anti-Flag.

VINNIE CARUANA—*THE MOVIELIFE, I AM THE AVALANCHE, SOLO ARTIST*

MATT: Being a New Yorker, you must remember Donald Trump from before his political career began, when he was just a local business tycoon. Was he notorious, even back then?

VINNIE: Yeah, he was always a celebrity. You wouldn't know who the other rich guys in the city were, but you knew who Donald Trump was because he was a socialite who liked to be in the papers. He liked people to know his name. And he liked to put his name all over buildings, too.

MATT: Was he ever popular in New York?

VINNIE: Certain people maybe got a kick out of him in a tabloid sense. But I just remember him as the loud mouth, brash guy that flaunted money. I'd always just be like, "He's that rich, loud womanizer." That was all. Then he ended up having the show *The Apprentice*, and that was basically how the rest of America found out about him. A lot of people knew the name Trump because he had it on casinos all over the country, but I think most of America outside of New York really got to know him through *The Apprentice*, which was a hugely popular, scripted reality TV show. And now he's the president of the United States of America. It's the worst thing ever.

MATT: It's mental, isn't it?

VINNIE: Yeah. It's a true American embarrassment. And to be American right now is a weird feeling. Life is fucking weird.

MATT: It is. It's not just you guys, though. We have it here too, with Brexit.

VINNIE: Yeah, that same sentiment and new world order of old shitty racism, and rich white folks being like, "All right, we gave you your time for progress. We're going to turn back the clock now."

MATT: It's like the 1980s all over again—on steroids.

VINNIE: It sucks.

MATT: At least some good art and music will come out of it. Although, I'm yet to see much in the way of engaging, powerful, political art—at least in the music world that I operate in. I thought more bands would be confronting these issues, to be honest.

VINNIE: I guess it really depends on where the writers and artists are coming from. The Movielife were never a political band, and the subject matter on this new record was a stretch for us. And it's not on the nose, but it's there. Do we care? Yes. Are we writing about it? Yes. But we're doing it in our own way. That's a record for Anti-Flag to write, you know what I mean? Not us. We're never going to be something that we're not.

MATT: What's it like in the States right now? Is there any objectivity in the media?

VINNIE: Well, CNN and those kind of left-wing places are reporting all of Trump's malfeasance. And they're reporting very, very closely on the Russian investigation that's going on right now. Those guys are guilty, and a lot of them are going to jail—although that's easier said than done, obviously. Then there's Fox News on the other side, which basically just churns out right-wing propaganda.

MATT: I bet it's not even thinly veiled propaganda, either.

VINNIE: Not at all. And listen, I'm not saying the left-leaning media is unbiased. But even when we're presented with stone cold facts, and I think, "This is the thing that's going to get him," half of the country is still like, "Fake news—because our boy Don says so."

MATT: That's his evil genius, sadly. So much of the news is fake, but he's twisted that to further his own bullshit agenda.

VINNIE: And that's straight out of the fascist's handbook. So we just have to smash that every chance we get.

JUSTIN SANE

MATT: Do you have any friends that voted for Trump? And do you let politics affect your friendships?

JUSTIN: This has been the hardest one for me because Trump is so obviously a sexual predator, a racist, a bigot, a xenophobe, and a nationalist. So I have a really hard time with anybody who voted for him. I stopped going to businesses that supported Trump because when you support someone who is that openly bigoted and mean-spirited, what does that say about you? I understand there were certain people that I know who voted for Trump because they felt like the neo-liberal politics of the Democrats had left them behind, and I totally agree with that. But I couldn't overcome the idea that Trump is a racist, and with your vote for him, you're actively endorsing systemic racism. You can't say "I'm not a racist" if you voted for Donald Trump.

I think what a lot of people don't understand about racism is you can have a Black friend and still be racist—that's not the whole crux of racism. It's a systemic issue, and there's a certain group of people that are discriminated against because of the color of their skin for the benefit of another group of ruling people. So, yeah, with Trump it's been very difficult for me. There's certain people that I avoid and have kind of written out of my life. But I've also tried to have discussions with certain people because I think that talking to people is important.

MATT: That was going to be my next question because, for me, there's too much of a readiness and a willingness in today's internet-driven society to shut people down—or even block or erase them—if they disagree with you, or hold a viewpoint that you don't share. And if you only surround yourself with like-minded people, then you wind up living in an echo chamber, which I think is both regressive and dangerous.

JUSTIN: Correct. I totally agree. I think that dialogue is very important and I've tried to have that dialogue before giving up on people. But anyone I decided I didn't want in my life anymore was someone that was already on the fence, you know what I mean?

MATT: I hear you.

JUSTIN: And I took Trump very personally because I see the impact that it's having on my Black, Mexican, Muslim, gay, and trans friends. And there are people in the refugee community, and the undocumented community, who are afraid to go to the police now if they have a problem, or there's violence in their life. Things like Charlottesville [the Unite the Right neo-Nazi rally] wouldn't have happened without Trump, either.

And look, I was not a fan of Obama—just look at his drone program, or his domestic surveillance program, or the fact that he didn't go after one single banker on Wall Street after the economic crisis. I have lots of reasons not to like Obama. And I wasn't a fan of Hillary Clinton, either. I think she was basically Obama Part Two. But with Trump, it's a whole other level of corruption and destruction, and a blatant disregard for people over profits.

MATT: What's the solution then? Is there one?

JUSTIN: Well, we write these heavy songs, right? We're Anti-Flag, and we're *serious*, and we're *angry*. But the reality is this: I'm actually really optimistic. We're on tour with Reel Big Fish right now, and we had a tour set up with them in the States, too—right after the Trump election. We went out on the road with those guys, and it was amazing how many people would track us down after our set each night. And a lot of the time, I would go out to the merch area and talk to people, and so many people would come up to me and say, "I was sleepwalking. I was apathetic. I didn't care. I care now. I'm awake. I'm engaged." That was really inspiring to see and hear.

There were five days of protests in Pittsburgh after Trump was elected, too. I think people wanted to send a certain message, and it's the message that on our new record—to me at least—is the most important message: "If you're one of the people that Trump is scapegoating; if you're one of the people that's being persecuted right now, we're not going to leave you on your own. We've got your back. We're there for you. And we're there to fight for you, and stand with you." I'm seeing so many people come out of the woodwork and saying those things. And that gives me a lot of hope.

If there is a silver lining to Trump—and this would really have to be a silver lining because make no mistake, Trump has done a lot of damage and a lot of harm to a lot of people already, and he's only just got started—it's that people are getting engaged *because* of him. I believe there's already a huge backlash against him, and that backlash is only going to get stronger.

We have an opportunity, right now, not just to go back to the way things were with Obama, but to have some vision and move beyond where we were with Obama. So let's work on healthcare for all people. That seems like a novel idea in the UK, but in the States that's a huge hurdle to get over. Let's talk about real gun reform, too. And let's talk about reeling in our military, so we don't have military bases all over the world in places where we don't belong.

MATT: Do you think these are achievable goals?

JUSTIN: I do. They're obviously huge issues to tackle, but the consensus with more and more Americans is that they're out of sync with what needs to be happening in our society. And I hear that message being expressed in places where I never thought I would hear it being expressed. Also, when you're working for progress, you quite often fail, and you fail, and you fail, and you fail…then you get a victory. When you look at a Martin Luther King [Jr.], or a Gandhi, they didn't win overnight. It took a long time. In my parents' lifetime, they lived in a segregated America where there were "Whites Only" water fountains. And a lot of people thought that would never go away. How could it go away? It was so entrenched in our society. But for progress to happen, we have to believe. And we have to keep fighting for change—even against the greatest odds.

CHUCK ROBERTSON—*MAD CADDIES*

CHUCK: There's no black and white. There's no left and right. There's really just the middle. I was reading some article a while back about how a few hundred years ago in your country, it was commonly believed that royal blood was superior, and anyone not born of royal blood was inferior—mentally, physically, in every way. Then some lord decided to do an experiment at some town fair in England, where he played a game called "guess the weight of this cow." What they found, and this is true today, is that the right answer was the common sum of everyone's answer.

MATT: The law of average.

CHUCK: Exactly. Some people were way off to the left, and other people were way off to the right, but *the law of average* proved to be correct: if they got enough people to guess, most people would guess close to the right answer. And that's the same with politics—and life in general. It's why we do better as a community when we all work together to solve problems. It all goes back to "how much does this fucking cow weigh?"

Of course, some people are brighter at math, or whatever. But everyone has a place in society. And people on the left can be just as crazy and extreme as the assholes on the right. But where we all meet is the middle: the common ground. What do we *all* need? What can we *all* agree on? Let's just start there.

MATT: That's where I stand: firmly in the middle, often looking out in amazement at all the madness on both sides.

CHUCK: Same. Both the right and the left have moved so far along the opposite ends of the spectrum that most of us are just waving our dicks in the middle going, "What the hell happened to common fucking decency?" When you look back at shit from the election in our country when Obama was running for president, you had people saying, "He's a Muslim." Then John McCain gets up there and he goes, "No. He's not a Muslim. He's a Christian. But even if he was a Muslim, it doesn't matter. He's a good man. You shouldn't be scared of him."

Now you've got the orange head up there, starting a fascist civil war in our country, and it's happening over here with Brexit, too. It's the same shit. White people only make up 30 percent of the United States now. So why are 90 percent of the people in power old white men? Women make up half of our country, but they're still massively underrepresented, and they should be equally represented. It goes back to the old mothers of the community who kept the peace.

We have a saying back home, and I'm sure it's a proverb all around the world: it takes a village to raise a child. It can't just be one or two people. You need the help of everyone to educate a young child how to love, and be empathetic, considerate, and compassionate to others. These are all things that are taught and learned, just like racism and ignorance.

MINA CAPUTO—*LIFE OF AGONY, SOLO ARTIST*

MINA: Everyone is preoccupied with Trump, but the political paradigm doesn't begin with Trump: it began thousands of years ago. We've just inherited this maniacal, twisted sense of self through all the institutions set into place by mankind, which isn't at all progressive for humanity. I think control always existed. I think if you have a virus like the human race on a planet, we seek to control the uncontrollable, whether it's a rash on our body or an STD, or a girlfriend or a boyfriend, or a child in the educational system. I believe there's all different kinds of elitists and globalists and corrupt things going on that we'll never really know about.

The internet was an idea invented by the military to harness thermonuclear power. I don't know all the details of it, but whatever was going on in that military industrial complex completely failed and the internet got into the hands of the people. Then the world became smaller, and now lots more interesting information is seeping through the cracks, whether it's fluoride in the water, how to preserve your pineal gland, or the Egyptians really being a forty-thousand-year-old culture rather than a five-thousand-year-old culture. The bought and sold scientists of today basically have this fake timeline going on. But then you have cats like Graham Hancock debunking this oversimplified idea of humanity. How do you explain the Vatican withholding fifty miles of ancient texts from the public? What the fuck are they hiding? God knows how many fucking bones are buried down there. I'll probably be shot after this interview, by the way.

JESSE MALIN—*HEART ATTACK, D GENERATION, SOLO ARTIST*

JESSE: I think we have to be more evolved to a certain point of understanding and respect, and I don't think we're anywhere near that yet, unfortunately. Some of the decisions that both of our countries and the masses have made in recent years have really reflected where their minds are at, who they believe in, and how they think things can be solved. If we're not careful, we going to burn this planet up. I know terrible things have been happening for years and we're still surviving, but it certainly feels like the time bomb is ticking right now. I recently saw *1984* on Broadway, and I'm not usually a big Broadway guy, but it was so relevant to what's happening right now. And once the play ended, everyone's head went right back into their cell phones.

A lot of the fear that the government and media push is set up so they can get away with certain stuff, and they're able to take away a lot of our liberties in the name of protecting us from these awful things that have happened in the past, and are supposedly happening more and more. Media manipulation and Trump coming into power all felt like interconnected propaganda to me. Even when you listen to the more liberal news, like CNN, you just know there's so much money behind all of it, and you're never going to get the full truth. The media really affects how people think, what they fear, and how they vote. It's a very hypnotic tool.

MATT: Is a lot of this what inspired your song "Meet Me at the End of the World"?

JESSE: Yeah, but that song is also just about living each day to the fullest, like it could be your last. Terrible things do happen all the time, but life can also be great; you can create your own world; you can have great friends and family; you can give love and get love back. That's always been my message. I've taken the PMA thing from the Bad Brains—I've put it on my guitar and a couple of T-shirts over the years—and preached that life is attitude, and respecting each other and the planet is important.

Good communal energy starts in your own circle. My mom used to say, "Show me who your friends are, and it will show me who you are." So surround yourself with good people and treat each other well, and try to do something positive with your time on this planet.

ROGER LIMA—*LESS THAN JAKE, REHASHER*

ROGER: Overall, the world is a good place. Wherever we go on our travels—Japan, Australia, the UK, wherever—we meet good fucking people. And I have faith in the world community. We have a very unique perspective, obviously, because we're going in to play music and people like music, so there's always a positive energy everywhere we go. I'm really fortunate to experience the world in that way. But it also makes me think, "It could be like this for everyone," because I think there's positivity everywhere. I really get behind that world community perspective.

You can go and see a punk rock show anywhere in the world, and it's not going to be that different wherever you go. I don't understand all these lines that are drawn. Maybe if you're like twenty years old and you still don't know what you're talking about, you might still think that racism makes sense, and you might not understand why this couple is two guys, or whatever. You're young, you're dumb—I get that. But after being around for a while, those lines should disappear. And traveling the world is a really good way to understand that we're all just the same. None of that other shit matters.

BRIAN FALLON—*THE GASLIGHT ANTHEM, THE HORRIBLE CROWES, SOLO ARTIST*

BRIAN: There are so many dividing lines between people: I'm a Republican, I'm a Democrat, I voted for Donald Trump, I voted for Hillary Clinton, I'm straight, I'm gay, I'm Catholic, I'm Protestant, I'm Muslim, I'm this, I'm that. There's all these lines that separate people, but I feel like at the baseline of humanity we're all just the same: everybody's got a heart, everybody's got problems, and everybody's got joy. It would help if people could see that more.

Of course, everyone should be an individual—I fully support that. But there's a commonality no matter what you say: everybody feels the same things. If you put on a Madonna song, everyone wants to dance. I've never seen anyone not want to dance to Madonna, I don't care where you come from. That's what music does: it unifies people. I think music is maybe the last thing that truly brings people together, and that's what's special about it.

There's a connection between human beings that I think has either been forgotten about, or no longer paid attention to. But it's there and we can't forget it. And that's what drives me to create. I would never want someone to not come to my show because they're Catholic and there's a Muslim there. That would really bum me out if I found that out. I think if people were just more accepting of each other and our differences, we definitely wouldn't be having the problems that we're having right now. But even while saying this, I can't help but feel stupid because I'm just an uneducated musician. What do I know?

MATT: Well, you have seen a lot of the world, and you've met a lot of people through touring and playing shows.

BRIAN: I have, but I still feel very unvalidated in my opinions. Every opinion that I have, I've built because that's what I think for my life. Who am I to be telling other people what to think? I don't know it all; I haven't found the truth or the bottom line in life yet. That's why I hesitate to make heavy opinions. All I can say is what I think. And people might disagree with me and see things in a different way, but that's cool. I respect that. And if you want to let me know how you feel, then lay it on me, and maybe I'll learn something. The only thing I do know to be true is that you can't separate people or choose not to like them because they're different from you. You learn that in the sand box when you're a kid.

When you meet someone, they start at one hundred percent: they're the best person you ever met in your life. Let them dictate whether it goes down. Their race doesn't do it, and who they go to bed with doesn't do it. Because guess what, buddy? You don't have to go to bed with them. And you don't have to go to the same church as them. It's none of your fucking business what anyone else does. So before you decide your opinion on anyone, how about you meet them with a little bit of sympathy? And if they want to talk to you and get real, then listen—just listen before you form your opinion. You have to try and see things from the other person's point of view; imagine the road they've walked to get to where you're meeting them today.

JOEY CAPE—*LAGWAGON, ME FIRST AND THE GIMME GIMMES, SOLO ARTIST*

JOEY: My religion is compassion and kindness. That transcends all of it; just be kind to other people and live your life that way. I don't believe in karma and fate or any of that stuff—it's not coming back to me, necessarily. But I believe that when you live your life that way, and you treat people with common courtesy, it makes your life a happier one because it feels good to be nice to people. Sometimes people forget that.

The thing that I find the most terrifying, which isn't so much the politics and the state of the world right now—although that's all terrifying, of course—is the diminishment of important pieces to humanity's survival, like empathy, compassion, and courtesy. All of those things are dying out, and I find that far more disturbing than anything else. I held a door open for this old man as I was exiting a building not too long ago. He was maybe fifteen feet behind me, but I saw him coming and he was very old, so I stayed and I held the door open for him because of course that's what you do. And he cried. He took me to the side and he said, "Nobody ever does that anymore." And he started crying. It broke my heart.

FRANK IERO—*MY CHEMICAL ROMANCE, LEATHERMOUTH, SOLO ARTIST*

FRANK: I desperately want to believe in something bigger than myself. If we could prove that we weren't just worm food after this, that would be a wonderful thing. But I feel like right now we're in dire straits because people are so concerned with what comes next in the afterlife, they're actually destroying what's around them. They don't treat the people that are here—or the planet that we're on—with any kind of respect because they're so concerned about the next realm. And it would be nice to know that there's something else out there, but it might also be nice to know that there's nothing else out there, and this is it. So stop fucking it up.

MATT CAUGHTHRAN—*THE BRONX, MARIACHI EL BRONX*

MATT C: Growing up, I went to church every Sunday. Religion was never forced on me—we were just a Christian family who believed in God. But I was relatively young when I saw it all for what I think it is. I went to Christian high school, and in Christian schools at that time— at least in the one I went to—there was a lot of hatred toward other people. That's one of the things that I hate about religion: it's meant to be this beautiful way of being in touch with the creator of the Earth and all that stuff, but the ugly reality is it's basically just a bunch of people saying, "My God is better than your God. We're going to heaven, but your group is going to hell."—all that finger-pointing shit.

CHUCK RAGAN—*HOT WATER MUSIC, SOLO ARTIST*

CHUCK: As a young kid growing up, religion was really pushed on me, and it just didn't feel right. I grew up going to religious, Christian schools, and I rebelled against everything and everyone. I really fought the church.

FRANK IERO

FRANK: I remember vividly being in fifth grade and being forced to sign a petition against a movie being released. It was a movie about priests molesting children, and it obviously portrayed the Catholic church in a very bad light. I remember the principal and the nun, who was my teacher at the time, saying that it was a requirement to sign it. And I remember, even in a fifth grade mindset, thinking, "This is ridiculous." That kind of sums up my feeling on organized religion. It's like they say: "You can count the atheists in the room by how many people went to Catholic school."

JUSTIN SANE

JUSTIN: I'm perfectly willing to respect everyone's religious beliefs, but to me religion just feels kind of silly. Santa Claus isn't real—

MATT: What?

JUSTIN: The Easter Bunny isn't real—

MATT: *What?* You're bumming me out, dude!

JUSTIN: I should've put a child disclaimer on this. I'm sorry, buddy. But it's amazing to me that people can disassociate from reality in that way. If you feel connected to a spiritual force, then I can almost relate to that. But what I can't relate to are the writings from a book that someone wrote down thousands of years ago that people are still holding on to as dogma. That just seems a little naïve to me. And I have a hard time, just from a standpoint of simple logic, understanding why people would buy into that.

The example that I have in my life that helps me understand is my mom and dad. Both of them tell me—and they would tell you the same if they were here—that they were brainwashed from day one, in the same way that people are brainwashed with nationalism. So I was really turned off religion from day one.

MATT: The thing about religion, and the stories contained within these ancient texts, is they're age-old fables clearly designed to give life meaning many years ago. And a lot them don't necessarily have any relevance to the world today.

JUSTIN: To give life meaning and social structure, sure. But also to keep elites in power. And now we have a new religion called capitalism, which also keeps the elites in power.

MATT: And that's overtaken any religion that came before it: Capitalism absolutely dominates modern-day society on a global scale.

JUSTIN: Yeah, and I think growing up poor and having it rough— whilst it wasn't a lot of fun at the time—really helped me to care about the situation of other people a lot more. When you go to school in the middle of winter without a proper jacket, it definitely helps you to have empathy for other people who don't have a lot. And I think it also helps you be grateful for what you do have.

MINA CAPUTO

MINA: It isn't even about money anymore because the abundance on the planet is infinite. Notice how these ages of Depression only ever hit the poor neighborhoods? They're all just games of depopulation. There's so much cryptic stuff going on. And institutionalized religion isn't about love, otherwise they wouldn't condemn people like me that are expanding and have something positive to teach and share.

Humanity is an ever-growing, free energy that's encased in a temporary physical manifestation. We're here and now, and then in a blink of an eye we go there—wherever there is. Even the portraits that they paint of their ideologies of death are corrupt. Death is probably the most magnificent experience that there is. I don't believe in the traditional idea of death, and I'm not afraid of dying. I actually look forward to it.

MATT: It's the great unknown, right?

MINA: It's the great unknown. And I believe in my own intuition, more than any scholar or anything that's been taught on this planet by any man. My intuition isn't any less than the Dalai Lama. Neither is yours, or the poor kid in Ethiopia, or the German Queen that you guys have here in England, or Johnny Lydon over in fucking Malibu. Our intuition is our source: it's that great breath that allows us to experience the beauty of what this planet and its people have to offer. It's all about frequency, energy, and vibration. You just need to tap into your own source—your own radio dial.

I think everyone knows when they look in the mirror, whether they want to look at their own self or not, that something bigger is going on. It's like what George Carlin said: "There's this big party going on, and we're not invited." There's a lot happening right now. But then there are things that are *really* happening, and you are what you focus on. My suggestion to people is just to focus on being happy. Don't be happy after you get the car in the garage; be happy now; watch love manifest around you; watch friendship manifest around you; watch whatever you want and desire manifest around you. That's how I live my life. And I'm not perfect. I have my ups and my downs, but that contrast and negativity is good. All these things are there to teach us. And my dog has taught me more about unconditional love than any institutionalized religion, be it Buddhism, Hinduism, Catholicism, Judaism, or Islam—which are all fear-based, barrier-based teachings. We're all growing, and we'll continue to grow because this is just preparation for the real growth, and the real growth is leaving the physical body.

The here and the now is the only moment that will ever truly exist or matter. That's all that we ever truly have. There is no future— John Lydon always had it right. It's just an illusion. It's all an illusion. But a lot of people on the planet don't have the ability to suss up that thought and feeling. They don't want to go there because they're more concerned about the new sneaker, or the new iPhone. My priority is health and happiness. The rest is just gifts. You need to be creative to live life. That's how you keep things interesting: you creatively experience the here and now. Once you start conventionalizing your own self-yearning, you're fucked.

ANDREW W.K.—*SINGER-SONGWRITER, PRODUCER, WRITER, MOTIVATIONAL SPEAKER*

MATT: I often think about the reason why we're all here on this planet. It's a trip, isn't it?

ANDREW: It's the trip of all trips. And there's no way to hide from the big questions like that. You can fool yourself into thinking that you're not thinking about them, or that you don't want to think about them, but you're facing it at all times. Even choosing to seemingly not engage with these questions is still a way of engaging with them. At some point, you just break down and turn yourself over to it, and maybe even not to get any answers, but just to stay up close in the questioning of it.

What's quite exciting, of course, is that for thousands and thousands of years, the greatest human minds have more or less devoted themselves entirely to these questions, and they have a lot of interesting thoughts on them. I find those who are so bold as to say that they had it all figured quite inspiring. Even if the answer isn't the right answer for you or me, the fact that they had the courage to dive in is inspiring. And almost every point of view has some validity: they all seem to ring true in a consistent way with one another's. There's a common thread of integrity, too, even in the most radical ways of looking at the question, "what is the meaning of life?" That commonality in itself seems to point to some sort of fundamental truth. But I don't know if we can ever really grasp it in the way that we would like to. That doesn't mean that it doesn't exist, or that we can't conceive of it, of course. But it's designed to be just out of reach to keep us striving for it.

MATT: There's that great David Bowie lyric from his song "Quicksand," which says, "Knowledge comes with death's release." Do you ever give the matter of death much thought?

ANDREW: As much as is possible. It's *the* definition of the great unknown. All other fears, all other mysteries, and all other anxieties that we have about unknown aspects of this world are just reflections or shadows of the ultimate unknown, which is that moment of entering into whatever death actually is. And we really have no idea. That's what's so terrifying about it. Some people feel confident that life just stops and that's it, but we really don't know.

MATT: Do you think everything just stops? I think there's so much energy in the universe, when the lights go out on life, that can't just be it.

ANDREW: I really don't know. I like to imagine that all of a sudden everything just makes sense in a way that's on the one hand mind-shatteringly new, but at the same time completely familiar, like, "Oh, of course."

MATT: Like it was right in front of us all along.

ANDREW: Yeah. I like the idea that it's like that; a depth of understanding that can't even be expressed; an understanding that's so deep that it's physical. That's what I imagine Christ is: a love that transcends love, where everything makes sense, and always had made sense, and the things that made the least sense now make the most sense because of this incredible understanding and order that's always been there. Those are things that you can fanaticize about. Of course, you can always slip back into an intellectual interpretation, but every now and then you get these physical glimpses of clarity where you actually feel it, and that's when it gets really powerful. That's sort of what music is: music takes these ideas and turns them into something tangible in the body, and not just in the mind.

MATT: Is that a sensation that you regularly experience when playing music?

ANDREW: That's the goal. All I can say is there's this certain feeling that's inside of me that I'm also looking for, that music is able to make real. And if music wasn't there, it would stay in this illusive spot. But music pulls it out from all these disparate locations where it's just floating around, and it centralizes it for that brief moment—in that chord change, or in that melody. It crystalizes it, and allows you to hold on to it, and say, "This is real." Then you can listen to it again, and it feels like that again, and it doesn't ever slip away. That's what's so incredible about music: you can listen to the same song for forty years and it can even increase in its ability to bring that special feeling out. Those are powerful forces, and they're not just thoughts or inklings passing through your head. It's raw emotion that's coming from a more fundamental place, and I don't even want to say a deeper place because sometimes they feel like they're coming from above you, or outside of you. They can prompt someone to alter the entire course of their journey.

EUGENE HUTZ—*GOGOL BORDELLO*

MATT: What do you think the meaning of life is, Eugene? Why are we here?

EUGENE: Well, the name of our new album, *Seekers and Finders*, kind of reflects the internal conflict at the center of all human existence, which is that the ironic part of the quest, despite what many teachings say, is this: in order to find the answer, you first have to stop seeking. Some cultures say, "To find, you *must* seek." But others say the complete opposite. What is the correct answer? I don't know. But as human beings, we have immense physic power, and it's either dormant or it's not, but we all have it. There's huge creative potential behind that, too.

Personally, I believe in the diamond body, which is the spiritual essence of life-force and has many different sides and dimensions. In each lifetime, we polish one dimension—in one lifetime, you might be working on patience, for instance. And in another lifetime, you could be working on empathy, or just a general sense of composition and getting the feng shui right. It's a constantly revolving door. I should also add as a footnote that I'm siding with the theory of reincarnation; I'm operating from that perspective. And I believe there's a diamond body at the end of all this that's indestructible.

MATT: So, the payoff at the end is all of those different lessons and learning experiences come together to create something whole?

EUGENE: Maybe there's payoff. Maybe there's not. But I think it's a worthy pursuit.

MATT: I like that idea.

EUGENE: I didn't invent it. I think it originally appeared in *The Tibetan Book of the Dead*. But it's the one that I resonate with the most. European existentialism kind of ends where it ends, with a gun pointing at your head. And I'm a big fan of Jean-Paul Sartre, but I was excited to surpass that state of mind.

STEVEN VAN ZANDT—*BRUCE SPRINGSTEEN AND THE E STREET BAND, SOLO ARTIST, PRODUCER, RADIO HOST, ACTOR, ACTIVIST*

STEVEN: I left the E Street band after *Born in the U.S.A.* because I had become obsessed with politics. I felt very successful at that moment: we'd broken through with *The River* and sold three million albums. And I thought to myself, "You can't sell any more than that." Little did

I know we were about to sell twenty million copies of *Born in the U.S.A.* But three million felt like an enormous success at that time. We were selling out arenas, and I thought that was as high as you could possibly go. So my consciousness started to break down this tunnel vision that I'd had all my life of trying to make it in rock 'n' roll, which was an impossible dream to begin with, but suddenly I was there. That's when I really started to think about the world for the first time in my life.

MATT: You were sitting on the pavement, thinking about the government.

STEVEN: That's exactly right. I'd mixed my medicine in the basement, and now it was time to think about the government. So I started reading every book that I could find on our foreign policies since World War II, and I was shocked to learn that we were not the heroes of democracy that I once thought we were. I felt like nobody was really talking about that, and that it needed to be talked about.

Again, in that search for one's unique identity, I thought perhaps it was my destiny to be the political guy. So I decided to pursue nothing but politics, and be very extreme about it.

MATT: Tell me about the "Sun City" project, and the inspiration behind it.

STEVEN: Well, South Africa was on my list of forty-four different conflicts around the world that America was involved in. I was studying all of them, and South Africa was the one that I couldn't find out much information about. It was strangely hard to understand. So I went down there twice in 1984, and I did all the research that I could do, and talked to everybody that I could talk to.

At that point, my identity had become this sort of artist/journalist combination, and I was trying to stay objective about everything; I hadn't really planned on getting involved. I was just sort of observing and reporting, and doing it in my art form, which happens to be more of an emotional communication than an informational one. And I started putting book lists on my records. I would write, "If this song interests you emotionally, and you want to know the details that went into it, then read these books…"

So I'm in South Africa talking to people, and it's a very interesting situation down there. The whole homeland policy was quite diabolical and devious. They were knocking down people's homes and carrying them off to what they called their "tribal homeland." I soon realized the whole idea behind this was to get all the Black people out of South Africa, declare the country a democracy, then bring them all back in as immigrant labor. It was a beautifully evil scheme, which they basically used our American Indian reservations as the basis for.

I was beginning to put all these pieces together. Then I got in a taxi one day, and we're driving along the road, and this Black guy steps off the curb. He was a good ten feet away from the car, and the cab driver swerved to try and hit him—for sport. "Fucking kaffir," he said, which means nigger in Afrikaans. My objectivity went right out the taxi window at that point. I actually had a bit of a nervous breakdown right after that, where I had to go to the hospital for a couple of days and I didn't know why. I realized then that this was destiny at work: this was not just going to be another song on my next album. I felt like I needed to organize, and I needed to bring this government down.

So I sat down, and I started to plan out how I was going to bring down the government. I went through a logical analysis of it, and I discovered a whole side of my brain that I didn't even know existed because most of my life up until that point was total chaos. And I think most artists spend their lives in chaos; that's one of the reasons why we do art in the first place—to try and make sense out of all the chaos.

They'd already put the sports boycott together, which had been very, very effective. And I realized the government was going to come down when an economic boycott was in place because they couldn't survive without the banks. And what was in between the sports and the economic boycott? The cultural boycott. That was when I decided I was going to get one person from every musical genre to sing on a record and release it as a song against apartheid.

MATT: What an amazing ensemble as well: Tom Petty, Pete Townsend, Run-DMC—

STEVEN: I actually didn't get Petty in the end. But there were about fifty others on there. And people kept asking me why I was putting all these rappers on the record—rap at that point was very new, and people thought it was just going to go away.

MATT: I guess it still wasn't an acknowledged musical art form at that point.

STEVEN: Not at all. This was 1985, and they were trying to kill it in its infancy. But I felt it was extremely important because it gave Black Americans the chance to express themselves properly for the first time. Marvin Gaye had experienced trouble trying to make his *What's Going On* record. Stevie Wonder had to fight Berry Gordy to express himself. Miles Davis had basically been attacked his whole life, as had Gil Scott-Heron. It was just not something that Black artists were encouraged to do. Suddenly, you had all these Black artists telling the truth—telling it like it is—and I thought it was fantastic. So I put people like Afrika Bambaataa, Run-DMC, Melle Mel, and Duke Bootee on the record, right next to Pete Townsend, Lou Reed, and Jackson Browne. I wanted to make a statement about that new art form being important, at the same time as making a statement about our own racism.

Radio refused to play it because it was too Black for white radio, and it was too white for Black radio. It was only when MTV played the video that we were able to break through with it. And we were able to get so deeply into the national consciousness that senators and congresspeople's children would come back to them and say stuff like, "Daddy, what's this South Africa thing?"

When the economic boycott legislation came up, [Ronald] Reagan predictably rejected it, but we had such a strong groundswell that it overrode his veto.

MATT: Which just goes to show that music really does have the power to change the world.

STEVEN: In that case, it really did. We got that economic boycott legislation through and the dominoes fell, just like I knew they would. Then the banks cut them off, and they had to release Nelson Mandela. Boom! That's how you bring down a government. It was one big effort that was really quite unified, and we all inspired each other. It was a truly wonderful thing to be a part of.

POLITICS & RELIGION PLAYLIST

ANTI-FLAG—"CHRISTIAN NATIONALIST"
VINNIE CARUANA—"BETTER"
MAD CADDIES—"SORROW"
JESSE MALIN—"MEET ME AT THE END OF THE WORLD"
LESS THAN JAKE—"GOOD ENOUGH"
THE HORRIBLE CROWES—"I BELIEVE JESUS BROUGHT US TOGETHER"
JOEY CAPE—"I KNOW HOW TO RUN"
MY CHEMICAL ROMANCE—"DESTROYA"
THE BRONX—"THE UNHOLY HAND"
HOT WATER MUSIC—"STATE OF GRACE"
ANTI-FLAG—"FABLED WORLD"
LIFE OF AGONY—"MEET MY MAKER"
ANDREW W.K.— "TOTAL FREEDOM"
GOGOL BORDELLO—"SEEKERS AND FINDERS"
ARTISTS UNITED AGAINST APARTHEID—"SUN CITY"

CREATIVE PARTNERSHIPS

"I hate him and I love him, just like a brother."

A S FAR BACK AS I can remember, I always wanted to be a gangster. No, wait, that's *Goodfellas*. As far back as I can remember, I always wanted to be in a creative partnership. It doesn't quite have the same ring to it, does it? But it's true. And I didn't really care what it was: a DJ duo, a comedy double act, a songwriting partnership, an actor-director relationship like Scorsese and De Niro—whatever. I just wanted to do cool shit with my friends.

I have enjoyed a few fun creative partnerships over the years; I drew cartoons in school with my mate Matt Harwood; I wrote punk songs as a teenager with my best friend Greg Gaiger; I started a *Jackass* knock-off in college (Bum Rat) with my great friend Andy Telford; I fronted a DJ crew (the Fuck Yoself Collective) in university with my partner Kim Calloway; and I made a few no-budget films with my brother Joel Carr. But nothing ever stuck.

Now, granted, a lot of these sound like childhood folly and adolescent pipe dreams, and not something you could ever make a living out of. But I've always been a dreamer. And who says you can't?

After discovering NOFX, the next life-changing moment for me was the breakthrough of *Jackass*. *Jackass* showed me that it was possible to combine a love of punk rock and skateboarding with a lack of any discernible skills or talent—apart from a lust for life and an appetite for destruction—and basically get paid to muck about with your mates. The first time I saw that show, I made a silent pact with myself to never work a real job in my life. And I've spent the last two decades doing exactly that: dodging the bullet. It's been a right laugh.

It does get a little bit lonely sometimes, though. All the gigs and roles that I undertake—DJ, presenter, writer, photographer, podcaster—are one-man jobs. That's not to say they aren't lots of fun. And I do come into contact with lots of interesting and amazing people. I just wish I had a buddy to share the experiences with. But it's like Neil Diamond says, "I'll be what I am: a solitary man."—you're damn right I'm down with Neil Diamond.

Thankfully, I get to live vicariously through the people that I speak to on my podcast, and hear all about the ins and the outs of their creative partnerships, and how those friendships and relationships have defined their lives and careers. Now, it's your turn to do the same. You're about to hear B-Real on Everlast, Doug Stanhope on Joe Rogan, Steven Zan Vandt on Bruce Springsteen, Nick Oliveri on Josh Homme, Kyle Gass on Jack Black, and Steve-O on Johnny Knoxville. But first up, it's Joey Cape from Lagwagon on the main man at Fat Wreck, and my musical hero—Fat Mike from NOFX.

JOEY CAPE—*LAGWAGON, ME FIRST AND THE GIMME GIMMES, SOLO ARTIST*

MATT: How did you and Fat Mike first get acquainted?

JOEY: I'd met Mike a few times at shows, but it was never a good experience because he was always short with me. The first time I met him properly was at a show in 1990—I can't remember which one—talking to the guys in a band called RKL [Rich Kids on LSD], who I used to play with. I was actually in the original version of RKL, who were a huge influence on NOFX. So I'm from that era. I'm actually older than Mike.

There was a weird thing happening in my world at that time, where I was writing songs that tried to marry RKL's riffy, bluesy metal with Bad Religion's *Suffer*. When I first heard that record, I was like,

"Oh, shit. We can do this." Because I wanted to hear harmonies. I love The Beach Boys and The Beatles, and that was where my head was at. And when I first met Mike, that's exactly where his head was at, too, which was really interesting and cool. I think that's why NOFX and Lagwagon have a very similar sound.

Mike had already set up Fat Wreck Chords by this point, but they only had the first NOFX 7-inch out [*The Longest Line*]. And I had a Lagwagon demo in the glove compartment of my car that night. I thought to myself, "Fuck it. What have I got to lose?" So I went outside and I got the demo, then I came back inside and gave it to Mike.

Mike called me the next day—I don't even know how he got my number because I was living at my dad's house at the time—and he was like, "Dude, do you want to do a record?" I said, "Yeah, but I have to call all the other guys, as we're kind of not a band anymore." I rang them all up, and I said, "Fat Mike just called me, and he wants to make a record with us. Are you guys in?" The next thing I know, we're in LA recording *Duh* with Mike producing, and we did the whole thing in three days—mixed and everything.

It said Section 8 on the reels because that's what we were originally called. And Mike hated the name. He said to us from the start, "You guys have to change your name. It's a shit name." We were all like, "Fuck you. Who are you? That's our name. We're a band, man. We don't need you." Because we were proud. And I liked the name.

What happened next was this: we went on a Pacific Northwest tour with NOFX, and at every town we played someone came up to us and said, "So you guys are that band that have that 7-inch, *Fat, Drunk, & Stupid?*" It turned out there was another punk band called Section 8 that already had this 7-inch out, and we didn't really want anything to do with them. Then we were in a record store one day around the time all the hardcore stuff by NWA was coming out, and there was a poster on the wall for this other band from Compton called Section 8. I saw the poster, looked at Derrick [Plourde], and said, "Well, that just about does it. I don't want to argue with those guys." So we changed our name to Lagwagon, and the rest is history.

MATT: Was Lagwagon the first Fat Wreck Chords band?

JOEY: Yeah. I consider us to be the flagship Fat Wreck Chords band, too. Our first album was the first full-length record they put out, and we're the only band to have put out all our records with that label. And we've never seen any reason to leave: we've always had the best relationship with the people that work there, and those people are my friends.

MATT: Why do you think the label had such a long and successful run?

JOEY: The thing that Fat Wreck Chords has always done well—that I've always understood to be their genius—is Mike knew from the beginning not to spend more than he was going to make. And that sounds so simple, but everyone gets the fever once things start going, and they all start saying, "If we want to jump to the next level then we've got to take some risks." But if you just stay and grow with the game, you're going to enjoy longevity. I understood that to be a wise decision, even back then. It's how I operate in every aspect of my life to this day. I've met a lot of guys that've been in giant bands over the years, and now have nothing. That's just ridiculous. Where did those millions of dollars go? So we never had a reason to leave Fat Wreck Chords. And I feel like everything I've ever done, creatively, is all in one place, which feels really good.

CHUCK ROBERTSON—*MAD CADDIES*

MATT: When did Mad Caddies sign to Fat Wreck Chords?

CHUCK: We got signed in '96, and *Quality Soft Core* came out in the spring of '97. It was originally just supposed to be a demo. We all borrowed a couple of hundred bucks from our parents, raised a couple of grand, then went to the local studio in Santa Barbara [Orange Whip Recording Studios] to cut the tracks. It was all done in four or five days, and I only had one day on vocals. Literally two days after we finished it, Fat Mike called Sascha [Lazor] out of the blue—

MATT: How did he find out about the band?

CHUCK: Lagwagon are from Santa Barbara as well, and they'd been recording in the same studio as us. We'd never met any of those guys, as we were all ten years younger than them, but Joey Cape came into the studio one day when the engineer was putting the final mix together, and he was like, "Oh, this sounds good. Who's this?" We weren't even called the Mad Caddies at this point: we were called The Ivy League back then. And Joey Cape said, "Fat Mike is looking for a ska band to sign. I'm going to send this on up." Mike called Sascha two days later and was like, "Hey, Sascha. It's Fat Mike." Sascha thought it was me fucking with him at first. He was like, "Shut up, Chuck. What do you want?" And Mike was like, "No, no, it's Fat Mike." Then he recognized Mike's voice from videos and stuff like that, and Mike said, "I just got your record. And I want to sign you guys." He came down a few days later and took us out to dinner. Then he signed us, bought us a van and some gear, and put us out on the road. It's basically been like that ever since.

MATT: Has Mike been a good friend and mentor to you over the various ages and stages of your career?

CHUCK: Oh, absolutely. I consider him a dear friend, mentor, and musical and business role model. He's a really, *really* unique individual, especially when it comes to lyrics, melodies, and songwriting. It's always nice to hear his opinion when we're working on a project.

MATT: What's he like in private? Who's the guy behind the guy?

CHUCK: The guy behind the guy is just Mike, man. He's just a little Jewish kid from a wealthy broken home. From what I've come to understand, his dad wasn't around much, so his mom pretty much raised him. And he was always super motivated to be successful. The character that you see of him is just his alter ego, which I personally think is put in place to hide some of his demons from kind of a sad, lonely childhood. But whatever shit people want to talk about Mike, he's a really lovely person deep down. He loves punk rock, he cares about his friends, and he really takes care of his bands. He's always coming up with creative ideas to do something new and different, too. And he always tries to share the profits with everybody.

MATT CAUGHTHRAN—*THE BRONX, MARIACHI EL BRONX*

MATT S: I feel like all bands *should* be a gang, but The Bronx really seem like a tight unit.

MATT C: Absolutely, man. That's just the way we roll: we look out for each other, we work hard for each other, and we hold each other accountable. The great thing about this band, and the thing that I think you want out of any situation—whether it's a working relationship, or a partnership with a significant other—is just to be yourself, and to not have to hide any side of your personality, for better or worse. We all work hard for each other, and we've been through some of the raddest stuff ever, so we're all very fortunate. I trip out at the talent that I get to be surrounded by on a nightly basis. Everyone in this band just rips, and we all still love what we do.

TIM McILRATH—*RISE AGAINST*

MATT: Bill Stevenson seems to be a key figure in the evolution of Rise Against. Where does that relationship begin?

TIM: Bill's role in Rise Against can't be overstated enough. He's like our sensei; he's our mentor; he's our guru; he's the fifth member of the band. We wouldn't be here in the way that we are without him. I guess it would be like if you showed up in a country speaking a different language, and he was the first person you met who understood you. As you said earlier, Rise Against straddles many musical lines, and Bill understood that right off the bat. We always loved his production work. And we ended up having two different producers fall through for our second record [*Revolutions per Minute*]. I'm so glad that they did, though, because then we met with Bill and decided to do the record with him—between Thanksgiving and Christmas in 2002. He understood our band from the get-go, which was amazing. And not just the music, but also the lyrics, and who we were and what we wanted to do. And because he was such a hero of ours from Descendents and Black Flag, we were excited just to be around him and hear his stories.

The band was getting a little bigger at that time, and as your band gets bigger, the circle of people that you trust gets smaller, and it all kind of closes in. Bill became somebody that I lived to impress—even to this day. I not only took his criticism, I craved it. And he would always shoot me straight. He was one of those guys that we really listened to. After *Revolutions per Minute,* we did *Siren Song of the Counter Culture* with Garth Richardson, but we had a bad experience with him and it made us long for Bill. Working with him was so great, and we took for granted that not every experience would be that great. After it wasn't great, we realized we'd struck gold with Bill, and that we needed to go back and work with him again. So we did: we made the next four records with him [*The Sufferer & the Witness, Appeal to Reason, Endgame,* and *The Black Market*], in fact.

B-REAL—*CYPRESS HILL, PROPHETS OF RAGE*

MATT: Talk to me about Everlast.

B-REAL: Everlast has been my brother through the thick and thin in both our careers. We've been good friends through all our ups and downs; we were at each other's weddings, and we practically live an identical life. I think that's why our bond has been so strong for these twenty-some odd years. We've been able to work together, tour together, and hang out as friends away from the business. It's been a dope friendship, man. I have a pretty decent circle of people that I can say are my brothers and sisters, aside from my immediate family, and he's definitely one of them.

MATT: Did you link him up with DJ Muggs?

B-REAL: In terms of them working together, yes. Everlast and Muggs already knew each other through this girl that Muggs was dating because she was friends with the girl that Everlast was dating. I believe the two women lived together in an apartment, or they were just that close that they'd always spend time at each other's spot. So that's how Muggs met [DJ] Lethal and Everlast, and I met Everlast through them.

MATT: What was your first impression of him?

B-REAL: I just thought he was a fucking cool dude. We got along right off the top. And at one point he was showing me the new style that he was doing, as opposed to the one that he'd been doing with the [Rhyme] Syndicate and whatnot, and I thought it was dope; I heard the potential there because he's a very talented dude.

At this point, I'd already been given the "Jump Around" beat from Muggs, but for some reason I couldn't come up with anything for it—it's one of the few times in my career where I pretty much got stumped by a song. I gave the beat back to Muggs, and I said, "For some reason, there's nothing coming to me off this." I think he got kind of bothered by that. He gave me the Muggs look, like, "*What? How dare you?*" But I said, "Look, I think if you gave it to Everlast, he can do something with it. He's got some cool shit jumping off at the moment, and I think he can make this one go."

To Muggs' credit, he was open-minded enough to play it for Everlast, and Everlast jumped right on it like I knew he could—and would. He fucking smashed it out of the park: it was a home run. I kick myself for not being able to come up with something as clever, but it was meant for him, and everything like that happens for a reason. Maybe if I had got on that song, it wouldn't have become the hit that it became with House of Pain. For me, that beat was something that was meant to be for them, and my part in it was suggesting to Muggs that he gave it to Everlast because I thought that he'd do something with it, which he did.

DOUG STANHOPE—*COMEDIAN, AUTHOR, PODCAST HOST*

MATT: You and Joe Rogan go way back, right?

DOUG: Yeah. I probably met him in the late nineties. I think he was still on news radio at the time.

MATT: What was the name of the TV show that you two did together?

DOUG: It was called *The Man Show.* Jimmy Kimmel and Adam Carolla hosted it first, and then they left. But Comedy Central still owned the rights to the show, so they just replaced them as hosts, which was a fucking terrible idea, especially with the way that they wanted it to go. It was a miserable failure.

MATT: Did you enjoy working with Joe, though?

DOUG: I enjoyed working with Joe, but I didn't enjoy doing television. It was a huge wakeup call for me. And I really don't need to live in LA. I want to do stand-up comedy. I don't want to do dog-shit TV.

MATT: Are you impressed by the whole comedy/podcast universe that Rogan has created for himself?"

DOUG: Yeah, he's a fucking monster. I just talked to him last night. He's doing fucking arenas now—like seven thousand seats.

STEVEN VAN ZANDT—*BRUCE SPRINGSTEEN AND THE E STREET BAND, SOLO ARTIST, PRODUCER, RADIO HOST, ACTOR, ACTIVIST*

MATT: When did you first meet Bruce Springsteen? And are you two the same age?

STEVEN: He's a year older than me. I think I was fifteen when we first met, and he was sixteen. We both had bands of our own at that point.

MATT: Were you the singer in your band?

STEVEN: Yeah. I led my own band, which was called The Source, and he led his band. And we'd always see each other at band battles, which my band always won—obviously.

MATT: Obviously.

STEVEN: There was only about a dozen bands in the entire area, so we all got to know each other pretty well. On the weekends, I'd go up to Café Wha? in New York City—which is still there, by the way—and on Saturday afternoons they'd have one band after the other perform.

So I'd sit there all day watching bands play. And I'd learn, and I'd learn, and I'd learn, because the bands in New York were like a year ahead of the bands in New Jersey. Then I started running into Bruce there as well.

MATT: You both always had that motivation to seek out the source, then?

STEVEN: Yeah. And we became even closer through that. But if you were in a band in New Jersey back then, you were friends with other bands anyway. And if you had long hair as well, then you were friends immediately.

MATT: What year did you start playing in a band together?

STEVEN: In 1975, on the *Born to Run* tour. The first two records [*Greetings from Ashbury Park, N.J.* and *The Wild, the Innocent & the E Street Shuffle*] hadn't done anything, and the third record was going to be the end. They were about to drop them from the record label, and if *Born to Run* hadn't have been as good as it was, then that would've been the end of Bruce's career.

MATT: What do you think it was that made the Jersey Shore sound so unique? Was it just your amalgamation of influences as musicians?

STEVEN: Yeah. You're looking for your identity, as I said before, and in those days you really had to have a distinct identity to be valid. With The Asbury Jukes, me, [Southside] Johnny, and Bruce had gone to see Sam & Dave perform live, and it was the greatest thing we'd ever seen. It was incredible. And me and Johnny said, "Okay, we're going to be the white Sam & Dave, but with rock guitars."

MATT: Because that hadn't been done at that point?

STEVEN: Right. We just kind of fell into that sound, and it felt kind of interesting. It felt like fun, too. It felt good. And it also happened to be original in its own way, which was a nice bonus. So that's where that sound of rock meets soul began. And in putting that together we kind of revolutionized what a bar band was. Before that, you had to play the

Top 40 hits, and that was the only way you could work in New Jersey. But we broke the mold.

MATT: How did you manage to get away without playing covers?

STEVEN: We discovered a club where the roof had caved in because of a hurricane, which they were going to close four weeks later. And we said to them, "Listen, man. We'll play for the door fee, and you take the bar. You're going to close anyway, so we're going to play whatever we want." No one had ever done that before. And that club was The Stone Pony. We played for fifty people the first week, a hundred people the next week, and two hundred people the week after that. Then they fixed the roof after the third week. And they expanded the club three months later, and went from a four-hundred-person club to a thousand-person club, and that's how it all happened. Suddenly, the phrase "bar band" became respectable. Even in the reviews, all the bands that came after us—Graham Parker, Elvis Costello, Mink DeVille, and Huey Lewis and the News—would be referred to as bar bands, and they meant it as a compliment for the first time. It was no longer an insult; the term became respectable.

MATT: You wrote the horn arrangement for "Tenth Avenue Freeze-Out" on *Born to Run*, which was the first song that you recorded with Springsteen. How did that situation come about?

STEVEN: It was a strange point in time because all the records of the 1950s and 1960s sounded great, and all the records of the 1970s sounded terrible—to me at least. I was in the studio visiting the band, as I'd known Bruce at this point since 1965, and this was 1974. We'd known each other a long time, and he was in the music business by this point, but I was still suspect about it, and being in that studio made me even more suspect about it. The band were in there recording, and this was supposed to be an exciting process—this was supposed to be the moment he'd been waiting and working for his whole life. But it just sounded terrible, man.

MATT: Did you have the kind of a relationship where you could just tell him that straight up?

STEVEN: Yeah. That was the period where the engineers took over and started close-miking and padding everything, and wanting to be in total control, as engineers often do. That's just their nature, God bless them. But that kind of separation, clarity, and control has nothing to do with rock 'n' roll. So I'm lying there on the floor, they're doing "Tenth Avenue," and they're recording some bogus horn chart, when Bruce says to me, "Well? What do you think?" They were in a desperate situation that I really knew nothing about. Their whole life depended on this record, and I really didn't care about anything at that point. So when Bruce asked me what I thought, I was like, "It blows. It sucks." There was a moment of stunned silence that followed, and then Bruce was like, "Well, go on in and fucking fix it, man." I said, "All right," and I went in. I didn't know these guys were the biggest session musicians in New York. But I wasn't intimidated because I didn't give a shit who they were. I just sang the parts and that was that. Job done.

CJ RAMONE—*RAMONES, SOLO ARTIST*

MATT: When you first joined the Ramones, how did you fit in with the rest of the band?

CJ: It's funny, when I first got into the band, I thought I was joining a gang. I'd always thought of the Ramones as a gang; I literally thought they were still hanging around together. So I had no clue. But I've never been the type of fan that wants to know what a band does when they're offstage, or anything like that.

When I got there in the beginning, I noticed that it was quiet in the van and there wasn't a whole lot of communication going on. But I just thought that was because they'd been together a long time. I didn't understand the situation between Joey and Johnny until later on. Then during some time that we had off from touring, I went for dinner at Johnny and Linda's apartment. And when I got in the van and said hello to everybody at the start of the next run of shows, I asked

Johnny how Linda was doing. All of a sudden, everything got quiet, and I was like, "Something's up."

We drove to the first show, and when we got there Monte [A. Melnick] pulled me out of the dressing room and into the hallway. He said, "CJ, you really have no idea about anything with Johnny and Joey and Linda?" I was like, "No. I don't have any idea." And that's when he told me, "Linda was Joey's girlfriend, and Johnny and her fell in love, and he kind of stole her away from Joey." I was like, "Oh, boy. Okay. I get it. I totally understand now." It explained a lot, and I realized at that point that it was going to be like a tightrope walk trying to be friends with both of them.

Johnny started showing me the ropes right away and telling me what was expected of me, so I communicated more with him at first. But Joey and I eventually became really good friends; I used to go to shows with him and stay at his apartment, and we would just hang out and listen to music together. Joey and I actually became close friends. Johnny was always my mentor, though, so he was more like a father figure to me. And he gets kind of an unfair shake for being a bit of a prick. And I'm not saying that he wasn't a prick—he was kind of tough, personality-wise. And he was very opinionated. But once Tommy was gone—and Tommy was the real creator of the Ramones—it was like the lunatics were in charge of the asylum.

You had Joey, who was mentally unstable. You had Marky, who was a really bad alcoholic. You had Dee Dee, who was a full-blown drug addict. And you had Johnny, and Johnny became the guy that had to keep those three tough characters in line. He had to make it all happen: all the day-to-day stuff was really all on him. That's kind of partially why Johnny was the way he was. And being that I'd just come out of the Marine Corps and was used to being told what to do, I had no problem with it. I didn't think he was a prick; I just thought he was very direct.

I really had to work hard to maintain relationships with Johnny and Joey. But I thought if I could be that in-between guy, then maybe

I could help motivate the band a little more to get things done. Of course, that was wishful thinking. But in a lot of ways, I think I really did help bridge some of the stuff between Johnny and Joey because they could both communicate through me. If Johnny said something to me, I would explain it to Joey in a way that I knew he'd understand, or at least be accepting of it—and vice versa.

It's crazy that they never made up. They literally took it to the grave. And it was definitely an uncomfortable situation. But that friction also created something really special, like Lennon and McCartney—they were both always struggling to be the guy.

MATT: Did Joey and Johnny clash over politics to the extent that it's been suggested that they did?

CJ: Politics didn't come up a whole bunch, to be honest. When it did, they always had opposing views, and I witnessed them have a little back and forth sometimes, but they were always both constructive in what they said. They'd be going at it, and Marky would say something to Johnny like, "Yeah, all right Nixon," and immediately everybody would laugh, and that would kind of diffuse everything. So it worked. It all worked—even with the stealing girlfriends and opposing politics and all that stuff.

We had good times. Were there tough times? Sure. But it's just like being in a family: you're going to have good times, and you're going to have bad times. That's just how it is. And no matter how cool your job is, after twenty-plus years of doing it, it's going to suck from time to time. But my experience in the Ramones was nothing but fun.

TOMMY VICTOR—*PRONG, DANZIG, MINISTRY*

TOMMY: Glenn [Danzig] is a little older than me, but we come from the same musical background. We were both into Sweet, T-Rex, Bowie, and The Stooges. And at the same time, we were both into Sabbath. Glenn goes even further back in his knowledge of 1950s music, though. He knows an unbelievable amount about old records. Still to this day, he'll go out on the road and buy hundreds of CDs. He's a music fanatic. And he knows every single Elvis song—who wrote it, who played on it, where they recorded it, all that stuff.

I don't agree with all of his methods, but I always understand where he's coming from, and that's why we've been able to maintain a relationship for all these years. The non-baby boomers don't really get it. But I have an older brother and three older sisters, so I grew up with that whole era. From as early as I can remember, The Rolling Stones, The Beatles, and Motown was in my head. It's all about how you grow up; you wind up working with people who have similar interests that you can relate to.

MATT: What's Danzig like as a dude? You hear a lot of contradictory stories about him.

TOMMY: He is contradictory because his dealings with people outside of the inner sanctum of the Danzig gang is completely different. He has a gang-like mentality: we're the core of this thing, and everyone else is the enemy. He definitely has an old-school 1950s attitude about a lot of stuff, including politics. But I totally understand where he's coming from because my brother has a lot of similar views. These are unpopular views in today's era, but I can relate to them. And I don't agree with everything that he says or does, but I understand where he's coming from.

MICHAEL MONROE—*HANOI ROCKS, DEMOLITION 23, SOLO ARTIST*

MATT: When did you first meet Axl Rose?

MICHAEL: Axl happened to be in New York when I was shooting the video for "Dead, Jail or Rock 'N' Roll" in 1989. He was walking by and he asked someone, "What's going on here?" They said, "Michael Monroe is shooting a video," and he came and introduced himself as a big fan of Hanoi Rocks. We started talking, and I'd guessed from his singing style that he liked Nazareth and was a big fan of Dan McCafferty. He actually didn't know that my song "Not Fakin' It" was a Nazareth cover. It was on *Loud 'n' Proud*, but that album apparently wasn't that big in the States. Once Axl found out that it was a Nazareth cover, he liked it even more.

MATT: It sounds like you hit it off right away.

MICHAEL: We got along really well. He was a really nice guy. Little Steven [Van Zandt] sings backing vocals on "Dead, Jail or Rock 'N' Roll" on the album, and I asked Axl if he wanted to do a couple of takes of Steven's parts with us for the video. He said, "Sure," and being the nice guy that he is, he let us use the footage for the video, which I guess got me a little more fame, and maybe I got him a little more street credibility in return. A mutually beneficial, truly great friendship started from there.

Axl and I had many great conversations over the years. He's highly evolved, very spiritual, and we talked about a lot of heavy stuff. He's a really interesting personality, and he's very smart. He'd always call me up whenever he was in New York and we'd go out to dinner, and he was never late. He was always a gentleman. I have nothing but good things to say about Axl Rose.

Later on, he asked me to play harp and saxophone on the song "Bad Obsession" off the first *Use Your Illusion* album. He told me over the phone that he'd never heard the Dead Boys, either. So I made a tape of their first album [*Young Loud and Snotty*] and the best of the second album [*We Have Come for Your Children*], and we listened to it whilst driving around Hollywood in Axl's car. That was when he first heard "Ain't It Fun." He was like, "Wow! We're doing a covers album next, and we have to do this song."

Guns N' Roses were already working on *The Spaghetti Incident?* at this point, and Axl suggested we do "Ain't It Fun" as a duet in memory of Stiv Bators, which we did. And that became the first single off the album. Axl really sounded like Stiv in parts of that song, too. After we'd finished recording the vocals, there was a piano in the studio, and I was sitting there playing it. All of a sudden, The Rolling Stones and Kiss pinball machines behind me started going off by themselves. When I got back into the control room, I asked Axl, "Do those pinball machines ever go off by themselves?" He said, "Oh, no. Never." I said, "That must've been Stiv getting his wings, then—like in It's a Wonderful Life. 'Every time a bell rings, an angel gets his wings.'" Axl was like, "That must be the sweetest thing I've ever heard anybody say."

On my way back to New York that night, I was taking the red-eye from LA to New York, and I was half asleep. When I came to, I asked the stewardess how far away we were from New York. She said, "We're directly above Cleveland right now," which, of course, is where Stiv Bators and the Dead Boys were from. I think that was a little sign from Stiv, too. And God bless Axl Rose for putting "In memory of Stiv Bators" on the record sleeve. I didn't want any money for my involvement in that song, I just asked that they mention Stiv Bators on the album to honor his memory, which they kindly did.

STEVEN VAN ZANDT

MATT: Did you witness Bruce Springsteen, from Born to Run through to Darkness on the Edge of Town and The River, evolve as a songwriter?

STEVEN: Oh, it was the most amazing thing I'd ever seen. One minute, he was struggling to get an album's worth of material—Born to Run had eight songs on it, and he'd only written about eight and a half—but for Darkness he wrote about sixty songs, and for The River he wrote about seventy songs. It's that thing that I was talking about earlier, about earning the release of your greatness. He was just about as focused as a human being could be. He was grinding it out, man. Bruce is the only guy I've ever met in my entire life that didn't ever have another job.

MATT: He's never worked an honest day in his life.

STEVEN: He's never worked an honest day in his life, and he'd be the first person to say that because it's true. He was completely able to stay focused on rock 'n' roll, and that was all he ever cared about. He's always been an inspiration to me in that way. And it really was a classic case of earning the release of his greatness. How else do you explain going from eight songs to sixty? And I mean sixty good ones, too. I'm not talking about some filler. The outtake album from *Darkness* is one of our best albums that never came out, and the outtake album from *The River*, I think, is our very best album ever.

MATT: Did you ever release those outtakes? Can people hear them anywhere?

STEVEN: Yeah, they came out with the rereleased album packages. They're incredible. The release had taken place and the songs came spilling out.

MATT: It sounds like a creative, prolific, magical time. You were obviously involved hands-on with the production on *Darkness on the Edge of Town* and *The River* as well.

STEVEN: Yeah. And *Darkness* was a real struggle, despite the fact that he was already beginning to write like a crazy person. That was part of the problem, actually: the first ten songs he wrote were fantastic, and we all knew it. We were thinking, "This is it. Let's go." But he kept writing, and writing, and writing. And that became frustrating because every song became a lost argument, and that continued right into *The River*. That two-to-three-year period was ridiculously prolific. Chuck Berry had it. Bob Dylan had it. And The Beatles had it. The Beatles wrote about 240 original songs in five years. That's an average of fifty great songs a year. And I mean *great* ones, too. The great artists hit those periods where they get so focused and there's this inner momentum that takes place, where suddenly everything you've ever heard and absorbed starts to get put together by your subconscious, and it starts spilling out in your own way. It's a truly wonderful thing to witness.

MATT: Do you think it was a wise move, reigning it in after *The River* and releasing a stripped-back acoustic record like *Nebraska*? Was that Bruce's way of consciously slowing it down?

STEVEN: Yeah, and I very much encouraged that. It was my idea, in fact. He played it for me initially as demos for the record that would become the *Born in the U.S.A.* album, and I'd never heard anything like it. He was playing me the thing and all I could think was, "This is an album." And he'd always had both of those sides to him, right from the very beginning. He always had a solo folk-like consciousness about him, in addition to the band thing. From day one, he always had those two sensibilities, and because he recorded *Nebraska* without any intention of releasing it—

MATT: There was a purity to it?

STEVEN: Yeah. And he'd really become those characters. All singers are actors—I don't know if people realize that, but we are. Every single singer is an actor: you're basically acting out the role of the lyrics to your songs. If you're good, it doesn't look like acting, which is why we're the most autobiographical art form—because people assume it's autobiographical whether it is or not. But Bruce had *really* inhabited the characters in these songs, which were very, very cinematic. I'm a producer first, so I know greatness when I hear it. And I was hearing greatness there. I said to him, "Listen, man. I don't know how to tell you this, but that ain't no demo. That's an album." He said, "What do you mean?" And I said, "I'm telling you right now, on that little 4-track cassette player, with your roadie hitting record, you've just created one of the most intimate and interesting records I've heard in a very long time." It was pure art, in the truest sense of the word.

CLEM BURKE—*BLONDIE, RAMONES, IGGY POP, JOAN JETT*

CLEM: My dad passed away right as Blondie was getting back together, and it was really gratifying for me that he knew that. I would've never thought off the top of my head that Debbie [Harry], Chris [Stein], and Jimmy Destri would have been there at my dad's funeral, right there at the graveyard with me. But they were, and that really meant a lot to me.

When Jimmy—who was the last remaining original member of the band—left Blondie in 2004, I came to Debbie and Chris, and I said, "You know what's going to happen now, don't you?" Debbie was like, "I don't always agree with Chris." I said, "Debbie, you've got to be fucking kidding me. It's fine, I get it. But it's like a fucking love triangle now." And that's kind of what it is. But as crazy and corny as it sounds, we're a family. And a lot of things have happened between us that have made our lives better in a lot of ways. We're good friends, there's no question about that. And we respect each other.

MATT: It's great that you haven't let the business side of things ruin your relationship, like so many bands do. Why do you think that's so often the case?

CLEM: I've been with Blondie since the beginning, and all the business stuff was set up to my satisfaction a long time ago, so I don't have any problem with that. Drummers often quit because they're not getting a piece of the action—I always tell young drummers that. And it is unfair: if a group all invest in a company, and they all put in the same amount of time and effort and that company becomes successful, but one person receives a smaller percent of the profits, then that's wrong. But that's really the dynamic of a lot of bands, and it's ongoing. I always point to two bands that really stood the test of time—one broke up and stopped performing on their own volition, and the other one's still going strong—and that's R.E.M. and U2. It's common knowledge that all the money is shared equally in both of those bands.

NICK OLIVERI—*QUEENS OF THE STONE AGE, KYUSS, MONDO GENERATOR, DWARVES*

NICK: Once upon a time, I made some real money playing music. I can honestly say that I did it once. I look back at some of the things that I appreciated then, but I didn't quite grasp that it could all end at any point, which of course it did.

MATT: Did you foresee getting kicked out of Queens of the Stone Age?

NICK: I didn't foresee what happened as far as getting cut out of something that was half mine. And I signed it away, which I didn't have to do. I signed over everything: I had half of the merch, and all the gear that we bought half of together is now all his. I was never fighting for the name. But he [Josh Homme] didn't want to play with me anymore, so I just signed it all away. And I've gotten to use his studio a few times over the years, so it's not like it's all gone. But it all belongs to him now.

I believe that I helped to build that name with him, though. It was worth nothing when we started playing together, and we made it worth something because we both cared about it. And I still care about it, to the point where I don't want him to stop doing it because I don't want the name to die out. I still believe in that name, and I still believe in that band.

MATT: Do you feel like the most creative times of your life have been with Josh?

NICK: Yeah. We got to do things that I never dreamt I would do. I don't know if Josh feels the same way—maybe he did at one time— but I know that my songs are better with him. I can make a good tomato paste, but when Josh is involved then basil and stuff is going in there and it becomes something nice. Josh would hear something I'd be doing, and he'd be like, "Dude, I've got this other part that I can add in there and bring something else to this." And it became better. He always added something great to my songs, and I believe I added something great to his songs, too. I like the songs that he writes on his own as well; I'm not taking anything away from his songwriting; he's a great songwriter. But I know I added something on top of it.

MATT: How did you find out you were being kicked out of the band?

NICK: The day I was kicked out of the Queens of the Stone Age was February 15, 2004. And I wasn't told I was kicked out of the band: I read about it on the internet. It's a shame because I'm still the same person that I was when I was twelve. I've never changed. I'm the same person that he knew as a kid, and he's the same person that I've known since he was a kid. I have recordings of every session that we ever did together; parts that never got used; vocals that never got used; lyrics that never got used. And I could've bootlegged that shit a hundred times over. But I've always stayed true to my army. Regardless of whatever beef Josh and I have had in the past, that's irrelevant to me when it comes to upholding that.

MATT: How's your relationship with Josh now?

NICK: I hate him and I love him, just like a brother. He can either be your best friend and the coolest guy in the world, or somebody that's a total dick. You usually have to know him for him to be a dick, though.

KYLE GASS—*TENACIOUS D, THE KYLE GASS BAND, ACTOR, CO-MEDIAN*

MATT: How did you and Jack Black meet?

KYLE: We both started out in The Actor's Gang, which was a political theater group led by Tim Robbins. We were young idealistic college students out of UCLA [University of California, Lost Angeles], just trying to make a difference in the world.

I'm nine years older than Jack, so he was the new kid on the block, but you could tell right away that he was special. And part of the package was his amazing voice. I was fascinated that he didn't play an instrument because I'd never met anyone that sang so well, and that was their only instrument. I was very impressed. It was a case of, if you can't beat them, join them. So I said to myself, "I better hook up with this guy."

At first, I thought we'd be like an Everly Brothers or a Simon & Garfunkel–type funny act. But it didn't take long for me to realize that Jack had to sing and I had to be his accompaniment—the straight man in the duo. He was just such a force of nature. But my goal was just to make it work, and I was willing to do anything to do that, and provide Jack with the platform that he needed to do his thing. That hasn't always been easy: part of the reason why I started The Kyle Gass band was so I could actually talk on stage.

MATT: When you become as huge and successful as an act like Tenacious D, does the friendship get corrupted by the business?

KYLE: Are you nuts? Of course it does. It's impossible to avoid.

MATT: Would you advise against going into business with your friends, then?

KYLE: Ironically, I only like to work with my friends. But the whole Tenacious D thing, combined with Jack's meteoric rise to superstardom, meant we went through some pretty heady times together, and I fell apart a couple of times during the process.

MATT: What time period are we talking?

KYLE: When we were developing *The Pick of Destiny*, and Jack went and made *School of Rock*. I was like, "Dude! You're doing a rock movie before our movie comes out. You're kind of stealing our thunder, don't you think? And it's with kids? I mean, what is that?" And, of course, *School of Rock* ended up being huge, and I wasn't in it. That was very difficult for me. And with Jack constantly working on movies, there was a lot of time away from the band, and I just became side-lined. But in a way that actually helped me because that's when I started doing side projects—I couldn't just wait around for Jack because I like playing too much. So I made some lemonade out of the lemons. And I really love my band now. We have a great time. It's not Tenacious D size, but what is?

MATT: Did you let Jack know how you felt whilst all this was going on?

KYLE: I think so. I mean, obviously I didn't want to kill the goose; I still wanted to work with him. And it was difficult because I also understood that's just what Jack does, and he's very good at it. I had to deal with that. And I still deal with that to this day. We could probably be on an endless tour right now, making lots of money and having lots of fun, but that's not the way it is, and I just have to accept that. I still enjoy it when it happens, and I think it's worked out for the best because we're still really good friends. What doesn't kill you makes you stronger, and right now our friendship is in the most comfortable and beautiful place it's ever been.

STEVE-O—*JACKASS, STUNT PERFORMER, ENTERTAINER, CO-MEDIAN*

MATT: What went down on the money front with Johnny Knoxville and the *Jackass* movies?

STEVE-O: I can't say for certain what the situation was, but the money was a joke from the beginning of *Jackass*. And when the first movie deal came around, they offered us an amount of money that we were totally excited about, not realizing it was a fucking joke. From what I understand, I think Jeff Tremaine would've been perfectly happy to give us what we were being offered. He was like, "They're fucking stoked, just give it to them." But Knoxville really put his foot down, and said, "I'm not going to sit in front of a camera for this project unless we take care of the cast with some backend percentage and profit participation." Considering there's a bunch of us, we didn't exactly do that well, but that's something that I understand happened and it's characteristic of Knoxville.

MATT: Taking care of his boys.

STEVE-O: Yeah. And I've never begrudged Knoxville for anything. There was a situation after the third movie [*Jackass 3D*]—like a genuine clerical error—that prevented any of us from getting paid for quite a while, and that upset me. I started running my mouth a little bit, and there was some resentment on my side of the street for a while. But it was a genuine clerical error and everything was made completely right. So if it ever seemed at one point like I was upset with Knoxville, that was a super temporary situation and it's completely rectified now. I love the guy. He's a fucking hero, dude.

CREATIVE PARTNERSHIPS PLAYLIST

NOFX—"THE LONGEST LINE"

LAGWAGON—"ANGRY DAYS"

MAD CADDIES—"DISTRESS"

THE BRONX—"HEART ATTACK AMERICAN"

RISE AGAINST—"PRAYER OF THE REFUGEE"

HOUSE OF PAIN—"JUMP AROUND"

BRUCE SPRINGSTEEN—"TENTH AVENUE FREEZE-OUT"

RAMONES—"WE'RE A HAPPY FAMILY"

DANZIG—"LET YOURSELF GO"

MICHAEL MONROE—"DEAD, JAIL OR ROCK 'N' ROLL"

GUNS N' ROSES—"BAD OBSESSION"

DEAD BOYS—"AIN'T IT FUN"

BRUCE SPRINGSTEEN—"HIGHWAY PATROLMAN"

BLONDIE—"DREAMING"

QUEENS OF THE STONE AGE—"YOU THINK I AIN'T WORTH
A DOLLAR…"

TENACIOUS D—"WONDERBOY"

MINUTEMEN—"CORONA"

THE HERO'S HEROES

"Rock 'n' rollers with a heart."

IN OCTOBER 2019, I HAD Perry Farrell on the podcast. I was extremely excited to meet to him, seeing as how he's basically the Godfather of alternative rock, and getting the chance to interview him was a dream come true.

Once our conversation was over, I phoned my friend Chris Dean to tell him how my afternoon with Perry had gone—amazingly well, obviously. And Chris referred to Perry as "the hero's hero." Personally, I'd never heard that phrase before—I'm going to credit Chris with its invention, though. And I thought that would make a great chapter for the book. So, here we are.

Growing up in a pre-internet age, you had to look at who musicians mentioned in their interviews to find out who their influences were, just as you had to look at who they thanked in their liner notes to discover bands that sounded similar—you couldn't just go on Spotify or Wikipedia. Now, call me sentimental, but there was joy in the art of discovery back then; you had to really work for it, and the payoff was infinitely more rewarding. Anyway, where was I? Ah, yes, the hero's heroes...

One thing I always do when preparing for an interview with any musician, actor, or comedian, is read up and see if they've worked with, or are friends with, an artist that I know has inspired them. If they have, or they are, then I talk to them about said artist, and try and get the lowdown on what they're like in person. Call me nosy, call me snoopy—call me what you like. I love hearing those stories, and my podcast is the perfect platform to share them.

We're losing legends at a rapidly increasing rate these days, and not all of them will get their own biographies or documentaries made, so I see it as my job to keep these oral storytelling traditions alive. That's been my modus operandi since day one.

Now, I'm not going to spoil the surprise by telling you who everybody's heroes are. But what I will do is list some of the icons coming up in this chapter, and you can try and guess whose heroes they might be. If you get them all right, give yourself the day off work. I won't tell anyone. Here we go: Black Sabbath, Brian May, Henry Rollins, Iggy Pop, Mike Patton, Mötley Crüe, Nick Cave, and Tommy Chong.

For those who are interested, my all-time hero is Little Richard. He once famously said, "Elvis may be the King of Rock and Roll, but I am the Queen." And you can add that to the long list of reasons why I think he's the greatest rock 'n' roll singer who ever lived. But don't just take my word for it...

MICHAEL MONROE—*HANOI ROCKS, DEMOLITION 23, SOLO ARTIST*

MICHAEL: Little Richard is the greatest rock 'n' roll singer of all time. If you listen to Elvis's "Tutti Frutti" and Little Richard's "Tutti Frutti," there's a big difference: they're like night and day. And God bless Elvis; he crossed over and combined the white and black thing and made a lot of progress with that. But when you listen to Little Richard's music, he's got punk, glam, and everything going on. He's the greatest rock 'n' roller of all time, no doubt about it.

MATT: Did you ever see him live?

MICHAEL: Yes, I saw him, and I got to meet him, too. Little Steven [Van Zandt]—who was my best friend in New York during the ten years that I lived there—knew Little Richard very well. When Steven got married to his wife Maureen, Little Richard did the ceremony because he's a minister as well. He married them, and they had Percy

Sledge sing "When a Man Loves a Woman" as their first dance. It was the ultimate rock 'n' roll wedding.

We both went to see Little Richard for his sixtieth birthday concert at a venue called Tramps in New York. He did three nights there, two sets a night. It was incredible: all the tempos were real fast like back in the 1950s, and he was really rocking. He could've been a stand-up as well. He was so funny. He had the audience in the palm of his hands. After the show, Little Steven took me backstage, and Little Richard came out of the dressing room with his minders, looked me up from top to bottom, and said, *"Oh, my!"*

B-REAL—*CYPRESS HILL, PROPHETS OF RAGE*

B-REAL: In the world of cannabis, and activism within that world, Tommy Chong is definitely my mentor. I've often told him that. He was the one showing us how to freedom fight. Him and Jack Herer—rest in peace—taught me a lot about the cannabis world, all the hypocrisy that exists within mainstream culture, and the reasons why it's been kept back for so long. I think Jack would be really proud to see how much more educated people are about cannabis culture nowadays, and all the politics around it.

Tommy Chong has been a very good friend to me over the years as well. We've done each other many favors and worked together on many things, and it's always cool catching a smoke with him. I watch what he's doing in the cannabis industry, and I really believe he deserves all the success and opportunities being afforded to him. He's put in all the work, and even served as a martyr when the government made an example of him by putting him in jail for the amount of time that they did. He didn't bitch and cry about it, either. He served his time like a man, and he did it for his son, so his son wouldn't have a mark on his record or his life.

Tommy didn't have to do that, but he took it upon himself to do so and the respect that I have for that man is beyond words. Him and Chuck D are my two mentors in two different lanes. They're the two guys that I have the utmost respect for and get to call friends. I get to smoke weed with one and wreck the stage with the other. Public Enemy were one of my biggest influences when we started Cypress Hill, so to share a stage with Chuck in Prophets of Rage is an incredible honor. I have the utmost respect for both Tommy and Chuck.

AL BARR—*DROPKICK MURPHYS, THE BRUISERS*

AL: Agnostic Front, in my opinion, are as legendary as Sick of It All. There wouldn't be American hardcore without bands like the Cro-Mags, Sick of It All, and Agnostic Front.

MATT: Tell me about Vinnie Stigma. He's a friend of yours, right?

AL: Vinnie is my uncle. Uncle Vinnie, man. Vinnie Stigma is one of the most interesting and entertaining people you could ever meet. There's many levels to Vinnie, you know what I mean? First of all, he's a musician; and he's a skin; and he's one of the original Lower East Side crew. But he's also one of the most thoughtful, generous, and polite people you'll ever meet—and that's if you don't know him. Then you get to know him, and he's got more heart and soul...

I've got so much love for Vinnie Stigma. I could go on about him for days. He's always been my friend, and he will always be my friend. I talk to him every year on the anniversary of Rick Wimert's—the rhythm guitarist from The Bruisers—death. Ricky was a good friend of Vinnie's as well. He'll call me, and he'll say, "You know why I'm calling you, right, kid? It's Flag Day. June 14. Flag Day."

When he still drank, he'd get on the bus and you'd be like, "It's going to be one of those nights." He'd be smiling, and he'd say, "All right, let's do the drinking song. Let's do Kenny first. Oh, drink, drink, drink, drink, drink / Drink, drink, drink, drink and be merry / My friends they just drink beer and wine / But me, I love my pal Kenny / Oh, all I can do is just drink, drink, drink, drink." Then he'd go on to the next guy, "Let's do Matty!"

So, there's that Vinnie. Then there's the guy who's been around hardcore for so long, and been a soldier for this music for so long. He's just one of those guys where you go, "Why hasn't someone ghost written a book for him?" Because he needs one. Vinnie's book has got be written, and there's got to be someone who writes that story because he's amazing. And what's even more amazing is he looks younger every time I see him. I'm always like, "What's going on with you?" I don't know what it is, but whatever he's doing, I want some because he looks fantastic.

DANKO JONES—*SOLO ARTIST, AUTHOR, PODCAST HOST*

MATT: I love the podcast that you did with Henry Rollins. How did that one come about?

DANKO: That was one of my favorite podcast interviews ever. I think Henry had perhaps heard of me already, but he didn't really know anything about me, and I sprung the podcast idea on him in the hotel lobby when we were both at Wacken festival in Germany. It wasn't something we had scheduled in, but he was cool enough to agree to it.

MATT: On the fly?

DANKO: On the fly. That was what was so cool about it. And he had a plane to catch—I don't think that's even mentioned in the podcast. When I noticed that he wasn't thoroughly into the idea of talking to me, I said, "I just need fifteen minutes." And in my head I was just going to splice it up with a talk that I had from years back with Ian MacKaye, which was about twenty minutes. Then I would've cobbled together an episode.

When we started talking, I just ran with what I knew he'd be into: records and record collecting. I knew I could hold a discussion with him about that. So we started talking about noise records, and hard-to-find records, and then I noticed he kind of let his guard down. When fifteen minutes was up, I was like, "All right, I got my fifteen minutes." And he just sat there and didn't say anything. So, we went for another fifteen to twenty minutes. It was amazing.

MATT: And he was present? Even though he had a plane to catch, he was there with you in the moment?

DANKO: Oh, yeah. And I feel like he opened up a little bit, too. I really appreciated him for that. I thought about how I'd be in that situation, and I don't even know if I'd be as nice as Henry was. It was very cool of him to do it. And it was one of my hard-won podcasts that I still love to this day.

JESSE LEACH—*KILLSWITCH ENGAGE, TIMES OF GRACE, THE WEAPON*

JESSE: I'm always proud of people when they approach me, and they do it in such a way where it feels like it's just a human talking to another human, instead of someone fanning out or being nervous—because I tend to have anxiety issues around people that I admire, too. When people come up to me and say that my music has affected them in a positive way, I feel that same way about other musicians; I'm equally as much a fan and indebted to music and musicians as my fans give me credit for. It's all part of the beauty of music. It just reciprocates.

We did the Soundwave tour in Australia once, and Mike Patton was on the bill with his band Tomahawk. His dressing room was next to ours the whole time, but I avoided him. Finally, on the last day, I walked passed him and he noticed I was wearing a Bad Brains T-shirt. I was like, "This is my moment." So I said to him, "Thank you for your work, not just with your music but the way you carry yourself, and your attitude. I don't want to fan boy out too much, but can I please have a photo with you?" He was like, "Sure." And that was it.

I recently met Barney [Mark Greenway] from Napalm Death, too. I've looked up to him since I was a teenager, and he was so disarming in the best possible way. Immediately, I was like, "Dude, you're a legend." I tried to refrain from treating him like my hero, but it was hard. He was so down to earth. He's a brilliant man.

JOE CARDAMONE—*THE ICARUS LINE, SOLO ARTIST, PRODUCER*

MATT: How do you know Nick Cave and Warren Ellis?

JOE: Warren and Nick are really cool guys. I worked with and for them for about a month on the *Lawless* soundtrack, and that's how

I got to know them. As soon as I met them, I instantly thought they were good people. And it's really nice to meet people who do stuff that you respect, and they turn out to be the coolest guys ever. Nick is fucking great. He's also one of the funniest dudes I've ever met.

MATT: No doubt. He wrote one of my favorite lyrics ever: "I'd climb over fifty good pussies to get to one fat boy's asshole." That's a dark canvas right there.

JOE: Totally. Warren is a fucking wizard, too. He's one of the sweetest, most generous human beings I've ever met. Whenever we came through town on tour with The Icarus Line, he'd let us sleep on his family couch and his wife would make dinner for the group. We'd eat dinner at the family table, you know what I mean? Real shit. Real people.

FRANK IERO—*MY CHEMICAL ROMANCE, LEATHERMOUTH, SOLO ARTIST*

FRANK: Having Brian May come out and play with us at Reading Festival was a dream come true. A couple of days before the show, we went to his house to rehearse and that was amazing. He was like, "Hi, I'm Brian. Do you want some tea? I'll make you some tea if you like." He was the most cordial, humble, and accommodating person I've ever met—just a beautiful soul. Certain people could really learn a lot from Brian May.

MICHAEL MONROE

MICHAEL: I love the Foo Fighters so much, and I'm so happy they're as big as they are because they really deserve it. Authentic rock 'n' roll like that is rare these days, and that's why we need people like the Foo Fighters. They're so good, so tight, and so right. They've got the right attitude, the right style of playing, great songs, a great style, and they pay homage to all the rock 'n' roll greats.

MATT: How long have you known those guys?

MICHAEL: Well, Chris Shiflett was playing in a band called Lost Kittens back in 1989, and they opened up for me on the *Not Fakin' It* tour in Santa Barbara, California. He even used to have the same kind of hair as me back then; he was really into Hanoi Rocks and my work as a solo artist. Apparently, he'd taken a fan picture with me a couple of years earlier in LA, around the *Nights Are So Long* time, but his friend had his finger in front of the lens and the photo didn't come out. Then we met properly for the first time in '89, when we played a show together.

The first time I met Dave [Grohl] and the rest of the band was when I opened up for the Foo Fighters in Helsinki in 2010. That was the first gig with Dregen [Backyard Babies] in my band. He had just joined, and that was his first show: in front of thirty thousand people. I met all the band then, and we got along great. We hit it off right away. We're the same kind of people.

MATT: Rock 'n' rollers.

MICHAEL: That's right. Rock 'n' rollers with a heart. They just played in Helsinki a couple of weeks ago, and I was there, and I had my harps with me. I said to Dave, "If you want a harp solo somewhere, I'm here." He said, "Okay, great." They ended up inviting me up on stage three times, which was a huge honor. I played "Best of You" and "The Pretender" with them, and they even invited me up to play "Let There Be Rock" by AC/DC, which was the last song of the whole show. I had such a great time. It was crazy.

FRANK IERO

MATT: In 2005, you supported Green Day on the *American Idiot* tour. It's hard to imagine a better support gig than that. How was it?

FRANK: It was insane. I was thirteen years old in 1994, and I remember buying *Dookie* on cassette tape and listening to "Longview" over and over again. The next thing I know, I'm hanging out with those guys and they're taking us to the movies and buying us lightsabers. Could you ask for a better tour to open up? There's no way. We learned a lot;

I watched them every night and they really had it down to a science. They took what they did very, very seriously. Their stage show was a craft. It was so meticulous.

Green Day were also the ones who told us we should talk to Rob Cavallo when it came to making *The Black Parade*. They'd just done *American Idiot* with him, and he was their go-to guy. They introduced us to Rob, and the rest, as they say, is history. We obviously ended up working with him on that record, and I don't think we could've made it with anybody else. It was a great partnership.

JESSE MALIN—*HEART ATTACK, D GENERATION, SOLO ARTIST*

JESSE: They're superheroes, those Green Day guys. They're on the right team. They've had great success and they fully deserve it because they worked so hard for it. They're a socio-political punk band at heart, but they also reach people in a mainstream way. And they've got all these great pop songs, but also something to say, like Bob Dylan, Bob Marley, and The Beatles.

MATT CAUGHTHRAN—*THE BRONX, MARIACHI EL BRONX*

MATT C: GBH have always been super cool to us. One of the very first tours we did was a US tour with The Bronx, GBH, and Circle Jerks. When you do a tour like that, you don't really expect to become friends with these people. You just think, "Wow! This is amazing. I hope I don't fucking piss them off." But we all became so tight after that tour, and to think that I can now call those guys friends is amazing. When you watch them play, they're still so fucking good, too.

ROBB FLYNN—*MACHINE HEAD, PODCAST HOST*

ROBB: Machine Head were on the Ozzfest tour one year, and Ozzy had to cancel a show at the last minute. So, Black Sabbath started talking to all the various singers to ask if they knew any Black Sabbath songs because they still wanted to play this sold-out show in Columbus, Ohio. And it was looking like they were going to have all the singers from the Ozzfest package come out and sing a song.

The Ozzy Osbourne band was playing as well; Ozzy was pulling double duty with Black Sabbath and the Ozzy Osbourne band. So I go into the Ozzy band room, and they're like, "We're going to do Ozzy songs with all these different singers, too. What songs do you know?" I said, "I'll do 'Crazy Train.'" Marilyn Manson was in there, too, and he was like, "I want to do 'Crazy Train.'" So I said, "Cool, let's do it together." And he was like, "Fuck yeah."

At that point, Tony [Iommi] and Geezer [Butler] came into the Ozzy band dressing room, and they asked me, "Do you know any Black Sabbath songs?" I was like, "Do *I* know any Black Sabbath songs? I'm your dude. I know every lyric and every melody." So they invited me to their dressing room to talk about what Black Sabbath songs *I'm* going to sing with Black Sabbath that night. I was sitting there, looking at Iommi and Geezer, flashing back to the album cover for *Sabbath Bloody Sabbath*—which I must have stared at for twenty hours of my life—thinking, "This is the fucking raddest album cover I've ever seen." It was a surreal, amazing moment that I'll never forget.

In the end, Black Sabbath decided not to play without Ozzy, but the Ozzy band did play, and I got up there and jammed "Crazy Train" with Marilyn Manson. Me and Dimebag [Darrell] sang "Bark at the Moon," too. It was fucking crazy, dude.

STEVE-O—*JACKASS, STUNT PERFORMER, ENTERTAINER, CO-MEDIAN*

MATT: Tell me the story of how you met Nikki Sixx and Tommy Lee from Mötley Crüe.

STEVE-O: I grew up in England, but during the summer I'd go and live in America, and on our visits to America my father would go out of his way to land us in a city that had a baseball game going on. He would arrange for us to stay in the hotel with the visiting baseball team, and I would just sort of hang out in the lobby and collect autographs from professional baseball players. So I was a little bit savvy to the idea that people like that stay in hotels—that's more information than anybody's going to give a fuck about, but whatever.

I was such a huge fan of Mötley Crüe, and the day before their concert in Toronto—where we were living at that time—I saw on the news that they'd gotten into trouble for something or other. I was electrified. I was like, "They're here! Oh, my God! The concert's tomorrow, but they're already here. And they're in a hotel, I know it." Thinking one hundred miles an hour, I was like, "Okay, I know all their real names: Frank Feranna, Vincent Wharton, Thomas Lee Bass, and Robert Alan Deal. But they're not going to check into a hotel under their real names. And they're not going to check in under their stage names, either."

My next guess was they were going to check in under the name of their manager. So I went racing to my room, and I went through all my tape cassette sleeves looking for the name of their manager. I remember thinking, "Please don't let there be a manager and a tour manager." But there wasn't. It was simple: it just said Doc McGhee— on every single one of them, including the *Girls, Girls, Girls* album, which was the one they were touring behind at the time.

So I had the name Doc McGhee, and I went running to the phone book and opened it up to the hotel section, and I preceded to call every hotel in the book. I didn't just go for the big ones that had ads out, either. I went through the whole fucking thing, starting at the top of the list so as not to miss any out. And this is the entire metropolitan area of Toronto.

What was crazy about it was my mom was sort of frustrated with me for tying up the house phone, and this was of course many years before call-waiting. But all my dad ever wanted was for me to show some initiative and apply myself, so he was thrilled with what I was doing. He didn't care that it was a heavy metal band. He told my mom, "Honey, back off. Let him do his thing." And I was allowed to keep calling. I probably called for two to three solid hours, and sure enough I got through.

They patched me through to a hotel room, and this guy answers the phone. He says, "Hello?" And I said, "Hello, is that Doc McGhee?" He said, "No. This is Doc's brother, Scott. Who's this?" I was like, "As in Mötley Crüe?" And I could sense right away that he was a little annoyed. He asked me, "How did you get this number?" And I said, "I called every hotel in the phone book." Then the guy went from being annoyed to genuinely impressed. He was like, "Wait a second: you called every hotel in the phone book? That's awesome!" He had never heard of that before. Then he said, "How would you like it if I put your name on the guest list with backstage passes to the concert tomorrow night?" And he also told me he could get me tickets in the fifth row, which was a godsend because I didn't actually have tickets to the show.

MATT: What a cool move on his part.

STEVE-O: What a way cool move, man. What a way, way cool move. So I went with my dad to the arena, and we got in line with all these cool media people with big camera packs and reporters, and everybody was going to get their press credentials. And sure enough, there was an envelope waiting there with my name on it.

When we went backstage after the show, which was amazing, and Mick Mars was roped off doing some kind of interview for *Guitar Magazine*. He didn't interact with anybody. And Vince Neil was nowhere to be seen. But Tommy Lee and Nikki Sixx mingled with everybody, and I got a hilarious picture with Tommy and a hilarious picture with Nikki. I ended up being the last person to leave backstage that night. They let me just hang around until the end.

MATT: Then years later you became friends with those guys, right?

STEVE-O: Sure. I linked up with Tommy and Nikki in a pretty meaningful way. It was 1987 when I first met them. Fifteen years later, in 2002, I was charged with two felony offenses in America, and I was facing eight years in prison because a kid got beaten up at one of my shows, and I had orchestrated the circumstances in which that had happened. I never intended for anybody to get seriously hurt, but what I did do was invite everybody to run onstage past the bouncers. So I was a principal to a battery in Louisiana, where this kid was pretty seriously injured. He went on to sue me for brain damage, too. I don't know how brain damaged he was, but he got paid.

I was then picked up in Los Angeles on a federal fugitive warrant out of the state of Louisiana for the whopping bond of one million dollars. They really threw the book at me. And I was under strict instructions not to do any drugs because if they tested me and it came back positive then it would really hurt my cause. So there I was at home doing no drugs, which made me really uncomfortable, just sitting around playing on my computer. I made my way onto Tommy Lee's website and onto his message board, and I wrote him this story about how we had met. I left my email on there, and sure enough a few days later I got an email back: "Tommy Lee here! Dude, you're in almost as much trouble as I've been in!" It was so cool, and we became kind of friendly after that. He was always there for me whenever I reached out, which was really cool.

Then in 2004, I got an email from Tommy saying, "Dude, call me on my house phone! Here's the number!" So I called the number, and I'm talking to him on the phone, which I just couldn't even believe. And he said, "Dude, I've been rehearsing with Mötley for the last two weeks. We're getting back together"—on whatever day it was in December 2004—"and we're announcing our new tour at the Hollywood Palladium. We're going to fly in on a helicopter, and it's going to be this epic press event, and I want you to announce us." This was the *Carnival of Sins* tour. It turned out they weren't able to fly in on a helicopter—that didn't happen—but they did have me go out there and announce them.

Tommy said to me right before I went out, "I want you to do something super fucked up when you announce us." So I went out there and I did my old light bulb trick, where I smash a light bulb over my head and the glass breaks, and I pick up a piece of broken glass and cut my tongue with it. I cut it pretty heavily that time, too. Blood was pouring out of my tongue, and I dipped my fingers in it and put the horizontal lines underneath my eyes like Nikki Sixx, and the diagonal lines on my cheeks like Tommy Lee. The blood was dripping everywhere and I was covered in it when I made the announcement: "Ladies and gentlemen, Mötley fucking Crüe!" It was the craziest full circle moment ever.

NICK OLIVERI—*QUEENS OF THE STONE AGE, KYUSS, MONDO GENERATOR, DWARVES*

MATT: I see you've got the Motörhead logo tattooed on your hands. What did that band mean to you?

NICK: Motörhead is a rock 'n' roll institution. I first saw them live with the Cro-Mags opening up for them, and both bands blew me away. That show was one of the main turning points in me knowing that I wanted to play music. It was in San Bernadino, at the Orange Pavilion, in 1986.

I never thought about going backstage as a kid. I never thought, "I'm going to go back there and meet the band." I'd just be like, "I'm going to get my ticket, maybe buy a T-shirt, and have some fun." But when Cro-Mags finished their set, they came out into the crowd and answered my stupid questions. They must've thought, "God, this kid's driving us crazy asking us all these questions about Lemmy." But they were cool to me, dude. They hung out and watched Motörhead with us, and it was an amazing night. After that, I knew I wanted to play music for sure.

Years later, I got to tour with Motörhead in my band Mondo Generator on their thirty-first anniversary tour, and on the last night of tour I shared some speed with Lemmy. It was like smoking weed with Bob Marley; if you get the opportunity to do that sort of thing, you have to do it. And I was flying back to the States the next day, so I couldn't take the speed home with me. Lemmy said, "I'll buy it off you." But I told him, "No way. This is for you. You already have bought it off me with all your music. In fact, I owe you a lot more than this if that's the case." He said, "Well, I'll make it up to you, then." Then Phil Campbell said, "How about he comes up with us tonight and plays second bass and helps us sing *Overkill?*" And Lemmy went, "All right."

I was like, "This is out of control. You don't need a second bass player. And I don't want to screw this up. How about I sing the second verse, do a stage dive, and then I'm out of there?" So that's exactly what I did. I have a video of it somewhere. I got to do speed and sing with Lemmy. I was doing cartwheels in my head, and I don't even know how to do cartwheels. After the gig, Lemmy shook my hand and he said to me, "You're a good bass player." It freaked me out, man. It meant the world to me for him to say that because I love Motörhead so much. Lemmy was like an old blues player. He played right up until he died.

DANKO JONES

DANKO: Lemmy embodied the mythological idea of an outlaw and a rebel. It was like he'd stepped straight out of a movie or a comic book. As a person, what I really liked about Lemmy—more than the music, even—is he didn't put any cool decorations on people like you or I would. And what I mean by that is he just took everyone at face value, and judged them on what he saw, not on what they looked like or how famous they were. I found that Lemmy could hang with anybody. He could see through people. That's what Lemmy meant to me. And I take that with me everywhere I go; I don't give a shit if you have the right patch on your fucking jean jacket. I really don't give a fuck.

MATT: It seems like everyone loved him, too.

DANKO: There's a great story that I heard, years before I met Lemmy, having to do with Geddy Lee from Rush. Being from Toronto, there's a lot of Rush stories abound in the city, and one story that I heard—and I don't know if it's true or not, but I kind of believe that it is—is that Geddy had invited Lemmy to his house, but Geddy's wife took one look at a picture of Lemmy and Motörhead, and she was dead set against it. But Lemmy came over and he charmed the living crap out of her. And that's exactly how I see Lemmy. He could probably charm my mom; he's just that kind of person.

MATT: Didn't you sing on stage with Motörhead once?

DANKO: Yeah. In my book [*I've Got Something to Say*], there's a four-page comic strip panel where I talk about singing on stage with Lemmy. It was illustrated by Gary Dumm of *American Splendor* fame, and that story is true. It happened on the Motörhead tour that we did with them.

MATT: What song did you do?

DANKO: "Born to Raise Hell." Of course, you might know a song., but if you were asked to sing it with the band who wrote it, do you really know all the words? I honestly don't. I'd probably have to run through it a few times, even if it's a song that I know really well. I've heard certain songs a million times, but I still don't know all the lyrics off by heart.

MATT: I've had that happen to me so many times at karaoke bars. I'll be like, "I know this. I don't need the words." Then you get up there, and you soon learn you don't actually know the words to anything apart from the chorus.

DANKO: Right. And "Born to Raise Hell" was one of those songs. I got asked to sing it that night, the day of the show, and I was never going to say no. You don't turn down Motörhead. But I started to panic. And to top it all off, Lemmy asked me to sing it in front of him, in his dressing room, just to make sure that I knew it.

MATT: What a surreal moment.

DANKO: It was one of the most nerve-racking experiences of my life. And I sang it right in front of him. As close as you and I are now, that's how close we were, and I sang the lyrics to "Born to Raise Hell" back to Lemmy, just to prove that I could get on stage and sing it with him. It was insane. Luckily, I passed.

MICHAEL MONROE

MATT: Talk to me about Lemmy.

MICHAEL: What a guy! Lemmy is my hero. He's like one of those old wild west outlaws. He was such a sweet guy, too. He had a heart of gold. And he was always consistent: his character never changed, no matter how much he'd had to drink. He was always the same guy. That's what I really appreciate in people because it's horrible when people get drunk or high and then they become like a stranger to you. But Lemmy was always the same. And he always had a sense of justice about him.

Opening up for Motörhead for three weeks on their thirty-fifth anniversary tour was the best tour of my life. They had the best catering and the best vibe: there were many generations of people working for them, and it was like a family. They were all really sweet people. I had such a great time on that tour. Motörhead are one of the best bands of all time. They had such a special, magical chemistry, and Lemmy was a total hero. God rest his soul. I really miss him. We had some great times, man.

After Razzle died, Lemmy said to me, "You know what, mate? We'll back you up." And he offered to have Motörhead back me up as a band because he was so upset about Razzle dying. I was like, "Woah! Do you know how much that means to me?" Talk about honor. I was so young and baby-faced back then, I'm sure his fans would have eaten me alive. But what a big heart he had. And he was always so consistent: he was always the same wonderful, lovely guy. I was very lucky to have known him. We always had a great friendship.

TROY VAN LEEUWEN—*QUEENS OF THE STONE AGE, A PERFECT CIRCLE, FAILURE*

TROY: When you look at Iggy Pop and the world of music, and how many of our heroes are going or gone, he of all people should have been gone a long time ago—especially considering where he was at a certain point in time. But he's still here. He's seventy years old, and he's still kicking everyone's fucking ass. That, to me, is inspiration. He bleeds every night, and he sings until he can't sing anymore. He doesn't ever really want to leave the stage. He's unstoppable.

MATT: You can also hear the inspiration that he's had on Queens of the Stone Age, even way before all the *Post Pop Depression* stuff.

TROY: Absolutely. The connection between *The Idiot, Lust for Life,* and *Post Pop Depression* is where Queens of the Stone Age lives, both sonically and creatively. Those records will always be an inspiration. And we didn't just interpret those songs when it came to touring them with Iggy: we literally copied what was on the records. Iggy even had notes of what Bowie played, what kind of keyboards and synthesizers he used—all that stuff. So that was fun putting all that together. And that's probably why you're hearing a lot of synths on our new record [*Villains*]—because we got into it. We literally had post-Pop depression after that tour.

MATT: I'll bet. What an incredible experience.

TROY: It was so special. Every night on stage, Iggy would need the key for "China Girl," and I would play the F-sharp so he could just come right in. Being on stage with him was always special. He actually came out to do the first rehearsal with us the day after Bowie died. That was heavy. It was one of the heaviest experiences I've ever had playing music, just dealing with those emotions. It affected Iggy deeply, and the inspiration and need to play was tangible. It was a real kick in the ass.

JESSE MALIN

JESSE: I first went to see The Clash at The Palladium in New York in March 1980. It was the *London Calling* tour, and they had Mikey Dread, Lee Dorsey, and The B-Girls on the bill. I was hanging out behind the venue waiting to see The Clash, and there was this other kid there in front of me. He had bondage pants and spiky hair and creepers on. The Clash came by, said hello to me, then took this other kid into the venue with them. A little bit later, I realized who this kid was: his name was Harley Flanagan and he was in this band called The Stimulators. He was twelve years old and already playing shows at Max's [Kansas City], which was the catalyst for me getting my band Heart Attack out of Queens and making that call from the payphone at junior high school to get the audition at CBGB, which eventually led to us playing there as an all twelve-to-thirteen-year-old band.

So I met The Clash briefly back then, and in time I'd get to know them personally through the D Generation days, which was a band that I did in the mid-to-late-nineties. Joe Strummer came down to a couple of our gigs at Coney Island High. This was before his solo career got relaunched, and he was in a quieter creative period. He'd just hang out and talk and drink tequila with you. There were many nights where we'd take over bars until 7:00 a.m., and Joe would start DJing and have everyone dancing up on the tables. Later on, when he started touring with The Mescaleros, his dressing room would look like something out of one of those Marx Brothers movies: "Come on in. We've got room on the ceiling." And Joe would be there, fresh off stage, no shirt on, all sweaty with his smokes and his spliff, giving so much of himself to everyone in the room. He was a really cool guy.

MATT: Tell me the story behind the Joe Strummer mural that you had painted outside your bar in New York.

JESSE: I used some money that I got from a record label advance to open up a bar with a couple of musician friends of mine. I wanted to have a little corner spot—like some kind of Frank Sinatra fantasy— where I could hang out with my friends and listen to good music when I wasn't on tour. And that Frank Sinatra fantasy bar became Niagara, which is located on Seventh Street and Avenue A, in the East Village.

Whenever I travel, I always want to go out to a bar after the show—if I have time. I want to hear a DJ spin records or talk to some folks, just to get a flavor of the town. And as much as I've seen alcohol ruin a lot of good people, I like bars, and I believe they hold an important place in our society. They're like churches to me: they're communal. And whenever I travel around on tour, I get hooked up with free drinks and stuff like that. So we had a policy: if you were a touring artist, come to Niagara and bring all your road crew with you, and we'll take care of you. That led to a lot of bands stopping there, and Joe Strummer came by after the first Mescaleros show at Irving Plaza [06/30/1999]. A few hundred people followed him there that night, including Shane McGowan, and it was a wild evening. Joe came by a couple of times after that, too, and people kind of connected that place with him.

The last time that I saw Joe was November in 2002, at the Cedar Tavern, which was this old beatnik kind of Ginsberg/Kerouac–type bar in Greenwich Village. I was about to head out on tour with Ryan Adams, and I wanted Ryan to meet Joe, so we swung by there to see him. There's a bunch of photos from that night. Bob Gruen was there, and Josh Cheuse was there also, who I'll get to in a bit. But that would be the last time that I saw Joe. He passed away on December 22, 2002. And throughout the Christmas period, fans and people who loved Joe started putting flowers and candles outside the wall of Niagara. I think they just needed somewhere to show their love and give their condolences. So, that was that.

A little time passed, and Josh Cheuse, who was a friend of Joe's and did the cover for many Mescaleros records—and every Jesse Malin and D Generation album cover for a while—was getting ready to shoot a video for Joe's last single, which was his cover of "Redemption Song" by Bob Marley. And in the neighborhood where Niagara is based, the Latino community have this tradition where if someone in their family or someone that they love passes away, they have an artist do a rattle can spray paint mural of them. It's just a beautiful way to celebrate their life. So Josh had this idea: let's take the side of Niagara, and get Dr. Revolt and Zephyr—who are great graffiti artists and friends—to paint this mural of Joe. Then we can have a street party carnival-type memorial for him, and that would be the video for the song. So, that's what we did. And Josh filmed the whole thing. I came by and put some flowers down. Jim Jarmusch came by. The guys in Rancid, Steve Buscemi, and a bunch of other people who all knew Joe came by, too. Fans and people on the street all got involved as well, and it was this whole magical thing. After we got done shooting, someone said, "Why don't you just keep the picture of Joe up?" So we did. And that's the story behind the Joe Strummer mural. It's still there now, too. People still come by and take about a hundred photos a day.

THE HERO'S HEROES PLAYLIST

LITTLE RICHARD—"TUTTI FRUTTI"

PROPHETS OF RAGE—"PROPHETS OF RAGE"

AGNOSTIC FRONT—"FOR MY FAMILY"

BLACK FLAG—"RISE ABOVE"

NAPALM DEATH—"SCUM"

FAITH NO MORE—"EPIC"

NICK CAVE & THE BAD SEEDS—"STAGGER LEE"

QUEEN—"WE WILL ROCK YOU"

AC/DC—"LET THERE BE ROCK"

FOO FIGHTERS—"THE PRETENDER"

GREEN DAY—"AMERICAN IDIOT"

GBH—"CRUSH 'EM"

OZZY OSBOURNE—"CRAZY TRAIN"

MOTLEY CRUE—"KICKSTART MY HEART"

MOTORHEAD—"OVERKILL"

MOTORHEAD—"BORN TO RAISE HELL"

IGGY POP—"CHINA GIRL"

JOE STRUMMER—"REDEMPTION SONG"

LIFE & DEATH IN THE STOCKS
"The reward is manifold."

WHEN I FIRST LAUNCHED *LIFE In The Stocks*, my goal was to make it the rock 'n' roll counterpart to *WTF* with Marc Maron. I *love* that podcast. I listen to it constantly to draw inspiration, and to up my game as an interviewer. I find it so inspiring. It's also extremely entertaining: the conversations that Maron conducts are raw, unbridled, and compelling. For my money, he's the best interviewer in the business.

One day I had a thought: wouldn't it be great to hear those types of conversations, but with people like Andrew W.K. as the guest? Many of the acts that've appeared on my podcast have also been on *WTF*, of course—people like Doug Stanhope, Tom Green, Steve-O, and Laura Jane Grace. But Marc Maron is unlikely to interview a lot of the people that've appeared on my podcast, and by extension this book.

Even *Kerrang!* and *Metal Hammer*, who do lots of great work in the world of rock music (I've written for both magazines in the past, and still have good friends who work at both now), are restricted as to whom they can have detailed discussions with. Primarily because of space in the magazine, but also because they have to reflect current musical trends and feature artists that are going to sell copies. And I completely understand that. It totally makes sense. But I don't care about the latest internet fad, or what's hot and poppin' *right now*. I'm interested in artists that have timeless stories to share, but rarely get the chance to share them. That's where *Life In The Stocks* comes in.

When I invite people on to my podcast, it doesn't matter who they are; I always approach the conversation with the same reverence as I would speaking to Bob Dylan or Elton John. That's just my way of showing respect. And when you show people respect, and you've done your homework, and you're the real deal, then they open up to you.

I pride myself on creating at an atmosphere of comfort and trust in my interviews, and I've been humbled and touched by the sensitive details that my guests have chosen to share. That's what this chapter is all about: weighty, intense, often difficult, but always important topics of conversation that you simply aren't going to hear or read about anywhere else.

Personally, this is my favorite chapter of the book. I believe it showcases the types of conversations that make my show special—if I can say so without sounding too full of it. Impending subjects include suicide, mental health, depression, gender dysphoria, sexism, feminism, and the #MeToo movement. You'll also read about the loss of band mates and family members, and the tragic deaths of internationally celebrated rock stars.

On top of all that, Vinnie Caruana provides a harrowing account of 9/11, Al Barr discusses the opioid crisis in America, Tom Green relives his battle with cancer, and Joe Cardamone lays his soul bare in an interview that still ranks amongst my all-time favorite episodes of *Life In The Stocks*.

This is the life and death chapter. It's a heavy one. But then life *is* heavy, and I've always found that talking about it helps. These conversations have served as therapy for me on more than one occasion, and I'd like to thank all the guests that appear in this chapter for being so fearlessly honest and vulnerable. I'd also like to give a special mention to my late friend, Amie Harwick. Thank you for everything that you taught me, Amie. The world is a darker place without you. I miss you.

NICK OLIVERI—*QUEENS OF THE STONE AGE, KYUSS, MONDO GENERATOR, DWARVES*

NICK: My father had some troubles, and he drove off a cliff in 1991. There's a picture of two greaser-looking dudes on the inside cover of

Blues for the Red Sun by Kyuss, and one of them is my dad. We dedicated that record to the memory of DJO: Douglas Joseph Oliveri.

Due to personal reasons, we weren't really getting along at the time, and we hadn't spoken in over a year. But he reached out to me a week before he died to say, "I've ordered your cassette." He lived out in Oakhurst, California, at the time, which is way up in the mountains by Yosemite. And he had to drive down to Fresno for over an hour to collect the tape that he'd specially ordered from the record store down there.

After he heard it, he called me up to say that he liked it and that he was really proud of me. That meant a lot to me when he told me that. It still does. Then a week later, I got a call from my brother to tell me that my dad had driven off a cliff, and he was dead. When I went to his funeral, I was going through all his cassettes, and sure as shit *Wretch* was right there in the tape player. That really meant something special to me.

CLEM BURKE—*BLONDIE, RAMONES, IGGY POP, JOAN JETT*

CLEM: Any time a close family member dies, a part of you dies. And when your parents pass, you become the family elder in a lot of ways. That's part of life's transition. Both my parents are gone. My mom died when I was seventeen, and I have no idea how I got into college because my last two years of high school were spent dealing with trying to care for her, and being involved in this whole cancer and death thing.

I really feel for people my age now who were lucky enough to have their parents live because many of them are now starting to lose their parents, and I have the empathy because I experienced that when I was much younger.

MATT: That must've been a difficult thing to deal with at that age. How did it affect you?

CLEM: Oh, it definitely affected me. I was in a daze. Luckily, I was always in bands, and that whole comradery and brotherhood—not to get all Springsteen on us—and the friendship and interaction that's involved with that is something that's fulfilling and positive and rewarding. Music is great therapy. I'd probably be an axe murderer or something if I didn't play music.

MICHAEL MONROE—*HANOI ROCKS, DEMOLITION 23, SOLO ARTIST*

MATT: Why did you decide to disband Hanoi Rocks?

MICHAEL: I made the decision to stop Hanoi Rocks to maintain the integrity of the band, and to show that there's at least one band out there that doesn't just do it for the money. The situation was such that we could've become this really big band, and it would've been even worse that way because people would've gotten to know the wrong version of Hanoi Rocks.

MATT: Do you think the band died when Razzle died, then?

MICHAEL: Yes, absolutely. Hanoi Rocks died with Razzle. That was the end of the band. What we had with Razzle was really special, you see. Then Sami [Yaffa] also left, so all of a sudden we didn't have a drummer or a bass player. It was just me, Andy [McCoy], and Nasty [Suicide], and they were all the way down there and I was all the way up there. There was no connection anymore.

To me, the most important thing was to end it, and maintain the integrity of the band. It was real, spontaneous, honest, and from the heart. And I wanted to maintain the memory of that. It's all about integrity: being honest and authentic, and singing and playing from the heart. A lot of people play from the wallet, and you can always tell. You can fool some people some of the time, but not forever. And I can go to bed at night with a clear conscience. My sleep is untroubled, and I wish everyone else the same.

JOE CARDAMONE—*THE ICARUS LINE, SOLO ARTIST, PRODUCER*

JOE: The last tour that The Icarus Line did was with Scott Weiland. It was the tour that he died on.

MATT: It was the one that he actually died on?

JOE: Yeah.

MATT: Did you know Scott before that tour?

JOE: No, I didn't know him. It was kind of some management/ booking agent deal, you know? *All Things Under Heaven*, which was the last Icarus Line record, had just come out. And it was weird because as I finished that record I kind of knew it was going to be the final statement from that group.

MATT: What sort of a headspace was that to occupy?

JOE: The way I felt when I finished it was just like, "This is what I've been trying to do with this thing the whole time." And boom! It was done, and I was finally at peace. I couldn't push a band format any further than that, at least right now in my life, and that was it. That's kind of how it felt.

MATT: Who put out the record?

JOE: We were signed to Sony, strangely enough. They put out the most uncommercial record I had made up to that point. Our management must've tricked them into putting it out.

MATT: Did Sony know what they were getting?

JOE: I don't think so. And I felt a little bit of pressure to at least show that I was going to promote it. So the Scott Weiland tour came up, and I was like, "Oh, fuck." I knew it wasn't the right tour for us, but whatever. Then right before the tour, Alvin [DeGuzman] got sick. It just happened like that: we're jamming, we finish the record, then right before the tour he called me from the hospital, and he was like, "Dude, I fucking woke up today, paralyzed." And he was paralyzed from the waist down, just like that—overnight. It was shocking and fucking upsetting. They found a tumor.

At that point, I didn't even want to go on tour because Alvin and I have been so close since third grade, which was when we started playing music together. The first person that I ever played music with was him, when we were sleepover age—that kind of shit. And we found out he had a tumor right at the base of his neck, in his spine. It was Thanksgiving, and I was at my parent's house when I got the call. I cried in the backyard away from everyone.

He started treatment immediately because he couldn't walk. All of a sudden he was bedridden—just like that. He woke up one day, and his roommates had to put him on an office chair and wheel him to the fucking emergency room.

MATT: And there were no warning signs?

JOE: Back pain. But who doesn't have back pain at thirty-eight?

MATT: Especially if you're a touring musician.

JOE: Exactly. I'm always complaining about my back. And he was complaining a little bit, but certainly not to the extent where we were like, "You're fucked." So Alvin's in a tight spot, and right before the tour he starts to fight and get his legs back. He's on a walker, and he's getting better, but he's not going to make it on that trip. So I threw together a skeleton crew of musicians, and besides my drummer and the saxophone player, no one else had played on the record. Everyone who had played on the record kind of went their separate ways. But I committed to doing the tour, so I put this group together and we get on it.

I think I saw Scott outside before the first show, which was kind of a warm-up gig for the tour in Hermosa Beach, just to like three hundred people. And I saw him, but I didn't really talk to him; I just let him do his thing. I knew the drummer Joey Castillo, though. He's a really cool guy, and it was cool to see him. I watched the show, and it was fine; the band seemed to have their shit together. It was weird for me to play without Alvin, though.

So, we did that show, and then we did maybe two other shows, and I think the third show was Halloween in Sacramento. At the end of that show, Scott was standing outside, and I decided to go up and say thanks for having us out. I tried to talk to him, but he was standing there having a drink, and he couldn't even talk. I saw this look in his eyes, and I've seen that exact same look before in other people that have died.

We did one more show in San Francisco, and then we were doubling back to LA to do House of Blues in Anaheim—or some shit like that. House of Blues is the worst. And then from there it was like a five-week tour. So we're in LA, and I call my manager, and I was like, "This is fucked up. If this guy dies—"

MATT: You saw it coming?

JOE: Yeah. I know it sounds crazy, but I did. I was like, "If this guy kicks it while we're on tour, what happens? Are we just fucked?" And my manager was like, "Yes." I would've had to pay the band out of my own pocket, as we weren't making any money on that shit, and if we got stranded it was going to be on me to pay for everyone to get home. He was like, "Look, man. If you don't want to do this, then I totally get it." He knew what shape Scott was in because he also managed him. So I said, "Yeah, I don't think I want to do this."

The last show of that tour for us, and the last show for The Icarus Line in general, was at the House of Blues in Anaheim, at fucking Disneyland. What a depressing setting to end it. And besides Scott's condition, the thing that really turned me off the entire situation was that maybe a month before the tour, some footage came out of him slurring his way through "Vasoline" on the internet, and it went viral because of how bad it was. So every night when the band would play that song, everyone's phone would come up to capture it.

MATT: That's fucked.

JOE: I know. I just felt like, "I don't want anything to do with this culture. Whatever this is, this is not why I'm here."

MATT: What's wrong with people?

JOE: They're fucked. They all wanted to be the one to capture it, so they could get likes on the fucking internet. You know what I mean? It's so wrong. And I took it personally to see that. I just didn't know what those people were really there for.

MATT: Do you think a lot of them were just there to watch the car crash?

JOE: Oh, yeah. And they were fans of his as well. It was all too much. So, that was the end for me: I dissolved the group right after that. There was no announcement or anything. I just wanted to wait for Alvin to feel better, and then assess things.

MATT: How many shows did Scott do after that, do you know?

JOE: Another week and a half. Then he died. Joey Castillo texted me a couple of hours after he found him on the bus.

MATT: Joey was the one who found him? That's heavy.

JOE: Yeah. I'm so glad I wasn't there for it. You don't want to be there for that kind of thing. And for me, that put the final nail in the project, not just for The Icarus Line, but for the rock band community in general. The format was already no longer exciting to me, and I looked out at the culture surrounding it—and of course there's positives— and I just felt like I didn't have anything to offer that world anymore. And it had nothing more to offer me.

TIM McILRATH—*RISE AGAINST*

TIM: Being a performer like [Chris] Cornell or Chester [Bennington] is not completely unlike being a lion tamer, and a good lion tamer will make it look easy. He'll make you forget that he's in some serious danger, and that those are lions with teeth that want to eat him, because through years of practice he's made it look entertaining and fun.

When you talk about Linkin Park and Soundgarden songs, you're talking about dark songs that deal with real demons. Chester and Chris—and other guys like myself who sing in these type of bands—all wrestle with these demons. But if you're good at it, and they were *good* at it, then you make it look easy; you make it look so easy that the audience forgets that those demons are still lions, and they're dangerous. Just because it's a top ten single, or the lyrics are on a T-shirt that they're selling that night, it doesn't change the fact that at the core of these songs, people's blood, sweat, and tears are poured into them. It's a scary thing, and when you add the distortion of drugs into that mix, it's really unpredictable what can happen. What's really sad, too, is I knew both those guys—I'd sung on stage with both of them—and out of all the people that I've met out here, they were some of the lightest of souls. And they seemingly had it all together.

Whenever I talked to Chester, it would always be at some huge show, and I'm sure there was always a lot of pressure on him to perform and be all that is Chester Bennington. But nobody was more relaxed or comfortable than he was. He'd walk into our dressing room about sixty seconds before he was due on stage, and his tour manager would be freaking the fuck out. He'd be like, "Chester, what are you doing?" And Chester would say, "I want to say hello to Rise Against. Give me a break." He'd just be calm and cool, and he'd tell me about some new band that he was listening to that I should check out. He'd just be floating, like he had it all together.

I've met people out here that I worry about. I've met people and thought, "That guy seems dark. He seems like he's in a dark place." I never had that feeling about Chester—or Chris for that matter. Chris was always such a warm-hearted, generous person who seemed all but unaware of his own celebrity. He just wanted everyone to have a good time and feel comfortable.

When I saw their deaths in the news, I thought they were both fake news. I thought, "No way. Not those guys. Maybe somebody else, but not those guys." That made it all the more shocking, especially in the case of Cornell; he'd survived so many of those grunge deaths; he made it through all the shit. I'm friends with the Audioslave guys, too, and I've heard lots of stuff about Chris. It seemed like his demons were all behind him. That's what makes it even more sad. But if nothing else—in the wake of their deaths—these are things that we can hopefully talk about and be more aware of, and not just be so quick to move on and forget. If something good can come out of it, hopefully that's it.

JESSE LEACH—*KILLSWITCH ENGAGE, TIMES OF GRACE, THE WEAPON*

JESSE: Depression runs in my family. My grandfather was manic—probably bipolar, even. But I don't know if he was properly diagnosed. He'd get on a high, and he'd be the king of the world, and he'd put on my grandmother's spring dress and go water skiing. He'd do crazy stuff like that and make people laugh, and just be this amazing figure that everyone was drawn to. Then he would disappear for weeks on end.

I remember seeing him lying in bed watching TV one day, and he wasn't even responsive. He barely even acknowledged I was in the room. It was dark. So I know it runs in my family: my sister also suffers from it. I used to be a lot worse, but thankfully through therapy, natural medications, and exercise, I've got a lot better handle on it. And I now have more tools to build upon to help come out of it as I feel it starting to come down on me. I can't always sense it coming, though.

For me, the big thing was talking about it. When I started to let people know on a very public level—on my Instagram and Twitter pages—and open up that dialogue, I began having so many conversations with fans and friends. And I feel like the more you know, the more you're able to help yourself. When I feel like I'm sliding into a dark place, I reach out to people and ask for help. And I think having that dialogue is the reason I'm able to function a lot better than I used to. I haven't had a suicidal thought in a long time, and when I was younger, it used to happen a lot. So I try to keep that dialogue open at all times. I almost wear it like a badge of pride because I know that it helps other people, and I talk about it as much as I comfortably can.

DOUG STANHOPE—*COMEDIAN, AUTHOR, PODCAST HOST*

MATT: There's a great bit that you do in the *No Place Like Home* special, which I watched the other night, where you talk about how the last group of people to not have anyone defend them are crazy people: the mentally ill.

DOUG: Yeah.

MATT: That's a really interesting observation because it's so true. You get in trouble for saying words like "retarded" these days, but you can say just about anything you want in regards to a crazy person, and no one's going to tell you off.

DOUG: Right. "That guy's a lunatic. That movie's crazy. This is fucking nuts." If you took all those words out of your vocabulary, you wouldn't be talking too much.

MATT: I love that you talk so much about your partner, Bingo, and her mental health issues, too. By turning those stories and experiences into comedy, it breaks down some of the taboos that still surround mental health. We need to have more empathy for these people who aren't well. What's the bit that you do where you talk about Bingo going to meet her mental health doctor?

DOUG: I talk about how she had to go past a VFW [Veterans of Foreign Wars] hall, a Second Amendment gun shop, and the Beast brewery to get to the mental health care center, and how the acronym of the building that she goes into is Community Intervention Associates, so it had CIA marked above the door where she went in. And there's no actual doctor in there, because we're so remote, so she'd have to talk via Skype to an RN [Registered Nurse] or an LPN [Licensed Practical Nurse], or some kind of fucking nurse. So she's talking to a TV set that's talking back to her.

MATT: None of those specifics sound conducive to someone trying to deal with mental health problems, do they?

DOUG: Not at all. And after I did that bit, within a short space of time they actually changed the name of the building to CHA: Community Health Associates.

MATT: Did they really?

DOUG: Yes. And I take full fucking responsibility for that. It's a small town, and if I put something like that out there, it's going to get back to them.

MATT: Who knew Doug Stanhope was such an influential figure in the local community.

LAURA JANE GRACE—*AGAINST ME!, SOLO ARTIST, AUTHOR*

LAURA: I talk about this all the time: I'm manic depressive. And depression is a mental illness that's separate and has nothing to do with being trans. But at the same time, when you're hiding a part of yourself and you're dealing with a part of yourself in a negative way, it certainly doesn't help the depression. For me, dysphoria in the past had been like these binge and purge moments, and there'd be periods of time where it would come on strong, and I'd give in to it. Then I'd say, "Okay, I'm swearing off this behavior now. I'll never do this again. I'm going to be a man."

Before I sobered up in 2005, I was getting fucked up all the time, and I was unable to control the dysphoria. I was giving in to behavior that made me ashamed of myself, so sobering up felt like my way of putting all that in the past. I said to myself, "I'm going to be a man. I'm going to commit to doing this band, we're going to sign to a major label and become famous and successful, and then I'll be happy and I'll be whole. And I'll never have to think about these things again."

In 2009, it really came back after things started to fall apart with the band. At the same time, I was still going through an arrest from 2007, and being stuck in the legal system is no fucking fun. So I had the normal pressures of being in a band, putting out a major label release, having to tour as much as we were touring, and making all the sacrifices that I was making in my personal life. Added to that were the charges that were hanging over my head, and all the legal bills that were coming in.

Immediately after getting arrested, we also got sued by our manager. So we had that lawsuit hanging over our heads as well. And there was the added pressure of knowing that our first record for Sire [New Wave] wasn't a hit. They had to put out the second record because we'd signed a two-album deal, but if that one didn't take off immediately then we were definitely going to get dropped from the label. So there was an incredible amount of pressure and stress on me at that time.

It was around this time that my wife took a trip to Belgium to visit her sister, and I was at home alone. That's when I gave in to the dysphoria again—if you want to put it like that. At the time, I just thought, "This is some weird thing that's happening to me, and once I leave home and go to LA to make the new record, then I'm done again." It felt like stress relief, in a way: I felt like I could actually breathe because I was being myself, and it was an escape in a way where I didn't have to compartmentalize something. Once I got to LA to start recording *White Crosses*, I swore off it again. But obviously that didn't last long.

By this point, I knew the word transgender and I knew what was going on, so I spent a lot of time researching and talking to doctors and support groups. But I was too scared to follow up on any of it. We had *White Crosses* coming out, we were due to be going out on tour, and we were still in a lawsuit. But as things got worse with the band and the lawsuit, it kind of became like a strength. It became the one thing that I had in a world where everything else was full of shit; I knew this to be true, and I knew that no one else knew about it.

MATT: When you finally did come out in 2012, how did that feel?

LAURA: I needed truth. I needed to know something that was true, and I needed to be honest with myself in a way that I hadn't been in a very long time. It was completely empowering. The second I said the words to my wife and my band mates, it was like this rush that I'd never felt before. And a lot of that was terror, but it was still just incredibly liberating. It was freeing in a way that I'd never experienced before. It was like a trust fall: I walked to the edge, turned around, fell back, and just hoped that someone caught me—and I didn't die.

MINA CAPUTO—*LIFE OF AGONY, SOLO ARTIST*

MINA: I love Laura [Jane Grace]. The latest Against Me! album [*Transgender Dysphoria Blues*] is amazing, and her songwriting just keeps getting better and better. I'm stoked for her; I'm so happy for all her success, and the paradigms that she's shifting. I can tell that she's simmering away. I was like a catalyst for her, in a way. I think when I came out it gave her that little extra boost and courage to take her as far as it's going to take her, and it's taking her far. It's a big process: we're constantly transitioning.

MATT: Is it an ongoing evolution?

MINA: Evolution and de-evolution. That's humanity: we're constantly transitioning. It's like we're shedding skin every day. And you don't have to be gay or transsexual, or whatever title you want to put on nonconformists or outlaws like me. It's just about letting it all out; being both; being neither; being everything—whatever.

For me, it's about three things: energy, frequency, and vibration. I'm a galactic being, and I hate being put into categories. I'm beyond society's idea of what society and culture should be. We're just this energy, frequency, and vibration that's constantly expanding, and there's never an end to it. That's how I view myself. That's how I view what's going on with me.

I'm paying homage to, and respecting the idea of the feminine, which has been repressed for thousands of years throughout our time as whatever we are on this planet. And it runs deep. Society likes to put things in black and white, but it's beyond that. It's simple, but it's complex, and the complexities are mystical and mysterious. We'll never truly be able to pinpoint exactly what's what and who's who. But don't listen to me; do your own research; find out about this stuff for yourself. You need to be a voracious reader. Exercise your imagination.

I chose to mutate and regrow because I wanted to become the change that I wanted to see, and I want to see more femininity on the planet. And what I mean by that is more tenderness, more compassion, more grace, more love, and more understanding. Basically, everything that our society fails to teach or encourage.

Before the Spanish Inquisition, when the Europeans basically raped and pillaged their way around the world, the Native Americans had over ten genders and different ways in which men and women would express themselves. But the Spanish Inquisition wiped that out with their European Christian beliefs. They wiped out the ancient ways, man. And if you don't seek it out, you're going to miss out on all this ancient knowledge. But it is remaining out there. I just wish the world could reach the part of their heart that will allow them to live as happily, openly, and courageously as they can.

DR. AMIE HARWICK—*THERAPIST, WRITER, MODEL*

MATT: Why do you think the #MeToo movement broke through now in the way that it did? What do you think it's achieved? And what do you think the long-term effects will be?

AMIE: I think they're all very valid questions. Why now? Why did it turn out the way that it did? How has this affected things? And I think there are a lot of positives: people are listening to women more, and women are getting fairer wages, especially in the entertainment industry. People are more hypersensitive to the treatment of women, too. But on the other side, I think that men are scared. I think people might be more hesitant to be themselves or do their jobs in the way that they've always done them. And for that reason, I think we should all be curious.

I was just at a diner reading the paper, and I noticed a story on a gynecologist who just had his license suspended. He was taking medical photos—they weren't for personal or sexual use—and apparently some women felt uncomfortable with some of the things that he said, like, "You have wonderful skin," or "Your skin is beautiful"—but in a nonsexual way. Now, when I saw the headline for this, it read, "Gynecologist suspended over possible harassment." And my initial thought was, "Oh, that sounds terrible. A person who's harassing a woman *should* be suspended." But when you read the fine detail, the facts presented in this article—and all I know is from what was in this article—suggested that this person was probably just doing their job.

If I had a doctor who told me I had great skin, in a nonsexual way, I think that's an objective observation. But because of this movement, I don't think if it wasn't at this time this doctor would've been suspended. So I do think that some of it goes a little too far, and we have to be cautious about what assumptions we allow ourselves to make, based on the limited information that we have about people.

MATT: And a lot of that responsibility is in the hands of the press, right?

AMIE: Absolutely. People like you. It all starts with you, Matt. But it's true: responsible journalism. And no matter what journalism you're presented with, or what information you're presented with, it's our responsibility as freethinking individuals to take that information, and say, "Is this a reliable source? Is this bias? Does this actually violate somebody?" Because there's so much misinformation and persuasive journalism out there. Everything is written to make you think or feel something, whether it's intentional as a persuasive article or presentation, or maybe it's an unconscious bias that somebody has because we all have them. Any information that we're taking in has been filtered through somebody writing it, and somebody presenting it, and we just have to be aware of that and take responsibility for our own perceptions and reactions.

MATT: It's just common sense at the end of the day, isn't it?

AMIE: It really is just common sense, yes.

MATT: I don't know about you, but I feel like common sense is dying out in today's world. I talk a lot about it on my show, and I often sound like a grumpy old man, but the way the internet works is an article will get shared online, but the headline is often the only thing that people read. And as you say, if it's a provocative headline, and the language is loaded, then your reaction is to go, "Oh, my God. That's awful. That person has done this, and now they're canceled. They're dead to me. Next." It almost becomes like an online witch hunt, for lack of a better word.

AMIE: Right. It has created some of that. On the one hand, more women are being heard for things that actually are happening, so there has been a lot of progress and that's great. But on the other hand, I think it's caused some people to pursue this kind of witch hunt behavior. And obviously if there are situations where there's people who are underage, or they're not consenting and there are violations or rape, then that's not even a question.

MATT: Of course.

AMIE: But there's a lot of gray area, as you say. And as a sex therapist, and a therapist in general, I hear a lot of gray area, and the gray area challenges us more because it challenges us to look at ourselves and our own behavior.

MONIQUE POWELL—*SAVE FERRIS*

MONIQUE: Back in the day—back in the 1990s—I was so focused on succeeding and fitting in that I didn't realize how rare my gender was on these stages. In 1998, when we first did Warped Tour, I was the only woman on that tour on any of the stages. Then when I came back in 2017, and I did the Warped Tour nineteen years later, I was the oldest woman on any of the stages. But there were quite a few more women by then, which was really inspiring and fun, and it was really nice to get feedback from the women in the other bands who expressed to me how much what I did meant to them. And that was a surprise because I never did what I did—

MATT: With that in mind?

MONIQUE: Never. In those days, in America, it was really unusual to look the way that I did, and have the size body that I had, and do what I was doing on stage. I experienced a lot of pressure and judgement from a lot of people.

MATT: From within the industry, from your peers, or from the general public?

MONIQUE: Everyone. There were some groups of evolved people who got it. And there were groups of people who needed it. I didn't quite realize how much we all needed it until I came back all these years later and got to hear the stories about girls that picked up instruments or liked themselves a little bit better because of my band.

MATT: That's what I noticed at the show yesterday. And for me—to go on kind of a tangent here, but also a related side-note—feminism is a very multifaceted concept, and people have different ideas of what being a feminist means. What I love about watching you do what you do, is your interpretation of feminism seems to be a celebration of the female form, and what it means to be a woman. Some women choose to suppress or conceal their femininity on stage, but you flaunt yours proudly for all to see.

MONIQUE: Right.

MATT: You're up there going, "I'm a woman. I'm happy and proud to be a woman. And this is what it means to be a woman."

MONIQUE: Yeah. I'm just different. There was a time when I was offended when a man would open a door for me, but I've grown up to be different now. Everybody has their own interpretation of respect and love for each other, and if that means you opening a door for me, then thank you. A lot of feminists think that that's offensive, but I don't.

MATT: For me, that's just a sign of respect. I'd open the door for a guy as well. It's just a nice thing to do for another human being.

MONIQUE: Right. And in my twenties, I just wanted to be one of the guys.

MATT: Because you were surrounded by guys.

MONIQUE: I was surrounded by guys. And in order for me to do what I wanted to do in this business, I had to learn how to speak this language with them. And I also really like guys: they're fucking cool to hang out with. But what I've now realized is that I don't have to succumb to the traditional view of masculinity in order to hang out with the dudes; I can still embody a traditional ideal of what a woman is *and* hang with the dudes. And listen, I can do anything that you can do, in heels.

MATT: No doubt.

MONIQUE: I've always said that: "I can do anything a guy can do, and I can do it in heels."

MATT: *High* heels as well.

MONIQUE: Oh, yeah. Last night I was in the kitchen, still in my hot pants and heels from the show, just cooking and barbecuing with everybody. They were like, "Don't you want to change?" And I was like, "No. That's going to take too much time." I was in full makeup, lashes—everything.

MATT: I love it.

MONIQUE: I learned in my twenties to act "as if": act as if I really liked myself, even when I had moments of terrible insecurity because what I was putting out there was far more important than what was going on in my heart. And eventually, if I acted as if for long enough, I would start to believe the things that I was putting out there. At forty-two years old, I really do like myself a lot. And I can go toe to toe with any of these guys.

MATT: I know. I've seen it.

MONIQUE: I'm not afraid of them. And I have to tell you, it hasn't been easy for me. The standards have definitely been different for me, compared to my peers in my part of the industry.

MATT: There seems to be a lot of interpersonal politics in the Orange Country music scene. Am I right in thinking that?

MONIQUE: I mean, everybody has history and stories when you've been doing this for as long as we have—over twenty years.

MATT: And you all came out of the same scene at the same time, didn't you?

MONIQUE: Yeah. It just comes back to the one simple thing that I've realized, which is that I was doing what the rest of the boys were doing, and then at a certain point we surpassed the bands from our hometown, and I don't know what happened after that. But it was very strange. Ever since the beginning, people's perception of me was really unrealistic and not based in fact. I managed and booked Save Ferris when I joined the band, and I helped in my own way make the band happen. But I just recently realized, in Orange County at that time, that wasn't the ladylike thing to do. It wasn't ladylike to take control, be in charge, and succeed. And whether or not any of these guys—

MATT: Were even consciously aware of that...

MONIQUE: Exactly. But there is this underlying acceptable misogyny that exists in my hometown. I went to school with the Reel Big Fish guys, you know. I was at their first shows, I dated the bass player [Matt Wong] for four years, I lived with them for a time, and we have a long history together. But it was never an inclusive scene—at least not from where I'm from. I don't know what the rest of the world is like, but the Orange County scene was never welcoming to me—ever. Those guys may have been my friends, but when I wasn't around I really don't think they were talking about how awesome I was.

DR. AMIE HARWICK

AMIE: There's so many different schools of thought with feminism. Even the word ends up being explosive for a lot of people because they have such strong ties to what the word means. Feminists, by definition, are people who want equal rights for men and women. And I can assume that most people want that; you want that, so that would technically make you a feminist. But a lot of people are scared to use that word. There are also different waves of feminism that have come across with different perspectives. The second wave of feminism was more conservative and women in that movement didn't want to exploit their bodies. It was more about burning your bra and letting your armpit hair grow. Then in the 1990s, culture was a lot more rebellious, whether it was the metal or the Riot Grrrl music that was coming out—

MATT: And even with pop groups like the Spice Girls, and the whole Girl Power movement.

AMIE: Right. Everything was in your face, and much louder, liberal, and more political. And the feminism that came out at that time was the third wave of feminism, which was really about how women should do what they want to do with their own bodies because it was their own choice. If that means you want to burn your bra and grow your armpit hair, or you want to be a sex worker with your cleavage showing, then both those lifestyles are equally valid, and you should have the right to do those things. Coming from that perspective, which is a belief that I hold—if you want to do it, do it—I think it's really important to be mindful of the cultural effect that your behavior could have, but ultimately it's your decision. Equal rights mean doing what you want to do because you want to do them, using your sexuality to your own advantage, as long as it's not harming other people, is totally fine. I definitely support women who want to be sexy and sexual, if that's part of what they want.

MONIQUE POWELL

MONIQUE: I've come back all these years later, and I make no apologies for who I am. I brought the band back in 2013 out of a desperate health diagnosis in which I thought I might never walk or sing again, and that story is so crazy that it puts all of this other bullshit to shame.

MATT: What happened?

MONIQUE: For ten years, my dad was like, "When are you going to get back on stage?" And I was like, "I don't think I'm ever going to get back on stage, Dad." Then I got this diagnosis where the vertebrae in my neck was disintegrating, my spinal cord was compromised, and I was losing my ability to walk. For the surgery that I had to have, they go through the front of the neck, and the amount of damage was so great that they would have to move the esophagus aside, which meant

I would never sing again. I had three doctors say, "So, do you want to walk, or do you want to sing?"

MATT: That was the choice: A or B?

MONIQUE: That was the choice. And one of the doctors said, "Well, when was the last time you put out a record anyway?" My sister was with me, and I remember we walked to the car and we sat there in silence for a moment. She said, "Well, what do you think?" This was the third diagnosis of a doctor saying the same shit. And I was like, "I can't imagine if I have kids one day, never being able to sing to them." I said, "We have to figure this out." And she was like, "We're going to figure it out."

We ended up finding a team of doctors that were daring enough to go through the back of my neck, and they sort of changed the game for my condition and the treatment of it. My neck was completely rebuilt from the back. Before I went under, as they were shaving my head and putting screws in my temples, I said to my dad, "If I wake up from this and I can still walk and sing, then I'll fucking bring the band back for you, Dad." When I woke up, I was like, "Oh, shit. I guess I'm doing this." So I did. And the original intention was to get all the guys back together. But that wasn't what happened, obviously.

MATT: Why was that? After you'd been through such a traumatic experience and miraculous recovery—

MONIQUE: Because none of that matters to any of them. It never mattered to them.

MATT: So friendship isn't on the cards with those guys?

MONIQUE: It never was. With me, there was always a different set of rules: you guys are homies and brothers, and that's Monique in the corner.

MATT: Do you think Gwen Stefani had the same experience in No Doubt?

MONIQUE: I don't know. All I know is that I just wanted everybody to like me, and I wanted to make everybody happy all the time. That was really all I wanted to do. And so I had this surgery, and the plan was to bring the band back, but for whatever reason the plan wasn't to their liking. And I don't know how else to explain it, except that it just didn't work out how I wanted it to.

MATT: But you tried?

MONIQUE: I did. But I also knew that I didn't have to fucking try. I was like, "If you guys are going to be assholes about it, and you're not going to have any respect for me, and you're going to try and hire your buddies to be our managers or booking agents to cash in and rip us off, then no. We're going to do this the right way, and if you don't like it then you don't have to come with me. I'm doing it regardless. But I want you there." Whatever happened after that happened, and I spent two and a half years fighting for it, but now I finally own the rights to the name. It wasn't easy, but I fought for it.

MATT: Not cheap either, I imagine.

MONIQUE: It wasn't cheap. But if something is meant to happen and your heart is in the right place, then the universe sees to it that you get what you need. And my heart was in the right place. When I woke up from that surgery and I said, "All right, Dad, I'm bringing the band back," it wasn't because I wanted to show the world that I could learn how to literally hold my head up again. It was because there were still people out there who loved Save Ferris.

I spent the next two and a half years fighting a lawsuit and writing an EP [*Checkered Past*]. While I was recording that EP, my dad came out and sang on one of the songs ["Goodbye Brother"]. That was a very proud moment for all of us, and we called that my dad's "last best day," because then he got really sick. I put out the record while he was in the hospital, and we recorded the video, then I went to show him the video in the hospital. But he didn't wake up that day, I didn't get to show him the video, and then he died. And I then went out on my first headline tour in fifteen years. Every moment since has been for him, and I don't care about all this other shit. It doesn't really matter to me.

I've always said, "I do this because this is the only thing that I *really* know how to do." And I love it more than anything in the world. I live to make people happy. Anything else that anyone has to say about me is really contrary to who I am in my heart. I'm not here to be a role model for other women. I'm just here to play great shows and create incredible experiences for people in which they feel really special for a minute. That's where I get my joy from, and it's so much bigger than Garden Grove, or Orange County.

MATT: Do you still consider the guys in Reel Big Fish to be your friends?

MONIQUE: I consider them all to be fucking brothers. They're all brothers, honestly. We have our differences, but that doesn't matter. At the end of the day, we tell a story that comes from the same place, and we're a family. All this other shit doesn't matter. If any of them called me tomorrow and said, "I'm in hospital, and I need a blood transfusion," I'd be like, "I'm there."

MATT: Do you think they would do the same for you?

MONIQUE: I don't know. But I don't have any expectation of that. I just know who I am, and if any of those guys ever wanted to bury the hatchet, then I'd be there. We're family.

MATT: And families have their differences.

MONIQUE: Yeah. And I think because there's been all of these movements for women—the #MeToo movement, and all of these other things—and women are speaking out about the lack of equality in the entertainment industry, I now symbolize something more to everybody. And I think that makes them more afraid, or maybe dislike me even more because now I'm calling everyone to task. In my twenties, that's not something I would've ever thought of doing because I just wanted everybody to like me.

MATT: That seems to be the general pattern, doesn't it? Women just wanted to be accepted and make progress on their respective fields, and not rock the boat.

MONIQUE: Yeah.

MATT: But now, which is great, women are saying that they've had enough, and this shit is no longer acceptable.

MONIQUE: Right. And you guys have daughters, sisters, mothers, and women in your life that are worthy of respect. So I'm calling every single one of these guys on these shows to task by saying, "I want you to think about how you treat us." I'm not asking anybody to treat me with any sort of special treatment. I just want you to treat me as an equal because I've paid the same fucking dues as the rest of you. So I'm calling you all to task. And this isn't just about me: this is about all women in this industry.

MATT: And all women in general.

MONIQUE: Absolutely. It's about bettering everybody's lives, and once you figure out how to communicate with women in the work place, then you understand how to raise a strong woman, how to treat her like an equal, and how to talk to her with a tone that says, "You can do anything that you want to do: be an astronaut, be a punk rock singer—it doesn't matter." Then all of a sudden you realize, "Wait a minute. Was I trying to empower this person and make them feel good about themselves? Or did I just say or do something that was sort of dickish?"

People are always asking me, "How does it feel to be objectified?" But I'm just going to put this out there as a disclaimer: I'm not the kind of woman who goes and complains to the management if some guy grabs my ass. If I don't like that, I will punch you in the fucking face.

MATT: I don't doubt that.

MONIQUE: Do you know what I'm saying?

MATT: Absolutely. It's difficult, as a man, to feel like I have any right in saying this, but I say do exactly that: if someone disrespects you, call them out then and there, to their face. Don't wait fifteen years and then go on social media, and say, "This person crossed the line back then." I accept the fact that some people might not have the courage to speak out in the moment. But if someone is an asshole to you, then you should address the situation immediately. And this is what we should be teaching all young people to do: call out bullshit right away.

MONIQUE: Exactly. I don't need a women's organization to come to my rescue. And I don't need a #MeToo movement to save me. I can save me. And most of the time, if a hot guy grabs my ass, I'm like, "Thanks." But I'm not afraid to take care of myself. And I know that there's a lot of people out there that don't feel strong enough, or don't think that they have the words. I was that person for a really long time. But after I had the surgery and my dad died, the game changed for me.

Everything that happened to me in my life up until that point you think would've made me a really tough person. But actually, I was never tough; I was always very sensitive, and I just wanted to please people. But now I have a voice, and I can teach you how to have a voice, too—whether you're a woman or a man. I can help you. Just watch me. Again, I'm not the type of person who goes to management and complains. And there doesn't need to be a security guard in the mosh pit just because I'm in there. Let's just fucking mosh.

TOM GREEN—*ACTOR, COMEDIAN, RAPPER, TALK SHOW HOST*

MATT: When you were at the peak of your fame and popularity, you got testicular cancer. That must've been a whirlwind period anyway, as a healthy person. So how did it affect you when you found out you also had cancer to deal with? And what did that whole ordeal teach you, looking back on it now?

TOM: It was really horrible timing. It's never a good time to get cancer, but that was definitely the worst time to get it. That's why I stopped doing *The Tom Green Show*. Not a lot of people know that. Generally speaking, people don't know that it was the number one show on MTV, and I quit at the peak of the show's popularity to go deal with my cancer.

When I finished battling cancer, I had several movie offers, so it's hard to sit here and complain about how horrible a time it was when I had four movie offers lined up, and I went straight from my cancer surgery right on to the set of *Saturday Night Live*, where I was hosting SNL. Then I went from movie set to movie set for the next two years, shooting films and doing incredibly well. So it's hard to sit here and complain, and say, "What a bad time to be sick." But it sucked.

It was extremely painful, physically. And emotionally, it's scary to think that you could be confronting death. But at the same time, it taught me that you can battle through horrible things and not let them destroy you. It also makes you very aware that life is fragile, and you have to be positive and enjoy and cherish every moment that you have. Not to sound cheesy, but all that really does come to the forefront of your mind.

On a daily basis, I'll have something pop into my head, and I'll think to myself, "At least I'm not in the hospital today." If I'm having a bad day, or something bad has happened, I just say to myself, "At least I'm not in the hospital right now, pumped full of morphine with tubes running into my spine, fighting cancer. Things could be so much worse." It's hard now to get really, really upset about little things; little things that would've been big things if I'd not been through that ordeal. So it's definitely been a positive experience overall.

I say in my stand-up show, "Sometimes, I think about my battle with cancer, and I think I wouldn't trade it for anything. But then I think actually, no, I'd trade it for my right testicle. I wouldn't mind getting that back." But it is true: I do think that I gained more than I lost. And they just took the right testicle. It's no big deal. I've still got the left one. It's fine; it's the middle one now—I'm just doing my jokes. But seriously, it was a good thing, and I took a lot away from it that ended up being very positive.

MATT: As a comedian, what did that experience teach you about laughter as a form of therapy? And because you're such a physical performer, did it slow you down or force you to change your approach to comedy in any way?

TOM: It was the reason I stopped doing *The Tom Green Show*. First of all, I'd been doing the show at that point for almost ten years, running round on the streets doing pranks. And I didn't want to go out and get into confrontational situations with people anymore because I was in a lot of physical pain. I had a lymph node dissection, so it was more than just a minor surgery, and it took me years and years to recover. I still feel physical effects from it, as far as pain issues and things like that. So for the first couple of years in particular, there was no way I wanted to go running around on the streets getting chased by security guards and things like that. I'd also done the show for so long, and I wanted to try something new. So I stopped doing *The Tom Green Show* and I started doing films instead. But does it still affect me now? Well, my stand-up show is very high energy, so I would say no.

MATT: Do you think there's more pathos in your material, though?

TOM: I knew there was another part to that question. I was just trying to remember what the question was. Yeah, I do a lot of material that's very dark in my stand-up show, and I talk a lot about death and morbid subjects, which to me is very cathartic. If I can laugh about dark, morbid subjects, then it helps me personally cope with the very present fear that I have of the end looming—for all of us. And I do think I think about that way more than the average person because I've been right there on the precipice of death: I've stared it in the face. I've been in that hospital bed, and the twenty-four-year-old kid beside me who had the exact same testicular cancer that I had died. He died. I remember the doctor saying, "The kid in the bed next to you is a fan of your show." So I went over and said hello to him, and we had a nice chat, and a year later he was dead, and I was alive. That makes you realize just how fragile everything is, and I wouldn't think about life in those terms if I hadn't had cancer.

MATT: What made you decide to do *The Tom Green Cancer Special*? That was an incredibly brave decision on your part, not to mention a brilliant piece of television.

TOM: Well, our whole staff had moved from New York to Los Angeles. People had given up apartments and moved their whole lives from New York to LA because the show was doing so well, and they assumed we'd be doing it for a few years at least. But a couple of months after we got to LA, I got cancer. So I thought, here's one last show we can do, which will take another month or two at least, so we don't have to send everyone home. That wasn't the main reason why we did it. But we were in the middle of production, and I did have the whole crew there, so it was easy enough to turn the cameras around on me.

It wasn't something that MTV instantly agreed to do. We had to really lobby them to let us film it, which eventually they did. And it aired so many times in the end, and raised so much awareness for testicular cancer, that here we are, seventeen years later, and at least once a week somebody still comes up to me after one of my shows and says that the reason they diagnosed their cancer was because of that show—especially in the United States, where the show was in such heavy rotation. The *Cancer Special* must've played on MTV a hundred times in the US, and so many teenage boys who would've never gone to the doctor went to the doctor because of that show. And that's when you get testicular cancer: fifteen–thirty-five years old, which was the prime age of viewership for MTV. At least a thousand people have come up to me and said that my *Cancer Special* saved their life. It's surreal. I don't think anyone really knows that. I don't think I've ever even said it before—at least not in that way. And that's just the people who've come up and told me in person. I can't even begin to imagine how many people actually went to the doctor because of it. I think MTV should air it every year.

JOE CARDAMONE

MATT: The film at the start of last night's show had me hooked anyway, but as soon as you walked out on stage looking like the fucking *Man Who Fell to Earth*, dressed like Ryan Gosling in *Drive*, saying, "I've lost my mind," I was just like, "Wow! I am *in*." It was intense, and unlike any live show I've seen before.

JOE: Thank you. That song is about me getting the call to say that Alvin [DeGuzman] was sick. That's literally how the set starts, with me getting the phone call—I didn't even realize that until right now. And that song kinds of sets up the whole thing, I guess, because I talk about that for a second, and then halfway through the song I talk about my best friend Annie waking up in the morning to find her baby dead. She lost her child around the same time that Alvin got sick: the child was born, then thirty days later she woke up in the morning, and the baby was dead. So a lot of things happened at the same time, and that song kind of sets up the scene of where we're going.

Alvin only died about seven days before I left for this tour. And I went to see him almost every day right up until the end. He was in bad shape: he couldn't see, and he really couldn't talk that well either, as he had a tumor in his mouth. It was fucked. I said, "Dude, I'll break you out of here. Do you want to go to the beach? What do you want to do?" I was desperate to fucking do something for him. But he was like, "No. I'm okay. We did it, man. We did it all. The only regrets that I have are the shows that we didn't play." And then he passed away. So I knew I had to go and do this tour because of that, do you know what I mean?

MATT: Because it's what he would've wanted.

JOE: Totally. So I picked myself up and I jumped on this tour. I haven't stop moving, basically, since his funeral.

MATT: What happens next? This is the end of tour, right?

JOE: Yeah. I go home, and I get to work. I have a record that I have to do as soon as I get home.

MATT: Are you going to stop at any point and allow yourself time to grieve?

JOE: I don't know. I've lost people before, but this is different. I don't even know what it means. I'll be honest with you, there was definitely a couple of nights on this trip where every once in a while I'd be alone, and I'd think about him and maybe weep a little bit. And on stage it was fucking crazy, man. I'm not incredibly spiritual, but I could definitely feel him—or at least the essence of him—around me at certain moments in the set. There's no stopping those things from coming to the front of my mind at that moment on stage, which is fucked. It's like, "I'm dealing with this shit in front of all these people, right now? *Fuck.*" That's been hard. It's been really draining. I almost dropped off the tour halfway through it because it's been so emotionally draining to relive some of the more horrific things that have been happening in my life over the last few years, every single night on stage. I don't have a detachment in this music. There's no wall whatsoever between me and my emotional wreckage. Some nights, people have really understood that that's happening, and they've really saved me and lifted me up. That's not something I've ever experienced before. This trip has been really transformative in that sense.

VINNIE CARUANA—*THE MOVIELIFE, I AM THE AVALANCHE, SOLO ARTIST*

MATT: What do you remember about 9/11?

VINNIE: We were on tour, and I can't remember where we played the night before, but we stayed at a hotel room in Connecticut. We turned on the television in the morning, and there it was. Both towers were on fire. It was so difficult to register what was going on. We were all in complete shock. My uncle had a business down there, where he and my older brother worked, and I worked down there with them when I was home from tour. My immediate reaction was to call his office, which was right in the shadows of the Trade Center. I called the number, and my uncle answered the phone hysterical. I then heard all the hysteria over the phone; it wasn't just on the TV anymore. Our immediate reaction was, "We need to get home. We need to get home." So we drove south to catch the ferry from Connecticut to Long Island, where we lived. We managed to get on with our van and trailer and we caught a ferry to Long Island. Then we got off the ferry, and we drove down the southern state to bring us back home. And you could see all the smoke. We live about twenty-five miles from the Trade Center, but you could see the smoke in the distance. We were like, "Holy shit. Holy shit. Holy shit." You just can't compute it. This was before anyone knew how to deal with terrorism on this scale. And I was young back then. I wasn't ready for it at all. I mean, who was?

My brother, who worked down there and was down there when the planes hit, had to run over the bridge to get home. Everyone just ran out of their buildings and then ran over the bridge to Brooklyn. I think my brother ran over the Manhattan Bridge. I don't really remember how he found his way home from the city, as I'm sure all the trains were fucked, but thankfully he found his way home. I was at my parents' house, just trying to understand what had happened. Then my brother walked in and he was very upset. I'd never seen him like that. It just kept sinking in and sinking in. He was telling us his story, then he got a call from our friend to say that his brother went up into the tower, and he didn't come back. They said they couldn't find him. That was when it became really, *really* real.

MATT: How, as a city, did New York move forward after that day?

VINNIE: I was a Long Island kid, so I was still living on Long Island and I wasn't fully in it. But it was still our city. And the city was closed below Fourteenth Street for quite some time, which was where all of us would spend time. That shit was on lockdown for a while. And you could only get past the police lines if you could show proof of residence to get into your place, if you were cleared to go back there at all. It just became this normal thing that you kind of got used to. Then there was the cleanup; the names kept coming; the death toll kept rising; the anxiety kept rising; and the feeling that things would never be the same started to solidify. I still probably haven't come to terms with it. I don't even know how you do wrap your brain around that. A lot of people from Long Island perished, and the closest one to us was our boy Matt's older brother. We really felt his pain.

MATT: Did you ever feel any desire to leave New York after 9/11?

VINNIE: It didn't cross my mind. We were on our little Long Island bubble, and I was twenty-one when it happened, and I still lived with my parents, so moving out wasn't an option for me. I was still getting paid fifty dollars a week to be in a band and play in people's basements. I actually don't know anyone who moved out of New York after that, though. Everyone stuck around because New York was our home. I still haven't left New York. My wife and I talk about moving to live somewhere else sometimes, but we never really have an answer as to where that would be.

AL BARR—DROPKICK MURPHYS, THE BRUISERS

AL: There's an incredible opioid and heroin problem in New England right now. We've lost so many friends and family members to drug overdoses. It's astounding. Since we've been out on this trip, Kenny [Casey] has lost another family member to an overdose. It's everywhere in America right now, but the state that I live in, New Hampshire, which is an hour north of Boston, is number one in the country for overdoses. Literally every single person that I know knows someone who's either overdosed or died. It's insane. The big pharma companies are stepping over bodies to cash their checks. They don't give a fuck. You know what I mean?

You take a kid in high school who's blown his knee out playing football, and you give him sixty OxyContin. He's in unbelievable pain, so he's taking it. And at the end of the cycle he feels like he still needs it, but he doesn't have another prescription, so he goes out on the street for it and it's fucking eighty to a hundred dollars a pill. Well, check it out, man: fifteen to twenty dollars gets you a bag of dope. And now they're fucking cutting it with fentanyl, which is what they use in hospitals to put you under during an operation, and it's a hundred times stronger than heroin.

Two years ago, my brother-in-law died from a heroin overdose. My sister was the one who found him. She didn't even know he was doing it, and when she opened the door and he fell into her arms, the needle was still on the floor, and it was full. He'd literally just hit a tiny little bit, and that tiny little bit of fentanyl killed him immediately. I just found out that's what killed Prince: he had a Vicodin prescription, and there are people out there taking opioids and basically pressing them to look like what you're getting is Percocet or Vicodin, but actually it's fentanyl. That's what Prince was taking, and it killed him. It's crazy, man. It's really, really scary. There's been a lot of heartache that's touched us all lately, hence the "pain" in our new album [11 Short Stories of Pain & Glory].

The song "Rebel with a Cause" is the perfect example. You take a kid that's got no hope in their life; they've got no job and no future, or at least they don't see that they have any future; then here's this fucking drug that comes along that makes you feel like a rock star, and you can do anything. Of course, you're not actually going anywhere. But it makes you feel that way. How are you going to tip the scales so that kid doesn't start taking that drug, with what I've just put out there for you? How do we get through to them and make them care enough to save their own lives?

I've got a friend who's head of an emergency room, and she works the night shift. She told me she literally sees the same people coming in every single week. They save their lives, they send them back out, and they're back again the next week because they've overdosed again. And they don't always save them, either. Now all the police officers and first responders now have Narcan, too. They can hit you with this Narcan pen if you're having an overdose, and it will save your life because it cancels out the effect of the drug.

I had a friend who's a cop tell me that a guy came out of dying from an overdose, and the guy started trying to strangle him. He was like, "You just fucked my high up, man." Actually, he just saved your life, kid. But they don't care. That's what this fucking shit does to people: they care more about the high than their own lives. But a song like "Rebel with a Cause" is talking about how there's still a heart and soul in there, and we can't just write these people off. We've got to do something, and there's got to be hope because you can recover from an addiction, and you don't need to die.

ANDREW W.K.—*SINGER-SONGWRITER, PRODUCER, WRITER, MOTIVATIONAL SPEAKER*

MATT: Life isn't always easy or elevated. Sometimes, you have to confront the difficulties and the hardships—

ANDREW: And stare them down, and look at them as a test. It's like, "Okay. Let's see what you're really made of now. You were doing fine when everything was going your way. Let's see how you do when things aren't going your way." Because that's when you really see what you're made of, of course. And most of the time I fail those tests, or at least have moments of failure within them, but then I try again.

MATT: It's a cathartic experience, when you build up the courage to deal with your demons, and you get through it. The reward is powerful.

ANDREW: And the reward is manifold because then you remember the next time that feeling comes along, "Wait a minute. I remember the last time I faced something like this, which I thought at the time was the end of everything, and not only did I get through it, but I was better from it." That's what's so strange: how can the worst thing that happened to us also be the best thing that happened to us? But I can say from my own experiences that some of the worst days of my life were also the best days of my life because of what came out of them. And that doesn't make sense: the way our minds prefer to work, things shouldn't work like that. Only good things are supposed to equal good outcomes, and only bad things are supposed to lead to bad things. But for better or worse, it's not that simple: it can all be useful, and ideally force us to grow. And to go back to your earlier question, if there is a meaning or a purpose to life, I think it's to develop these skills. People have been saying that since the very beginning: we're here to pass these tests, and not just act like idiots the whole time.

JESSE LEACH

JESSE: Through suffering and experiences that are difficult, you often find out who you are, what you're worth, and what you're really made of.

LIFE & DEATH IN THE STOCKS PLAYLIST

KYUSS—"GREEN MACHINE"

HANOI ROCKS—"DON'T YOU EVER LEAVE ME"

STONE TEMPLE PILOTS—"VASOLINE"

LINKIN PARK—"IN THE END"

AUDIOSLAVE—"LIKE A STONE"

KILLSWITCH ENGAGE—"CUT ME LOOSE"

AGAINST ME!—"TRANSGENDER DYSPHORIA BLUES"

MINA CAPUTO—"IDENTITY"

SAVE FERRIS—"GOODBYE BROTHER"

JOE CARDAMONE—"DEAD BEFORE DAWN"

I AM THE AVALANCHE—"BROOKLYN DODGERS"

DROPKICK MURPHYS—"REBELS WITH A CAUSE"

ANDREW W.K.—"EVER AGAIN"

THE WEAPON—"NO SURRENDER"

OUTTAKES

"Tommy is the man."

W E'RE APPROACHING THE END, my friends. I hope you've enjoyed the ride. We've explored childhood; musical awakenings; DIY culture; the highs and lows of fame; alcohol and substance abuse; spirituality; politics; the ins and outs of artistic relationships; icons and legends; mental health; death; and the great beyond. But there's still a few topics left—no stone left unturned and all that.

Don't be misled by the chapter title, though. These aren't outtakes from my podcast. (Sorry if any long-term *Life In The Stocks* listeners have landed here expecting to hear untold stories; they're all already out there, I'm afraid.) Instead, these are passages that wouldn't fit neatly into any of the other chapters, but I still feel are worthy of inclusion.

This isn't B-roll material, though. Think of it more as "miscellaneous." (Perhaps that's what I should've called the chapter. Balls to it. Outtakes sounds better.)

Parenthood and social media are two recurring themes in my podcast. I don't talk about them all the time, and there wasn't enough material to warrant chapters entirely devoted to either subject, but there are some choice segments coming up. Social media is an inescapable aspect of twenty-first century life, after all, so it makes sense to talk about it. And whilst I'm not a parent myself, a lot of the artists that I interview are, and many of my listeners are, too.

Environmentalism is another universal theme that affects all of us, and I'll get to talking to Chuck Ragan about that momentarily.

As for switching up set lists, and the lasting legacy of the Ramones, perhaps those topics aren't quite as vital. But then you have made it this far through a book based almost exclusively on rock 'n' roll stories, so you're probably a lifelong music lover like me. And stuff like that *is* important—at least to us.

This book is dedicated to all the lifers out there: the ones who are in it for the long haul, and doing it for the cause. Thank you for reading. Thank you for listening. As they say in Llandow, "ciao for now."

CHUCK RAGAN—*HOT WATER MUSIC, SOLO ARTIST*

CHUCK: When I'm not on tour, I'm just a fly-fishing guy.

MATT: What does that involve?

CHUCK: Well, I'm a licensed coast guard captain, and I take people fishing back home—from beginners all the way up to experts. I run three different boats, and I work at about nine different fisheries.

MATT: How long have you been doing it?

CHUCK: I've been running the boats and fishing for years and years and years. And I've been actively licensed—insured and bonded and everything like that—for about three years now.

MATT: And that's your full-time gig when you're not on the road?

CHUCK: Yeah, it's like fifteen-hour days. And the thing about that kind of work is you don't clock in and then leave your job and go home. That work comes home with me because I'm always maintaining my boats and my gear, and I'm either on the phone or on email contacting and coordinating with clients. And it's constant in the sense that there's always licenses and permits to obtain in the areas that I work in. But I love it, man. The thing about guiding is you never know who you're going to get. For the most part, it's hired, skilled labor; it's very similar to being an independent contractor. And for the most part, being an independent contractor means there's very little security, in the sense that you don't have this big company or corporation that kind of has your back, or helps cover medical expenses and sick days, or anything like that.

MATT: And there's no paycheck coming at the end of the month, unless you get out there and hustle it for yourself.

CHUCK: Yeah, you have to chase it. And some days, it's green lights all the way, and you're getting paid and everything's working. And some days you get a hole in your boat, or your engine blows up, or something happens and everything just comes to a grinding halt, and you have to fix it, and you have to pay for it. And the sooner you do it, the sooner you're back up and running.

At the same time, you're almost in this kind of service industry, and it's your job to accept whoever is walking into your establishment; it's down to you to take their pain away and give them the best experience they can possibly have. I feel like—in the position that I'm in—it's not only my duty to give people a great experience and uplift their spirits and teach them the art of fly casting, but also to teach them the opportunities that we have to make this world a better place.

The conservation efforts are already in place, they just need more support to keep our water cleaner and basically sustain all the wild places that we love. I get a lot of messages where people contact me, and they're like, "How could you kill all these fish?" But the truth is, I release 99.9 percent of the fish that come on to my boat. The only reason we ever kill any fish is if they swallow a hook or something like that, which rarely happens. For the most part, it's all catch and release.

MATT: As you said earlier, it's all about making a difference on a small scale in the immediate area around you, and just trying to do your best. And if everybody does a little better, that ripple effect spreads.

CHUCK: Yeah. In the guide business, a lot of us teamed up with Klean Kanteen, who make stainless steel water bottles and food canisters for camping and everyday use. And we joined this campaign called Kick Plastic. The whole idea was to get rid of all the plastic water bottles from off our boats.

Any time I take clients on a fishing trip or an excursion, I usually take two people, and I'll normally bring anywhere from twelve to sixteen water bottles—sometimes even more. For the most part, people would have maybe six to eight throughout the day, and on a summer day, all those things would be gone. So we started this campaign, and I've been doing it for a little over two years now, where we made a pact to rid all the plastic water bottles off our boats.

Now, each individual gets a clean and sterilized twenty ounce bottle full of filtered water. They get it at the beginning of the day, and it has to serve as your bottle for the day. And I have sixty-four ounce growlers—big stainless steel jugs—full of water to refill them. Over the past two years, for the amount of trips that I've done and what I normally take, I've saved using over 1,500 water bottles. And everybody's been happy because the water actually tastes better.

MATT: And you're on a boat, so you want that outdoor experience; you don't want to drink out of a plastic bottle like you would do in the city; you want to drink water out of a canteen because it feels more authentic.

CHUCK: Yeah, exactly. And it works. I probably barely make a dent out there with what's happening in the grand scheme of things, but if everybody would just do a little bit to make their surroundings and the world a better place, that's when it turns into a tidal wave, and that's when it turns into real change. I've actually been talking to Klean Kanteen about trying to implement that same ethic and mindset into the touring business.

MATT: When you think of the waste that goes on in this industry—

CHUCK: Oh, my God. It's unbelievable. And the amount of money and the carbon footprint that it takes to make one plastic bottle is astounding. This is a relatively new thing, too. None of our parents ever thought about buying water. These businesses are making hand over fist selling something that should be free. It should be free. And it is. It just needs to be cared for and cleaned, like it was for generations before us. Hopefully, we can implement something in the touring world where it would lessen the footprint and make a little bit of a difference there, too.

DAVE HAUSE—*THE LOVED ONES, SOLO ARTIST*

DAVE: We switch up our set list every single night. For me, not only is that great for the band because you stay challenged and on your toes, but it also respects the audience in a meaningful way. If you know what song your favorite band is going to open every single show with, it gets old. You want to be challenged—within reason. It's also important to recognize that people are in a different mood on a Monday to a Friday, and if you're going out on a Bank Holiday weekend then you're looking for one thing, and if you're going out on a random Wednesday then that's a different set of circumstances altogether. These things do make a difference.

MATT: You're right. That was one of my favorite things about scheduling music on my old radio show: each day is different, and each time of day is different, too. And if you take those factors into account, there's creativity and fun to be had.

DAVE: I agree. And that goes back to the whole autumnal versus summer records conversation we were having earlier. All those things are meaningful; they've always been meaningful over the course of my life; certain records mark certain times of year. I'd like to think that's happening with my audience, too, and I have to respect that and take it into account. Switching up the set list and keeping it exciting is all part of that.

I'm lucky enough to have fans that come to multiple shows, and they want to hear the deep tracks and the weird, off-the-wall songs. And that's exactly what you hope for: you never write a song and think this will be buried deep in the album, so I'll just slip it past the goal post. You never think about songwriting in that way. You work hard on all of them, and you want them all to count. So to get that, and have the fans get that, is a real treat. And you want to stoke that fire, whilst all the while knowing there's this peripheral of people who also want to hear the well-known songs. You want everyone together, and that's an exciting part of any live show. The trick is to push them as far as you can without pushing them away.

CHUCK ROBERTSON—*MAD CADDIES*

MATT: Where does the New Orleans jazz influence come from in your music?

CHUCK: Sascha [Lazor] is the one who brought the New Orleans sound into the band, on our second record *Duck and Cover.* Between *Quality Soft Core* and *Duck and Cover*, his fucking hand was crushed by a giant boulder whilst he was hiking. And it was his right hand: his strumming hand. A rock came loose and fell on it, and crushed like ten bones in his hand. He's got like fifty pins and metal plates and all that shit in his hand. And he couldn't play guitar for like six months. He had a full cast on. So, he taped a pick to his right hand and starting learning banjo. Over the next six months, he learned to play the banjo and totally fell in love with New Orleans Dixieland jazz.

MATT: That's like the story of how Tony Iommi developed the heavy metal sound of Black Sabbath.

CHUCK: It totally is. He just discovered it. He was like, "You know what? Since I'm just sitting here, I might as well learn to pick a banjo." And he discovered the Preservation Hall Jazz Band through doing that. The Squirrel Nut Zippers were on the radio a little bit later with their whole Dixieland jazz throwback thing, too. And you had Cherry Poppin' Daddies and Big Bad Voodoo Daddy, and that whole swing revival that was very short lived.

MATT: *Swingers* was a big movie around that time, too.

CHUCK: Exactly. Everybody was zoot suiting and all these bands were like, "Oh, yeah. We're ska *and* swing." But we never wanted to be the swing guys because that shit was going to be over even quicker than ska. We play Dixieland jazz, punk, ska, and reggae. That's what we do. And we're the only band to really ever claim that—to this day. No other band has ever really said, "Yeah, we play Dixieland jazz and punk mixed together." It's like, "What? Who does that?" Well, we do. And with the *Dirty Rice* album, we wanted to make the adult sound of the stuff that we were going for earlier on, with songs like "Monkeys" and "Road Rash." We wanted to refine that into something more mature.

MATT: What's the story behind "Shoot Out the Lights," because that's a heartbreaker of a song right there?

CHUCK: I'm proud to say that song is one of my favorites to sing in the set right now, and I didn't write the lyrics.

MATT: You didn't write the words?

CHUCK: Not one. Our drummer Todd [Rosenberg] had written the chords, and a dear friend of ours called Logan [Livermore] wrote the lyrics. He's played in some local bands, but he's never really done anything musically. He's always been an amazing lyricist, though. I love his lyrics. He collaborated with me on the song "Last Breath" off the *Just One More* record, too. Logan just happened to be in the studio one day when Todd came up with the tune, and he just started writing these lyrics. Then when I came in a couple of days later, I was like, "This is fucking great. What's this song about?" Logan was like, "Gay people trying to get by in a third world country."

MATT: That's what the song's about?

CHUCK: Yeah, the song is about gay lovers hiding from people who want to fucking kill them, just because they're gay.

MATT: Wow! I thought there was a bit of a *Romeo and Juliet* thing going on.

CHUCK: Yeah, whether it's a man and a man, or a woman and a woman, or a man and a woman—whoever you want it to be. It's a song about forbidden love. And it's one of my favorite songs to sing each night, and I didn't write a fucking word.

TROY VAN LEEUWEN—*QUEENS OF THE STONE AGE, A PERFECT CIRCLE, FAILURE*

MATT: How did what happened with the terrorist attacks in Paris influence the recording process and the overall tone of the new Queens of the Stone Age record? That incident, and the whole aftershock surrounding it, must've had a profound impact on Josh [Homme].

TROY: What happened in Paris affected all of us. We're all pals and we're all family, and when you have a family member that's in a situation like that, the worst feeling is when you can't do anything about it, and you can't get in touch with them to see if they're alive. That's something that we'd never dealt with before. And the idea that you'd be at an Eagles [of Death Metal] concert, which is the most fun rock 'n' roll show you could ever go to, and have that interrupted by carnage like that, it's the worst thing I can possibly think of. As a performer, it terrifies me. It's seriously heavy duty.

I talked to Josh right after I heard the news. He was like, "I'm handling it." He jumped right into action to make sure everyone was safe, and that takes a lot of coordination when you're on the opposite side of the world. So that incident has definitely added some anxiety to what we do, and it's made everyone feel like life's too short. We're also lucky to have this great life, and we shouldn't focus too much on the negative side of things. So let's try to be positive and get up and do something before we run out of time. That's the core of where we're at right now. When it came to recording *Villains*, it was time for us to be a band again, and do what we do best, which is making music.

MINA CAPUTO—*LIFE OF AGONY, SOLO ARTIST*

MINA: I really unplugged from all of it when the Eagles of Death Metal were out here and that whole thing happened out in Paris. I lost some friends in that, and I really started to unplug from all of it after that. All the idiots on Twitter are just regurgitating hatred. It's no wonder all our children are being bullied: all the adults are bullying the adults.

JESSE LEACH—*KILLSWITCH ENGAGE, TIMES OF GRACE, THE WEAPON*

JESSE: Facebook feels like a constant commercial to me, and I can't stand TV. I watch it on tour when I just need to be numb, but the brainwashing and negativity on Facebook have triggered some really dark places that I've gone to in my head, just seeing people's ignorance and hatred. When the politics started to get really stirred up in the States was when I was like, "I can't do this anymore." I'd go on there and try to be positive and fight against the wave of ignorance and hatred, but it was so overwhelming. I decided that I had to take care of myself because it was affecting me in a really bad way, and making me dislike people that I'm close to—even some family members. I also think the disconnect of face-to-face contact and body language creates passive aggressiveness and this forum of bullshit that's just fake. You don't know who's being true or not, and I think that's a poisonous way to be. Facebook gives you a false sense of bravery and a false sense of safety, and people say things they would never say face-to-face to people on there. It's the same thing with the comments on YouTube; I stopped reading that shit years ago. I liberated myself from all of it, and it's one of the best things I've ever done.

BRIAN FALLON—*THE GASLIGHT ANTHEM, THE HORRIBLE CROWES, SOLO ARTIST*

BRIAN: I'm really into cats. I like cats a lot. In the jungle, big cats wait, and they stalk their prey, then they pounce. And when they pounce, it's vicious. They'll crush your skull. It's a planned-out thing. I feel like that's the way people are on the internet: they just sit there and wait for somebody to slip up, and not even in a big way. And you know who's usually the first people to pipe up? Rich, overeducated white kids. They're always the first people jumping on everybody, and they're often jumping on people who are on the same side as them. I don't have time for any of that shit. I'm too busy: I'm out here working, trying to make the world a better place.

EUGENE HUTZ—*GOGOL BORDELLO*

EUGENE: I read an article in *The Guardian* just today about how social media is tearing society apart. But that's not news to me: I've been writing about it for years, before it even appeared. "From screen to screen, them travelin'," is the opening line from "Wonderlust King," and that song is about precisely this: people stare at a screen as soon as they wake up in the morning, then they go to another screen to do their job, then they return home and stare at another screen, and that's their life. They're living in the matrix of a Nazi zombie existence. And when you say stuff like that, it sounds like humorous science-fiction—

MATT: But it's actually our present-day reality.

EUGENE: Yeah. And a lot of people's attention is just not available, which is why you have to take them out of it and present them with something raw, physical, story-orientated, and rambunctious in every way. That's the whole Gogol Bordello gist: tell the story in such a way that it rattles all your cells.

AL BARR—*DROPKICK MURPHYS, THE BRUISERS*

AL: When I first joined this band, there wasn't any fucking social media. There weren't even cell phones back then. The antenna cell phone thing came along, but it wasn't like it is now: there wasn't this internet phenomenon. Now, you walk off stage and you can see what people thought of your show, which is kind of cool. But sometimes it's not so cool if they thought you sucked.

Sometimes, I'll go through and read the comments, and I'll see a picture of a kid and know he's in fucking high school, and he's saying, "I miss the days of the old Dropkick Murphys." What the fuck are you talking about? Are you talking about eighteen years ago, when you weren't even alive, when you were dripping in your dad's fucking ball sack? That's like me saying, "I miss the Sex Pistols days," you know what I mean?

MATT CAUGHTHRAN—*THE BRONX, MARIACHI EL BRONX*

MATT C: I hated social media at first. I've kind of embraced it now, though. And not because I've been forced to, but because I'm really starting to enjoy it. I really enjoy the aesthetics and the visual side of Instagram, and I think it's cool for people to have an insight into what their favorite band is doing outside of music. It's a bit frustrating, as a human being, having to spend all this time updating your social media. But really it's not that big of a deal. That's just the way it is now: it's the modern era, and that's how people access information. So fuck it, just get with the program.

JOEY CAPE—*LAGWAGON, ME FIRST AND THE GIMMES GIMMES, SOLO ARTIST*

JOEY: Kids these days were born into it. They don't know any other way than making connections and communicating through social media. It's difficult, philosophically, to be a parent in this time because your children only know this world. I make jokes with my daughter and her friends when I see them all sitting in a room together on their cell phones. I say stuff like, "What's your high score on that?"

MATT: Classic dad joke.

JOEY: I like to make fun of the whole followers thing, too. I go, "So how many friends do you have? Do you guys hang out or go to the movies?" And they hate it. I tease them all the time because it's ridiculous. But it's not their fault. It's all they know.

CHUCK ROBERTSON

CHUCK: My son's three and a half, and he'll say to me, "Papa, please don't sing and play guitar right now. I'm trying to play with my tractors." Or I'll be rocking out on his drum kit, and he'll say, "Papa, can you play some jazz right now? That's a little loud. Could you just play some jazz instead?" And I'm like, "Sure, bud. No problem."

MATT: This might sound weird, and I promise I'm not stalking you, but I noticed your Instagram bio says "Father" before anything else.

CHUCK: Absolutely. That's my number-one job right now, and forever. I had plenty of time to be a selfish rock 'n' roll dude in my twenties and thirties. Once I became a father, it changed everything. That's my number-one job, for sure.

MATT: What changes inside you when you have a kid?

CHUCK: You can't explain it to anyone who hasn't had children. It's a biological change. I haven't seen him in about a week now, and every night I'm having dreams, like, "Where's Charlie? Shit! I've lost him." It's biologically in me now; I'm a father number one, and a singer-songwriter number two. I'm having a few legal troubles with my ex-wife at the moment, who's trying to move my kid away, and I was telling my lawyer, "I've been an original musician in my own band for the last twenty-three years, writing the music I want, and playing the art that I want to play. But if it meant that I had to stay home and start a wedding cover band to keep my kid—"

MATT: And that, for you, would probably be the most soul-destroying thing ever, right?

CHUCK: I would start an all-Eagles cover band, and I fucking hate The Eagles, man. I fucking hate them. And my lawyer started laughing. He was like, *"Big Lebowski.* I get the joke. And now I know how passionate you are about being a father." I took a year and a half off when my son was born, and I didn't tour at all during that time. I just stayed home with him whilst my ex-wife went back to work, and I was a stay-at-home dad. I loved it. Apart from needing to get out of the house for a couple of hours a day to go do some man stuff—like hang out with the boys, or whatever—I'm completely at peace being home with my son, just raising him and being a father.

MATT: You mentioned a moment ago that your son has a drum kit... Your son has a drum kit? And he's three years old?

CHUCK: Yeah, and he's a really good drummer already.

MATT: Do you think he's going to follow in his father's footsteps and become a musician?

CHUCK: That's the dream. Our drummer Todd [Rosenberg] has a daughter and she's a sick singer. So our drummer's daughter is going to be the singer, and then the leader singer's son—my son—is going to be the drummer. We're like, "Man, when the kids are old enough, we won't even have to go out on tour anymore. We'll just send them out, and they can be the new Mad Caddies."

MATT: Gene Simmons would approve of that idea: The Mad Caddy Juniors.

CHUCK: The Mad Caddy Juniors. That has a nice ring to it. No, I would never wish this life on my son, unless it was what he wanted. I'd never put pressure on him to do it.

MATT: If you could go back in time, would you have gone down a different path?

CHUCK: Hell no. It's been too much fun.

ROGER LIMA—*LESS THAN JAKE, REHASHER*

ROGER: Being a dad is so cool, and having a kid is such a unique experience. I feel like it's part of life, and we're all meant to go through it. It changes you instantly. I understand that it's not for everyone, but for me, having a kid has been fucking awesome.

ROBB FLYNN—*MACHINE HEAD, PODCAST HOST*

MATT: How have you found being a dad?

ROBB: Everything in your life changes. I was number one with my wife for years before we had kids. But when you have kids, you go from the center of the universe to like number ten on the list. You're like, "What the fuck?" And it's all really subtle, you know what I mean? There's never a big change. It's just a bunch of little changes along the way. Then one day you look back, and you're like, "Wow! I've really changed." I never swear at home anymore. I swear like crazy on stage and in my songs, but when I'm home, I don't want my kids hearing me swear. And I don't want them going around swearing, either. Everybody probably already looks at me and thinks, "That guy's kids are going to be terrible." But they're not at all. My kids are good.

BRIAN FALLON

MATT: How's becoming a father changed your outlook on the world?

BRIAN: It's taught me that I don't know anything. It's definitely taught me that. It also gives you a restart in life. If your job is to teach a child how to be a human being, you have to assess your own life, and say, "What are my preconceived notions and biases that I need to change and address?" Because whatever you put into that child, they're going to carry that into their adulthood. And you want your kids to have a blank slate. You want to give them the best chance that you can to go forward. Being a parent has made me see humanity through my kid's eyes, as new and unbiased.

JOEY CAPE

JOEY: I remember before we had our daughter, my wife and I talked a lot about Christmas. There's a lot of practical questions that you have when you're about to become a parent, but you still haven't been hit by the reality truck, and you still have your ideals. We're both atheists, and we look at Christmas as kind of a consumer holiday. We also didn't want to lie to our child and say that there's a Santa Claus when there isn't. But the big problem there is you're immediately ostracizing that person and taking them out of what happens with all of their friends at Christmas. And then there's the other side of it, which is that Christmas is a fun thing for a child to think about and look forward to. We ended up doing it in the end, but I maintained all along that I was sort of an agnostic when it came to Santa because I knew when the jig was up, I was going to be like, "What's up now? Who's the good parent here? Your mom, not so great." But the analogy there is that you have to let your kids enter the popular world; they have to be a part of those things to help with their development as a human being.

MATT: How did she take the news when she found out that Santa Claus wasn't real?

JOEY: I'm the worst liar ever, and she point-blank asked me as I was driving along one day. She said, "Dad, is Santa Claus a person? Is he real? And we all know you can't lie." I was like, "I plead the fifth. You have to talk to your mother about this one."

MATT: She sounds like a smart kid.

JOEY: She is. She's smarter than me, that's for sure. Luckily, I'd read somewhere about a month before this that the day your kid finds out that Santa Claus isn't real, this is what you should do: you sit them down, and you tell them, "Here's the deal. You've got to pick one of our neighbors, and we're going to buy them a thoughtful gift and put it on their porch, but you never get to take credit for it. You can never tell them it was you. They just get a nice gift at Christmas, and that's what you do each year from now on. So, you're now a Santa. And there are many Santas out there. Me and your mom are Santas, too. That's how it all works."

MATT: I've never heard of that before. That's the magic of Christmas right there, Joey Cape.

CHUCK RAGAN

CHUCK: Being a father is the most wonderful and terrifying thing you can imagine. It's exciting and terrifying all at the same time. My kid is my hero, you know. Every chance I get to be around him, I'm just overwhelmed with joy and admiration. It's one of those things where until it happens, it's hard to even fathom it. But it's where I've truly realized, "This is why I'm here. This is why *I* was born." Last month, I lost my father, which was rough. But at the same time, when I'd start to break apart and realize that he's gone, and I'd get beat up and really upset, I'd turn around and see a kid in his underpants with a bucket on his head, screaming and running around and tugging on my shirt, and I'd start to laugh.

MATT: The circle of life.

CHUCK: The circle and cycle of life: out with the old, in with the new. And I think my dad would laugh at that, too. It's such a beautiful thing. I was right there helping out when he was born, too. It all unfolded right in front of me, and it was the most intense and amazing thing I've ever experienced in my life. I'm completely overwhelmed by how strong women are. It's absolutely amazing. My respect, love, and admiration for my wife grew so much during all this, and nobody ever told me that would happen. Everybody talks to you about the baby, but I didn't realize quite how much I was about to fall in love with my girl all over again.

MATT: I guess that's because you've made this amazing thing together. You've made the ultimate thing together, in fact: a human life.

CHUCK: Totally. His name's Grady Joseph, and he'll be three at the end of May. I swear the development that happens between the age of two and three is astounding as well. It's nonstop. I went away for one weekend, and I came back and there were all these new phrases and new faces, and this whole new sense of humor. And all these things just happened overnight. It's such a joy and such an honor to have this opportunity. I just want to do the best that I can, and teach him everything that I know, and encourage him to find even more knowledge after that, and just keep fighting the good fight and being the best person he can be. That's all any of us can really do. It's an absolute thrill, and a huge responsibility. It can be terrifying, especially when you look around; this world can be an ugly and brutal place at times. And sometimes that gets a little scary because right now he's just living inside this beautiful bubble where everything is wonderful. That hit me not long ago, and I thought, "Wow. One day he's going to have his heart broken, and one day he's going to have his mind twisted—just completely confused." And that's a little scary. But you just have to take it one day at a time, and deal with the rest later on.

JESSE LEACH

MATT: Is parenthood something you've considered? It strikes me as strange that someone like you—with so much love to give, and wisdom to share—isn't a father already.

JESSE: I absolutely adore children. I'm actually one of those guys who will walk around when I'm out on tour, and when I see kids playing I get filled with joy watching the way that they act, and hearing the things that they say to each other. I love kids: I have two nephews and a niece, and I adore them both. But I have to say, I'm quite happy that I don't have any of my own. I enjoy being spontaneous and not having anything to tie me down. When I get home from tour, I can just get up and go on an adventure somewhere, and being out here on the road and living this life, I can't imagine having a child. I don't know if I would do well with being away from them for as long as I'm gone. So, I see it as a blessing that I don't have kids. But I do love them; they make you see the world differently; they're just pure joy and emotion.

ROBB FLYNN

MATT: What are you listening to at the moment, Robb?

ROBB: You know what I'm really into these days? Podcasts. I'm into Howard Stern. I listen to Howard Stern every fucking day. If I get in my car and I'm driving to practice, I don't want to listen to some fucking band. I want to listen to Howard Stern; the fucking interviews are so good, and all the drama between the cast and crew is so fucking funny. Or I'll listen to Joe Rogan, or *WTF* [with Marc Maron], or the Alec Baldwin podcast.

MATT: Hang on…Alec Baldwin has a podcast?

ROBB: Yeah. It's called *Here's the Thing*.

MATT: Does he interview people?

ROBB: He interviews people, yeah. It's super good, dude. He had David Letterman on there recently, and the fucking David Letterman interview was jaw dropping. I couldn't believe some of the shit he got him to talk about.

MATT: What about TV? Do you watch a lot of TV?

ROBB: I watch a lot of TV. I watch *Game of Thrones, Breaking Bad, House of Cards*—all that shit. TV, to me, is so amazing right now. *Game of Thrones* is fucking great. It's the best shit. It's got violence, brutality, treachery, and sex galore. It's funny, it's fantasy, and there's even gay sex in there. Renly Baratheon is getting blown by Loras Tyrell, and you're like, "What the fuck is going on?" They're just pushing every envelope. It's amazing. It's ten times more entertaining than any metal band, that's for sure.

TOM GREEN—*ACTOR, COMEDIAN, RAPPER, TALK SHOW HOST*

MATT: I feel like *Freddy Got Fingered* got a bit of a beating when it first came out. Do you feel like the film has been reassessed in more recent years?

TOM: *Freddy Got Fingered* has always had a huge fan base. The only reason people think that it doesn't is because it was cool to write that it was an unsuccessful movie. The movie wasn't unsuccessful at all: it cost fourteen million dollars to make, and it made that back in its opening weekend. Then it made thirty-five million dollars in DVD sales. So it's a huge financial success. Most movies struggle to break even, and a lot of them actually lose massive amounts of money. So by Hollywood standards, *Freddy Got Fingered* is a very successful movie. That's something that never gets written about. No one ever says that—except for me right now, obviously. And that's frustrating for me because it's disingenuous to call the movie unsuccessful. Even now, seventeen years later, literally not a day goes by when somebody doesn't throw a line from the movie at me: "Daddy, would you like some sausage?" or "The backwards man." People don't come up to me with lines from *Stealing Harvard*.

MATT: Do you get ever *Road Trip* lines quoted at you?

TOM: A little bit. People say, "Unleash the fury, Mitch," from *Road Trip*, and, "I'm not liquid, John," from *Stealing Harvard*. But it's nothing in comparison to *Freddy Got Fingered*. People seem to know every single line from that movie. I guess it's such a bizarre and nontraditional film; it's one of those movies where if you like it then you love it, and if you don't like it then you either hate it or you haven't seen it. And most people who think they hate it probably never even saw it. There's obviously going to be a lot of people who saw it that do hate it because it was designed to make people hate it; if you're an uptight, old conservative person who doesn't want to see somebody swinging a bloody baby around by the umbilical cord, of course you're going to hate it. That's why I was swinging the bloody baby around by the umbilical cord—I wanted to piss people off. But most people who've seen the movie understand that it's completely insane, and they like it.

MATT: Do you feel like the negative reviews were unfair, then?

TOM: That movie singlehandedly made me learn to have complete distrust for the media. People write the story that they want to write regardless. They always have their own agenda.

CJ RAMONE—*RAMONES, SOLO ARTIST*

CJ: There's a part of the Ramones legacy that really bothers me, and it's one of the few times that I was really disappointed in Johnny [Ramone]. I was disappointed in Johnny for the decision, and I was disappointed in Joey [Ramone] for not standing up to Johnny and doing the right thing.

MATT: What happened?

CJ: Our record deal with Sire was up, and Brett Gurewitz, who was having huge success with Epitaph Records at the time, was hardcore shopping the Ramones to sign to his label. He had an unbelievable lineup of bands at that time. And he flew into Amsterdam to come watch us play. I watched him pitch to Joey and Johnny, and he nearly begged them to come on board at Epitaph. There was no doubt that Brett wanted to give the Ramones the success that they'd not had, and I knew that entire label would be working for them. I said to Johnny, "That guy loves the Ramones. I know he does. And he's going to do everything in his power to make it happen." Johnny said, "We've decided to go with Gary Kurfirst's label instead."

Gary Kurfirst was getting his own label—through Sire, I think—called Radioactive Records, and my head almost exploded. I was like, "Johnny, are you kidding me? First off, I know you're a good business man, and the conflict of interest in being on your manager's record label is overwhelmingly outside of anything logical when it comes to business. But besides that, you've already given that guy some of the greatest rock 'n' roll ever recorded, and he couldn't bring it home for you." I just couldn't understand it. I was like, "John, this is your opportunity to have the commercial success that you never had, to be respected like you never have, and really finish your career at the level that your entire career should've been at. After all these years, don't you want that?" His response was, "When you have as many years in the business as I have, then you can tell me what to do." And that was a hard thing to argue with.

In the end, we went with Radioactive Records, and put out what I consider to be a comeback record for the Ramones: *Mondo Bizarro*. And it sold the same 30–40,000 copies that they usually did. It made no sense at all to me. I was unbelievably disappointed in Johnny, and in Joey for not trying to fight to make that move. Of course, what I found out years later was the decision had already been made on when the Ramones were going to retire, and there were all kinds of backdoor deals where Joey and Johnny were going to make a lot of cash. Gary was going to get big cash advances for the records, they'd spend a little bit of money making them, then those guys would split the cash. Basically, what they decided was they were just going to sell out at the end of their career for a couple of hundred thousand dollars, just to get an amount of money that they wanted to save before they retired.

MATT: What a disappointing end to what should've been a far more celebrated career.

CJ: It was an unbelievably hard pill for me to swallow. But for them, it just made sense. And they'd already been promised so much by so many people in the record industry; they no longer had any faith in anybody. Johnny realized that they just had to get in the van, play shows, and sell T-shirts, and that was their business model: just get in the van and go.

There's so many things about the Ramones that went unrecognized, and even now go unrecognized. There's so many things that are common to most bands now, that the Ramones pioneered, engineered, and were the first ones to do. And they'll probably never get the credit that they deserve. But everybody will be doing it, and the Ramones probably did it first. Eventually, their legacy will become like Elvis, where there'll always be people who love the music, but what really took place and what really happened will kind of be forgotten.

There's some parts of the Ramones history that have only come to light in the past few years, that I hope will now get a little bit more life, like the fact that Tommy [Ramone] really was the guy. Tommy is the man. I had an unbelievably great conversation with him the first time that we met. I'd listened to all the Ramones albums many times by this point, and I'd started to look for where they'd gone off course. By the time they put out *Subterranean Jungle*, I was like, "Oh, my lord." There were moments of greatness on there, as there was with any Ramones albums, but it was a very uninspired record. So I started to look back through the Ramones's career at what made them great in the time periods when they were really great.

Too Tough to Die was a great record, and that came after *Subterranean Jungle*. So, what was great about it? Ed Stasium and Tommy produced it—they were back in the production seat. And if you work back from there, the next truly great record, side for side, song for song, is *Road to Ruin*. And what's great about that? Tommy and Ed, again. That's when I realized that Tommy and Ed really are *the guys*. It's almost like the Ramones were a boy band. You could almost say that, except that Dee Dee is one of the greatest rock 'n' roll songwriters of all time—in my opinion.

Once I learned this, I was waiting for the opportunity to someday meet Tommy and tell him, "I know the secret." And I finally got to do that at a party at CBGB. I said to him, "Tommy, I just want you to know that there are people out there who know who you are in this band, and they know what you did." He was like, "What are you talking about?" And I said, "I deconstructed the Ramones's entire career going back, and in all the bright spots, you and Ed Stasium are there."

Linda Stein, Arturo Vega, Tommy, and maybe Joey were all sitting at the table, and Tommy looked over at Arturo, who just shrugged his shoulders. So I followed it up by saying, "And just so you know I'm not totally full of shit, Johnny started talking about you one day, and about what you did for the band, and I asked him about the importance of your role, and he agreed. He said it was all Tommy and Ed." I really hope all the Ramones fans come to understand that one day.

OUTTAKES PLAYLIST

HOT WATER MUSIC—"NEVER GOING BACK"
DAVE HAUSE—"BURY ME IN PHILLY"
MAD CADDIES—"SHOOT OUT THE LIGHTS"
QUEENS OF THE STONE AGE—"FEET DON'T FAIL ME NOW"
LIFE OF AGONY—"A PLACE WHERE THERE'S NO
MORE PAIN"
KILLSWITCH ENGAGE—"STRENGTH OF THE MIND"
BRIAN FALLON—"A WONDERFUL LIFE"
GOGOL BORDELLO—"WONDERLUST KING"
DROPKICK MURPHYS—"GOING OUT IN STYLE"
MARIACHI EL BRONX—"CELL MATES"
LAGWAGON—"ONE MORE SONG"
LESS THAN JAKE—"THE SCIENCE OF SELLING YOUR-
SELF SHORT"
MACHINE HEAD—"HALO"
TOM GREEN—"DADDY WOULD YOU LIKE SOME SAUSAGE"
CJ RAMONE—"TOMMY'S GONE"

AFTERWORD

IN THE WORDS OF Porky Pig, "That's all, folks." If you enjoyed the conversations in this book, and you've yet to hear it, be sure to check out my podcast, *Life In The Stocks*. It's available on all major podcast platforms—notably iTunes and Spotify. As I write this, there are 180 episodes available, and they'll likely be many more by the time this hits the shelves.

As well as the guests in this book, I've also interviewed a bunch of UK artists, like John Lydon (Sex Pistols), Shaun Ryder (Happy Mondays), Steve Diggle (Buzzcocks), Pauline Black (The Selecter), Frank Turner (Solo), Ginger Wildheart (The Wildhearts), Barney Greenway (Napalm Death), Penny Rimbaud (Crass), Boz Boorer (Morrissey), Hugh Cornwell (The Stranglers), Jake Burns (Stiff Little Fingers) Jaz Coleman (Killing Joke), and actors from TV shows like *This is England* and *Game of Thrones*.

Keep your eyes peeled for the follow-up book, too: *Life In The Stocks: Veracious Conversations with Musicians & Creatives, Volume Two*. In that one, you'll be hearing from Gene Simmons (Kiss), Tommy Lee (Mötley Crüe), Perry Farrell (Jane's Addiction), Tom Morello (Rage Against the Machine), Chuck D (Public Enemy), Buzz Osbourne (Melvins), Casey Chaos (Amen), Jesse Hughes (Eagles of Death Metal), John Feldmann (Goldfinger), Jim Adkins (Jimmy Eat World), Keith Buckley (Every Time I Die), Walter Schreifels (Rival Schools), and a whole lot more.

With all that shameless self-promotion out the way, all that's left for me to say is *thank you*. I really appreciate you taking the time to read these stories. If they've provided you with even half as much education and entertainment as they have me, then this book has done its job. And the next one promises to be even better.

Amie Harwick at her LA office on May 16, 2018. The last time I saw her alive.
Rest in peace. X

Dave Hause and Captain Stocks backstage at Reading Festival in 2014. Good times.

Me and Matt Caughthran backstage at Reading Festival in 2015.
"Two Matts are better than one."

With Brian Fallon at Reading Festival in 2016.

Me and Jesse Malin hanging out on the balcony of Jesse's hotel room in Camden on September 18, 2019. Thanks for writing the foreword, Doctor.

Clem Burke photographed at the Laslett Hotel in London on April 31, 2017.

CJ Ramone photographed at the Redrum venue in Stafford on August 29, 2017.

Joey Cape photographed ahead of a Me First and the Gimme Gimmes show in Birmingham on February 24, 2017.

Me and B-Real in his hotel room in London on November 13, 2017.

With Steve-O on his tour bus in Oxford on November 30, 2016. Shortly after recording the first ever episode of Life In The Stocks.

With Danko Jones at the Grafton on Sunset in Los Angeles on May 16, 2018.

Me and Tommy Victor at Bloodstock Festival in 2014.

Me and the lovely Monique Powell in Glasgow on
September 25, 2019. Love you, Mo.

On stage with Frank Iero at All Saints Church in Kingston-upon-Thames on September 10, 2016. We did a Live Q&A in front of five hundred diehard My Chemical Romance fans.

Nick Oliveri photographed backstage at The Flapper in my hometown of Birmingham on February 28, 2017. After we drank a bottle of Jack Daniels.

Troy Van Leeuwen doing his best impression of a James Bond villain. London circa 2017.

Me and my pal Jesse Leach ahead of our Live Q&A together in Birmingham on August 8, 2018. A night I'll never forget.

Me interviewing Robb Flynn at the Gibson Guitar Showroom in London on November 1, 2017.

Michael Monroe photographed at the old Universal offices in Kensington on June 27, 2017. Note the Hanoi Rocks tattoo on his deltoid muscle. This was such a fun day.

Me and Doug Stanhope on the roof of the Hilton hotel in Paddington on June 2, 2018. It was a baking hot day, I'd been up all night partying, and Doug had the shits from being on tour.

With Tom Green in Birmingham ahead of his stand-up show on June 14, 2017. This interview still ranks as one of my all-time Top 5 podcasts, and I was delighted with how deep the conversation went.

Eugene Hutz photographed at the K West Hotel in Shepherd's Bush on December 13, 2017.
Taylor Hanson from Hanson was knocking about that day.

Vinnie Caruana photographed outside The Library in Highbury & Islington
on November 15, 2017. Shit library. Great pub.

Me and Al Barr at the Gibson Guitar Showroom in London on November 17, 2016.
We look like extras in a Guy Ritchie movie. Nothing but respect for Uncle Al.

Me and Laura Jane Grace shortly after recording an interview and live session for Team Rock Radio back in November 2014. We've been good friends ever since.

GUEST LIST

(In Alphabetical Order)

AL BARR
Al Barr founded The Bruisers in 1988. He's the lead singer and last remaining original member of the band. In 1998, he also joined the Dropkick Murphys, where he continues to share lead vocals with bassist and band leader Ken Casey. (Episode 002—02/02/2017)

DR. AMIE HARWICK
Amie Harwick was a therapist, writer, model, activist, feminist, and friend. She died on February 15, 2020. This book is dedicated to her memory. (Episode 061—06/27/2018)

ANDREW W.K.
Andrew W.K. is a singer-songwriter, multi-instrumentalist, producer, writer, and motivational speaker. He's what you might call a modern-day Renaissance man. (Episode 049—03/12/2018)

B-REAL
B-Real is one of two lead rappers in Cypress Hill. The group helped pioneer West Coast rap during the 1990s, and have sold over twenty million albums worldwide. From 2016–2019, he also fronted rap rock supergroup Prophets of Rage alongside Chuck D from Public Enemy. (Episode 040—01/01/2018)

BRIAN FALLON
Brian Fallon served as lead vocalist and rhythm guitarist in The Gaslight Anthem from 2006 until the band broke up in 2015. He's since

become a solo artist, releasing three studio albums to critical acclaim. (Episode 011—04/23/2017)

CHUCK RAGAN

Chuck Ragan is the front man in Hot Water Music, and a prolific solo artist on the side. He's also a fully licensed fly-fishing guide, which is his full-time gig when he's not on tour. (Episode 066—07/30/2018)

CHUCK ROBERTSON

Chuck Robertson is the lead singer in the Mad Caddies, who formed in California in 1995. Their sound incorporates a broad range of influences, from punk rock and hardcore to reggae and ska, and a healthy dose of Dixieland jazz. (Episode 067—08/06/2018)

CJ RAMONE

CJ Ramone joined the world's most famous band of brothers in 1989, replacing original member Dee Dee Ramone on bass. He remained with the band for the final eight years of their career. Since 2012, he's been touring and recording as CJ Ramone. (Episode 036—11/19/2017)

CLEM BURKE

Clem Burke has been the drummer in Blondie since 1975, but he's also kept the beat with the Ramones, Iggy Pop, Joan Jett, The Eurythmics, The Romantics, Pete Townshend, Bob Dylan, and many more. (Episode 015—06/06/2017)

DANKO JONES

Danko Jones is the lead singer and guitarist in Canadian garage rock trio Danko Jones—see what he did there. When he's not making music with his band, Danko is busy writing books (*I've Got Something to Say*) and hosting podcasts (*The Official Danko Jones Podcast*). He's a man after my own heart. (Episode 069—08/21/2018)

DAVE HAUSE

Dave Hause made a name for himself as the lead singer in The Loved Ones: a punk rock trio from Philadelphia, who formed in 2003. In

2009, Dave broke out as a solo artist. He's released four studio albums to date. (Episode 029—09/19/2017)

DOUG STANHOPE

Doug Stanhope is a comedian, author, actor, and podcast host. He's best known for his aggressive wit and biting social commentary, and can usually be seen sporting secondhand thrift shop attire. He also likes a drink and a smoke—a lot like me. (Episode 058—06/04/2018)

EUGENE HUTZ

Eugene Hutz is a Ukrainian born singer, musician, actor, and DJ. He's best known as the front man in Gogol Bordello, who are responsible for the popularization of gypsy punk—a style that combines punk rock with traditional Romani music. He also starred in the film *Everything Is Illuminated* alongside Elijah Wood. (Episode 043—01/29/2018)

FRANK IERO

Frank Iero is the rhythm guitarist in My Chemical Romance. The band rose from the East Coast underground scene to the forefront of modern-day arena rock during the early 2000s. They broke up in 2013, before reforming in 2019. Frank also fronted the post-hardcore band Leathermouth from 2007–2010. And he's released three solo records. (Episode 004—02/20/2017)

JESSE LEACH

Jesse Leach is the lead singer in Killswitch Engage, who formed in Westfield, Massachusetts, in 1999. They were a key band in the New Wave of American Heavy Metal, and helped pioneer metalcore music during the mid-2000s. Jesse also sings in Times of Grace and The Weapon. (Episode 005—02/27/2017)

JESSE MALIN

Jesse Malin is a singer-songwriter from New York City. He started his first band, Heart Attack, when he was just twelve years old, before going on to form D Generation, then continuing as a solo artist.

He's worked with Bruce Springsteen, Lucinda Williams, and Billie Joe Armstrong, and doubles up as a DJ on *Little Steven's Underground Garage*. (Episode 019—07/13/2017)

JOE CARDAMONE

Joe Cardamone was the leader of The Icarus Line from 1998–2015. After quietly breaking up the band in 2015, he began touring and recording as a solo artist, which he continues to do alongside his production work for acts like Queen Kwong. He also starred as himself in the movie *The Icarus Line Must Die* in 2017. (Episode 052—04/10/2018)

JOEY CAPE

Joey Cape is a singer, songwriter, musician, and producer. He's best known as the front man in Lagwagon, who formed in California in 1989. He also serves as guitarist in Me First and the Gimme Gimmes, and moonlights as a solo artist and record producer. (Episode 026—09/06/2017)

JUSTIN SANE

Justin Sane is the singer and lead guitarist in Anti-Flag, who formed in Pittsburgh, Pennsylvania, in 1988. The band is known for its politically charged lyrics and activism. They've released twelve studio albums to date, and show no signs of slowing down. (Episode 042—01/15/2018)

KYLE GASS

Kyle Gass is a musician, actor, and comedian best known as one half of the Grammy Award-winning musical duo Tenacious D—the other being his long-time friend and collaborator, Jack Black. Kyle also has his own group, The Kyle Gass Band, and has appeared in dozens of films and TV shows, including *Bio-Dome*, *The Cable Guy*, and *Elf*. (Episode 006—03/06/2017)

LAURA JANE GRACE

Laura Jane Grace is best known as the founder, lead singer, songwriter, and guitarist in Against Me!, who formed in Gainesville, Florida, in 1997. She's also a published author, following the release of her autobiography, *Tranny: Confessions of Punk Rock's Most Infamous Anarchist Sellout*, in 2016. And she has two solo albums to her name. (Episode 003—02/09/2017)

MATT CAUGHTHRAN

Matt Caughthran is the front man in both The Bronx and the Mariachi El Bronx. He also sings in The Drips, and has contributed guest vocals to songs by Biffy Clyro, Every Time I Die, and Trash Talk. He also has a great name. And two Matt's are better than one. (Episode 012—05/07/2017)

MICHAEL MONROE

Michael Monroe is a Finnish singer and multi-instrumentalist. He rose to fame as the front man in the hugely influential glam group Hanoi Rocks. After breaking up the band in 1985, following the death of their drummer Razzle, Michael soldiered on as a solo artist. He's released nine studio albums to date. His friends and fans include Alice Cooper, Dave Grohl, and the late Lemmy Kilmister. (Episode 023—08/15/2017)

MINA CAPUTO

Mina Caputo is a singer and artist best known as the lead vocalist in Life of Agony. The band formed in Brooklyn, New York, in 1989, and have released six studio albums to date. Mina has also released several solo records, including studio albums, live recordings, EPs, and collections of demos and rarities. She's a force of nature both on and off the stage. (Episode 035—11/13/2017)

MONIQUE POWELL

Monique Powell is the lead singer and last remaining original member of Save Ferris, who first formed in Orange County, California, in 1995. The original lineup broke up in 2003, and Monique reformed the band with a new lineup in 2013, after being legally awarded the rights to the name. She also appeared as herself in the movie *10 Things I Hate About You* in 1999, alongside the late Heath Ledger. (Episode 062—07/08/2018)

NICK OLIVERI

Nick Oliveri is a singer, songwriter, and musician. He's best known for his work in Kyuss and Queens of the Stone Age, but also plays in Mondo Generator and the Dwarves, and has collaborated with the likes of Masters of Reality, Mark Lanegan, and Slash—to name just a few. (Episode 007—03/27/2017)

ROBB FLYNN

Robb Flynn is the guitarist, lead vocalist, and chief songwriter in Machine Head. The band formed in Oakland, California, in 1991. They were part of the second wave of thrash metal bands to emerge during the 1990s, but have experimented with sounds such as groove metal and nu metal over the years. They've released nine studio albums to date. (Episode 037—11/28/2017)

ROGER LIMA

Roger Lima is the bassist and co-lead vocalist in third-wave ska punk band Less Than Jake. He's also the lead singer and guitarist in Rehasher, and has produced records for Less Than Jake, Masked Intruder, and The Suicide Machines. (Episode 013—05/14/2017)

STEVE-O

Steve-O is a TV personality, stunt performer, actor, comedian, and writer. He rose to fame in *Jackass* in 2000, and would go on to appear in all three *Jackass* movies, and the spin-off TV series *Wildboyz*. He's since segued into stand-up comedy, and has appeared in TV shows like *Happy Together* and *The Eric Andre Show*. (Episode 001—01/31/2017)

STEVEN VAN ZANDT

Steven Van Zandt is a singer, songwriter, musician, producer, actor, and activist. He's best known as a member of Bruce Springsteen's E Street Band, and for his role as Silvio Dante in *The Sopranos*. He also has his own band, Little Steven and The Disciples of Soul, and he runs his own radio station, *Little Steven's Underground Garage*. (Episode 045—02/12/2018)

TIM McILRATH

Tim McIlrath is the lead singer and guitarist in Rise Against. The band formed in Chicago in 1999, and are known for their outspoken social commentary and advocacy of progressivism. They've released eight studio albums to date. Tim is also known for his promotion of PETA and straight-edge ethics. He's one of life's good guys. (Episode 041—01/08/2018)

TOM GREEN

Tom Green is a Canadian comedian, actor, filmmaker, rapper, and talk show host. He rose to fame off the back of *The Tom Green Show*, which first aired on MTV in 1999, and paved the way for *Jackass* and all the other stunt-based TV shows that followed. He also starred in a number of Hollywood films, like *Road Trip*, *Charlie's Angels*, and *Freddy Got Fingered*, which he also directed. He's since reverted back to his first love: stand-up comedy. (Episode 024—08/21/2017)

TOMMY VICTOR

Tommy Victor is the lead singer and guitarist in Prong, a band he formed in New York City in 1986. He's also toured and recorded with Ministry and Danzig, and has collaborated with the likes of Trent Reznor, Marilyn Manson, and Rob Zombie. And he was the sound engineer at CBGB back in the day. How about that? (Episode 008—04/03/2017)

TROY VAN LEEUWEN

Troy Van Leeuwen is a musician and producer best known as the guitarist in Queens of the Stone Age, a band he joined in 2002. Prior to that, he played with Failure and A Perfect Circle, and over the years has contributed to a number of Queens of the Stone Age side-projects, including Eagles of Death Metal and The Desert Sessions. (Episode 032—10/15/2017)

VINNIE CARUANA

Vinnie Caruana is the lead vocalist in The Movielife, and the lead singer-songwriter in I Am the Avalanche. He also tours and records as a solo artist. He lives in Long Island, New York. (Episode 044—02/05/2018)

ACKNOWLEDGMENTS

FIRST AND FOREMOST, I'D like to thank Clive, Hilary, and Helena Stocks. Everyone else in my life gets to tap in and out as they wish, but my family are stuck with me forever. Lord knows I've put them through some shit over the years. We've all put each other through our fair share, to be honest. But we're stronger, closer, and better because of it. I love you guys. And I wouldn't change you for the world.

Next up, I want to thank my oldest and closest friends and confidantes: Greg Gaiger, Josh Duffy, Derek Robinson, Joel Carr, Steve Howard, Paul O'Flynn, Loz Payne, Rob Grey, Andy Sawers, Andy Telford, Michael Lewis, Ben Bolton, Mark Davies, and James Whitehurst. I don't get to see some of you half as much as I'd like, but our friendships date back to the early 2000s and you've been like brothers to me over the last two decades. I wouldn't be the man that I am today if I hadn't grown up with you boys. (The jury's still out on whether or not that's a good thing.) Locals only.

I'd also like to thank my flatmate, Lauren Amelia Roberts. We've been friends for over fifteen years now, Lozza, and I'm going to miss living with you. Good luck with your move to America; I wish you all the joy and happiness in the world. Thank you for keeping me sane during lockdown. You are, and always will be, my sister. I love you.

Special thanks, as well, to Rosi Croom and Kim Calloway. I want you both to know that I wouldn't be where I am today if we hadn't met each other at Exeter University. You were the fire that ignited my passion to agitate and create, and I'm eternally grateful to the pair of you for inspiring me to start DJing back in 2006. Literally *everything* that is good in my life can be traced back to our initial meeting of hearts, minds, and souls, and I'll never forget that. You're my family. FYC forever.

Speaking of family, I have to say a big thank you to my surrogate big bros Matt Pritchard and Lee Dainton. If I hadn't met and befriended you pair, my life would look a whole lot different right now. You were my heroes growing up—Dirty Sanchez inspired me to pick up a video camera and start messing about with my mates—and now you're two of my best friends in the world. Thank you for helping me take my podcast to the next level. You're still the top two most downloaded episodes. Mental!

Of course, I have to say a heartfelt thank you to each and every one of the guests in this book as well. Thank you for appearing on my podcast in the first place, and for giving me your blessing to be featured in this book. And I need to say an extra special thank you to Jesse Malin for kindly agreeing to write the foreword, and for being so generous with his compliments and praise. You're the original doctor, Jesse, and there's no one quite like you.

I have to thank Tyson Cornell from Rare Bird for giving me this incredible opportunity, too. Writing a book is something that I've always wanted to do, and you made that happen, my friend. You took a chance on me, and it's been a long time since anyone has done that. I owe you everything (apart from my fee; you can't have that back), and I really can't thank you enough. Thank you to Hailie Johnson for all your help with the editing and proofing, too. The final version of this book is infinitely superior to the original draft that I submitted, and that's all because of you. Thanks for making me look good.

Finally, I want to thank everyone who's listened to *Life In The Stocks* over the last four years. Your support of my little DIY project has allowed me to pursue what I love for a living, and I couldn't have done it without you. The podcast has given my life purpose and direction, and helped me through the darkest of days. I genuinely don't know where I'd be without it. Thank you for your loyalty, encouragement, and support.

I really am a lucky guy. And the harder I work, the luckier I get. I'm also living proof that you can do anything you set your mind to. Never let anyone tell you any different. And never be afraid to follow your dreams. You never know, they just might come true.